Seminar in Physical Education

From Student Teaching to Teaching Students

Susan K. Lynn, PhD

Florida State University

Darla M. Castelli, PhD

University of Illinois at Urbana-Champaign

Peter Werner, PED

University of South Carolina

Stephen L. Cone, PhD

Rowan University

D1016456

Human Kinetics

Library of Congress Cataloging-in-Publication Data

Seminar in physical education: from student teaching to teaching students / Susan Lynn . . . [et al].
   p. cm.
   Includes bibliographical references.
   ISBN-13: 978-0-7360-5609-0 (soft cover)
   ISBN-10: 0-7360-5609-2 (soft cover)
   1. Physical education and training--Study and teaching--United States. 2. Physical education and training--Vocational guidance--United States. I. Lynn, Susan, 1956-
   GV365.S46 2007
   613.707--dc22

2006037748

ISBN-10: 0-7360-5609-2
ISBN-13: 978-0-7360-5609-0

The Web addresses cited in this text were current as of November 22, 2006, unless otherwise noted.

Acquisitions Editor: Bonnie Pettifor; **Managing Editor:** Jacqueline Eaton Blakley; **Assistant Editors:** Bethany J. Bentley and Jackie Walker; **Copyeditor:** Annette Pierce; **Proofreader:** Julie Marx Goodreau; **Permission Manager:** Dalene Reeder; **Graphic Designer:** Fred Starbird; **Graphic Artist:** Yvonne Griffith; **Photo Manager:** Laura Fitch; **Cover Designer:** Nancy Rasmus; **Photographer (cover):** Tom Roberts; **Photographer (interior):** © Human Kinetics, unless otherwise noted; **Art Manager:** Kelly Hendren; **Illustrator:** Lyndsey Groth; **Printer:** Versa Press

Printed in the United States of America   10   9   8   7   6   5   4   3   2   1

Human Kinetics
Web site: www.HumanKinetics.com

United States: Human Kinetics
P.O. Box 5076
Champaign, IL 61825-5076
800-747-4457
e-mail: humank@hkusa.com

Canada: Human Kinetics
475 Devonshire Road Unit 100
Windsor, ON N8Y 2L5
800-465-7301 (in Canada only)
e-mail: orders@hkcanada.com

Europe: Human Kinetics
107 Bradford Road, Stanningley
Leeds LS28 6AT, United Kingdom
+44 (0) 113 255 5665
e-mail: hk@hkeurope.com

Australia: Human Kinetics
57A Price Avenue
Lower Mitcham, South Australia 5062
08 8372 0999
e-mail: liaw@hkaustralia.com

New Zealand: Human Kinetics
Division of Sports Distributors NZ Ltd.
P.O. Box 300 226 Albany
North Shore City
Auckland
0064 9 448 1207
e-mail: info@humankinetics.co.nz

Contents

Chapter **3**   **Constructing a Professional
Development Plan 39**

PART
II   **Collaboration. 57**

Chapter **4**   **Developing Advocacy Skills 59**

Chapter **5** **Personal Professional Development. 79**

Chapter **6** **Using Community Resources. . . . 97**

Chapter **7**   **Establishing Productive Relationships 117**

PART
III   **Curricular Implementation. 137**

Chapter **8**   **Reducing Liability and Risk 139**

Preface

The changing teacher preparation landscape served as a primary motivator for this project. Four major issues affect preservice teacher preparation programs:

1. The disappearance of many organization and administration courses—fewer than half of the Teacher Education Physical Education (TEPE) programs now include such a course, possibly a casualty of the time-to-graduation dilemma

2. Time-to-graduation discussions and the resulting credit-consolidation requirements experienced by many programs, where faculties are asked to consolidate courses to reduce or control the total number of credits in a student's program

3. The implementation of capstone or seminar courses, many conducted in conjunction with practicum or student teaching–field experiences or both

4. The increased visibility of National Council for Accreditation of Teacher Education (NCATE) accreditation, where standards focus on student disposition, knowledge, and demonstrated performance

The project's breadth and depth were ambitious and challenging. The significance of such a text and its contributions to preparing physical education teachers are without question. As a result, a team was assembled to bring a richness and quality of perspectives and experiences to facilitate the connection between content and learner.

Dr. Susan Lynn, Florida State University, brings perspectives on teacher career development; effective teaching and learning; middle and secondary school physical education curriculum design, theory, and development; and gender issues in sport and physical activity.

Dr. Darla Castelli, University of Illinois at Urbana-Champaign, contributes knowledge about the effectiveness of physical education programs, implementation of physical education programs, purposeful integration of technology, and standards-based education reform and accountability.

Dr. Peter Werner, University of South Carolina, and I had previously worked together, and his expertise in teacher preparation is well known. His sage perspectives include thoughts on advising and teacher preparation, understanding the accreditation process, developing an interdisciplinary approach, and curriculum development and implementation.

Dr. Stephen Cone, Rowan University, offers thoughts on leadership and advocacy, K-12 curriculum and instruction, program management and implementation, connections across the curriculum, and developing a comprehensive teacher preparation program.

The team would also like to acknowledge Dr. James H. Conn, Central Missouri State University, for his review contributions to chapter 8, Reducing Liability and Risk.

The purpose of the book is to help students understand and reflect on the educational experience. The book will also assist faculty as they address the specialized professional association (SPA) standards and requirements established by the National Association for Sport and Physical Education (NASPE), which serve as guidelines to address the NCATE accreditation requirements. The text provides information and resources through content, examples, and projects that will assist in teacher preparation, as well as the accreditation process.

The National Standards for Beginning Physical Education Teachers (NAPSE, 2003) provide references for determining the performances (skills), knowledge, and dispositions expected of beginning physical education teachers. These standards have served as the touchstone for this book's content. The 10 standards are as follows:

1. Content knowledge. Understand physical education content and disciplinary concepts related to the development of a physically educated person.

2. Growth and development. Understand how individuals learn and develop, and provide opportunities that support physical, cognitive, social, and emotional development.

3. Diverse learners. Understand how individuals differ in their approaches to learning and create appropriate instruction adapted to these differences.

4. Management and motivation. Use and have an understanding of individual and group motivation and behavior to create a safe learning environment that encourages positive social interaction, active engagement in learning, and self-motivation.

5. Communication. Use knowledge of effective verbal, nonverbal, and media communication techniques to enhance learning and engagement in physical education settings.

6. Planning and instruction. Understand the importance of planning developmentally appropriate instructional units to foster the development of a physically educated person.

7. Student assessment. Understand and use the varied types of assessment and their contribution to the overall program and

the development of the physical, cognitive, social, and emotional domains.

8. Reflection. Understand the importance of being a reflective practitioner and its contribution to overall professional development and actively seek opportunities to sustain professional growth.

9. Technology. Use information technology to enhance learning and personal and professional productivity.

10. Collaboration. Understand the necessity of fostering collaborative relationships with colleagues, parents or guardians, and community agencies to support the development of a physically educated person.

National Standards for Beginning Physical Education Teachers, 2nd Edition (2001) reprinted with permission from the National Association for Sport and Pysical Education (NASPE), 1900 Association Drive, Reston, VA 20191-1599.

The text is further structured to enhance the reflective-thinking process, facilitate portfolio development, offer separate chapters that facilitate focus, and emphasize the connection between preservice education and involvement in the greater education community. The content enables discussion and direct connections to the standards through questions and assignments.

The text is divided into three parts. Part I focuses on reflection (NASPE Standard 8) and includes three chapters. These chapters expose the student to the reflective cycle, identifying and using available resources and constructing a professional development plan. Part II investigates collaboration (NASPE Standard 10) and communication (NASPE Standard 5) through the content presented in four chapters. These chapters address advocacy skills, participating in the physical education professional community, accessing and using community resources, and establishing productive relationships within the school and community. Part III explores curricular implementation, which addresses parts of NAPSE Standards 1, 2, 3, 4, 5, 6, 7, and 9. The five chapters cover topics such as reducing liability and risk, decision making and managing resources, addressing technology, enhancing professionalism and professional growth, and developing a portfolio.

The chapters are divided into manageable units for use during a seminar-type course, covering one chapter per week. Each chapter begins with a brief vignette and ends with key terms, discussion questions, suggestions for professional portfolio content, and resource offerings. This structure was designed to facilitate connections between content, application, and standards.

We trust that this text will provide a framework through which students and professors can address the critical teacher preparation elements. The future of our profession will be in good hands and will continue to grow and move positively into the future if professors and students use this framework and reflective process. As the Fram oil filter commercial from the 1970s offered, "You can pay me now, or pay me later." Effective and well-trained physical education teachers acknowledge the value of prevention and maintenance as a low-cost approach to providing high-quality programs that lead to a healthy, active lifestyle. We must continue to take the lead and contribute to a healthful future.

Stephen L. Cone

I

Reflection

An educator must continually reflect on and evaluate decisions and practices in order to change the knowledge, skills, and dispositions appropriate for a high-quality education. The educator must understand how these decisions and practices affect colleagues, students, parents, and other learning community professionals. Chapter 1 explores the implementation of a reflective cycle in which goals, assessments, and new directions are identified. Chapter 2 addresses the use of available resources to help the educator recognize that he or she is not teaching alone but is associated with valuable information to enhance teaching. Chapter 3 introduces the concept of a professional development plan and suggests processes and benefits associated with its use.

1

Implementing
the Reflective Cycle

STANDARD 8: *Reflection.* Understand the importance of being a reflective practitioner and its contribution to overall professional development and actively seek opportunities to sustain professional growth.

OUTCOME 8.1: Use a reflective cycle involving description of teaching, justification of the teaching performance, critique of the teaching performance, the setting of teaching goals, and implementation of change.

While driving home after a good but relatively uneventful day teaching middle school physical education at your new job, you find yourself thinking about a negative, less-than-enthusiastic comment one of the less-active students made when you announced that the class would perform a particular task. Although you took it as grumbling, something all kids in this age group tend to do, you find that the comment is still nagging at you. Realizing that the student may have verbalized what other students feel but may be afraid to comment on, you reach into your pocket and extract the handheld tape recorder or PDA that you keep on hand for times when writing is impossible. You record your thoughts on what the student said—and what the comment may really have meant—while it is fresh in your mind. You remind yourself to think about the changes you could make that would make the student's—and other students'—physical education experience more rewarding.

Later, after the evening's activities have quieted, you replay the tape, make notes about the event, and begin to think about and list the changes you plan to implement to try to enhance the student's class experiences for the benefit of all.

Your first few days on the job as a teacher in a new school can be overwhelming. You find yourself in a completely unknown environment. You are consumed with details, paperwork, and unfamiliar faces. Nervous about looking professional, maintaining authority, learning your way around, fitting in, and learning the names of your students and colleagues, you can barely remember the real reasons you came to work in the first place.

As a new physical education teacher, you are eager to take charge of helping hundreds of young people learn to take full advantage of their physical capabilities and to make the best of their opportunities for health and fitness. You are also the master of the gym and playing field, ready to help your students have great fun.

But all those goals can get lost in the early days of teaching. Sometimes physical education class looks and feels like pandemonium. Fortunately, there are ways to make sense of the events that occur every day and to make yourself a better teacher in the process. Reflective teaching is the name professional teachers give to a process that can help you build your teaching capability out of the seeming chaos of your early days in the classroom.

Reflective teaching is a concept used throughout the teaching profession. It originated in the writings of John Dewey in the early 20th century. Dewey considered reflection to be a moderator between teachers' theoretical knowledge and classroom practice.

Reflective teaching refers to the constant self-evaluation that good teachers use to respond to changing classroom conditions. The steps involved in reflection can be broken down and analyzed, but teachers should keep in mind its ultimate goal: adjusting teaching methods to meet student needs while compensating for enrollment and demographic shifts and the threatened priority status of physical education curriculum. Reflection can be a solitary, introspective process, but its result is a dynamic response leading to action.

Educators of all subjects and levels consider reflection a highly desirable part of teaching, and physical education is no different. Outcome 8.1 of the National Standards for Beginning Physical Education Teachers says that teachers should "use a reflective cycle involving description of teaching, justification of the teaching performance, critique of the teaching performance, the setting of teaching goals, and implementation of change" (NASPE, 2003, p. 17).

This standard is a call for physical education teachers to use the reflective cycle, observing their own practices and their students' responses. The opposite of reflection is the utilitarian approach (Ross, Bondy, & Kyle, 1993): adapting teaching methods only to keep students quiet and on task, with no regard to whether they're learning or not. Equally perilous is the tendency to avoid change altogether and repeat the same lessons, using the same methods, year after year (Reiman, 1999). The essence of Standard 8 demands that physical education teachers change with the times and adapt to the needs of their students. Adopting this standard early in your career sets the stage for creative, responsive teaching.

WHAT IS THE REFLECTIVE CYCLE?

Kemmis and McTaggart (1982 in Ross et al., 1993) provided a model for the *reflective cycle* (see figure 1.1) as a continuum that begins with a teacher planning for change, acting on this plan, observing the results, and judging the success or failure of the attempt to change. These are the basics of the reflective cycle. *Planning* begins when you recognize a problem and devote yourself to solving it. Perhaps a particular lesson doesn't work well with one group of students, and you need a quick way to prepare for the next time you teach it. Or perhaps while reading over your journal entries, you notice a long-standing pattern that you want to

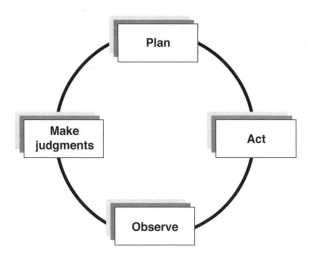

Figure 1.1   Kemmis and McTaggart's cycle of reflective teaching model.

Ross, Dorene D.; Bondy, Elizabeth; Kyle, Diane W. *Reflective teaching for student empowerment: Elementary, 1st Edition,* © 1993. Reprinted by permission of Pearson Education, Inc., Upper Saddle River, NJ.

overcome. In the planning stage of the reflective cycle, you find a problem and put a name on it so that you can move beyond it. You use your observations and skills as a teacher to plan a solution.

Ross, Bondy, and Kyle (1993) note that the next three steps of the reflective cycle, although distinctive, "most often occur simultaneously" (p. 22). You *act* on your plan, *observe* the results, and assess your success or failure. You *make a judgment* about how well you handled this particular opportunity for improvement, and you define future goals based on your progress.

Wuest and Lombardo (1994) give an example of actions a teacher could take based on an idea developed through the reflective cycle. Their example concerns a PE program in which the teacher has decided that the students should be more engaged in the curriculum. The teacher's next step is to think of ways to put this change into practice. In this case, possible changes include soliciting student input through suggestion-box-type activities and adjusting the social environment in the gym to reduce intimidation and extreme competitiveness. Genuinely reflecting on a problem can spawn a variety of solutions.

As you gain more teaching experience, you will be less likely to think about reflection in terms of its components. Reflection truly becomes a cycle: You *plan, act, observe,* and *make judgments* without thinking about passing through those stages. You spot problems and solve them in the ordinary course of your work. Instead of letting them nag you for months on end, you learn to tackle your long-term issues step-by-step.

In another study, a student teacher returned to an internship after taking a semester off to play professional football. After watching videotapes of himself teaching high school students to play badminton, he caught himself showing favoritism toward higher-skilled students. "I was not at peace with myself because of my inability to develop an appropriate lesson for the high and low skill level students," he wrote in his reflective journal (Langley & Senne, 1997, Connecting Stories section, para. 16).

Through reflection, he realized that he was expecting perfection from his students, perhaps without teaching them every step they needed to know to learn badminton in the first place. He became determined to spend more time writing his lesson plans, making sure he was prepared to individualize tasks for lower-skilled students and to provide time with them and feedback to them rather than spending so much time with the higher-skilled students. Using the reflective cycle can lead to your becoming a teacher who changes as the situation demands. Whether you need to quickly adapt your methods during class or make a lasting change to your outlook on working with students, reflection can help you help your students.

WHY IS REFLECTION IMPORTANT?

Reflection is a way of being your own teacher. Through your study of physical education, you have learned the profession's latest practices and examined the research that supports them. But in the real world, conditions change every day. As Wuest and Lombardo (1994) note, "Schools are places of great ambiguities and ill-structured problems that have multiple solutions" (p. 255).

Schools deal with growing or shrinking enrollment and changing demographics. Physical education teachers specifically deal with their subject's often-threatened priority status in the curriculum. The amount of money and equipment available to PE teachers and the quality of facilities vary considerably from one school to another. Researchers find new ways for PE teachers to work and learn new things about children's physical development. No one can predict these changes, but everyone will have to face them.

This is where reflective teaching can make a difference. Although you will receive direction from your supervisors, you are on your own in developing your personal teaching methods. Staying current on the latest research in your field can help—in fact, it is part of Outcome 8.2, and we discuss it in the next chapter. However, research cannot account for every situation, nor can it help you deal with problems in real time.

Simply put, there is no substitute for experience. Reflection ensures that you will learn from your experiences and put the lessons you learn into practice quickly.

GETTING STARTED

Reflecting on your work is as simple as it sounds. Look back on each day of teaching. Think about what went well and what didn't. Then use your own knowledge and experience to find ways to improve the situation the next time you face it.

There are several ways to reflect on your teaching practices. Keeping a daily log or journal of events that occurred throughout the day, free-association writing (jotting things down as they occur), critiques from colleagues and mentors, self-evaluations, video analysis of your class or activity, student feedback, and observing other teachers in the field are a few examples of how you can become more reflective.

An easy and popular way to start using reflection in your work is to write about problems. Use a journal, much as you might in your personal life, to put your problems on paper. Then step back, read what you have written, and see the solutions you tend to overlook during a high-pressure day in the classroom.

ANATOMY OF A JOURNAL

Researchers have created several templates or methods for compiling reflective journals. You can examine the approaches they offer and find the one that fits you best. Over time, you will develop your own habits for reflective writing. But remember, it is not as simple as writing in a personal diary. Your goal is to apply the thoughts you put on paper.

You can use a journal to reflect on the outcome of a whole lesson or class session. You can also use it to focus on a problem with an individual student or group. Any success or stumbling block can form the basis for a journal entry. As you write, remind yourself to see the situation from multiple points of view (Ross et al., 1993), increasing the likelihood that, on later readings, a way to improve your teaching will occur to you.

An example of reflection from a different point of view comes from a research study conducted by McCollum (2002) involving a physical education teacher who was evaluating a small obstacle that developed during class. The teacher noticed that first-grade students did not understand instructions that asked them to stand "four feet away" from their partners. Perhaps realizing that the students might be too young to process "four feet away," the teacher changed the wording, asking students instead to take "four giant steps back" from their partners. Immediately, the students understood. Reflecting on the situation, the teacher was reminded to speak in terms the youngest students could understand.

In a study by Langley and Senne (1997), student physical education teachers used journals to reflect on their early teaching experiences. Researchers asked the beginning teachers to write about specific situations in story form, making themselves the main characters. They were to begin with a problem and write through to the solution.

This approach to reflective journaling will require you to consider your own personality and past influences as you write. It's a personal approach and one that the researchers felt helped the student teachers place their experiences in context. Langley and Senne (1997) note that "the structure implied in storytelling—a series of connected events over time—forced the preservice teachers to view their decisions and actions in light of their personal histories" (p. 22). You may also find that storytelling helps you see the beginning, middle, and end of a problem you're trying to work on.

If you decide not to base your journal on the elements of fiction, you can find another writing style that fits you. Try starting with any of the following questions:

- What did you set out to teach?
- Were you able to accomplish your goals?
- Was your lesson teacher dominated?
- What kind of teacher–student interaction occurred?
- Did anything amusing or unusual occur?
- Did you depart from your lesson plan? If so, why? Did the change make things better or worse?
- Would you teach the lesson differently if you taught it again?
- What do you think students really learned from the lesson?
- What did they like most about the lesson?
- What didn't they respond well to?

Also, adopt a writing schedule that fits your needs. Some experts recommend jotting down a journal entry after every lesson or every day. If the unpredictable school environment makes that impossible, you may write less often. If you have not written in a while, an out-of-the-ordinary event can send you racing for your notebook and pen.

After you write, be sure not to leave your journal on the shelf. Reflecting really begins when you take time to read what you wrote about your own experiences and consider how the situations you face can help you improve as a teacher. Reflection involves analysis, so read with a critical eye.

Ask yourself questions as you reread your journal. Richards and Lockhart (1994) suggest several questions to get you started:

- What principles and beliefs inform my teaching?
- Why do I teach the way I do?
- Should I teach differently?

The exchange of reflective journals between student teachers and their professors is a well-regarded technique in college classrooms. When working from your own classroom, you may not always have easy access to your mentors, but you can adopt some of the same practices they would use in evaluating the comments you make in your journal.

- Have you noticed your own feelings and the students' feelings and described them in your journal? Emotions are part of the classroom experience. Acknowledge your feelings and use them to help you understand what has happened.

- Do your entries demonstrate self-confidence, or do they betray doubts about your abilities? Take time to encourage yourself and to work on the skills that will help you overcome your doubts.

- Are you actually reflecting on the teaching and learning process, or are you just recording information about what happened? If you're not doing the former, try expanding on these areas. Think beyond "What did I do?" to "Did it work?" "Why?" or "Why not?" And finally, answer, "What would I do differently if I taught the lesson again?"

These are some characteristics of journal entries designed for teacher educators reading interns' journals in a college setting (Reiman, 1999). However, you can use them to prompt responses to your own journal. Reflection makes you your own best teacher.

EXPANDING ON YOUR JOURNAL

As a physical education teacher, you will often work independently. If you find that collaboration is missing from your professional activities, forming a journal-writing group is a good way to reconnect with other teachers and work on being more reflective at the same time. Find a few others who share your goals, meet regularly, and review one another's journals. If you have trouble viewing your own journal with a critical eye, working with a group can help you develop that skill.

ALTERNATIVES TO JOURNAL WRITING

Writing in a journal is an excellent reflective activity, but some people may find it too open ended. Researchers have created several frameworks for writing that may help. Outside of writing, there are several other ways to record your own performance and reflect on it.

A writing approach with more structure than a traditional journal is the *reflective framework for teaching in physical education,* or RFTPE. It is also a method for writing down and reflecting on your thoughts. First proposed in 1994 by Tsangaridou and O'Sullivan, the RFTPE asks you to think about the classroom incident you're evaluating in terms of a specific set of categories: technical, situational, and sensitizing (see figure 1.2). These reflection categories are of equal importance and are interconnected (Tsangaridou & O'Sullivan, 1994). McCollum (2002) evaluated the RFTPE as a bridge between theory and practice and found that it helped preservice teachers become more reflective.

According to McCollum (2002), *technical* refers to your own learned teaching skills and methods, such as setting up a curriculum of study and daily lesson plans. Reflecting on past experiences and using theory are other examples of tools to use in the technical level of reflection (Taggart & Wilson, 1998). The *situational* category, also referred to as the *contextual level* (Taggart & Wilson, 1998), deals with unexpected events that happen during class, creating the need for decision making and alternative practices beyond lesson plans. A simple example of an unexpected event may be an outdoor tennis class needing to join you in your indoor volleyball space because of inclement weather. *Sensitizing* reflections—also known as the *dialectical level,* according to Taggart and Wilson (1998)—cover social constructions such as race; gender equity; and ethical, moral, and other issues that deal with cultural and political differences in the classroom.

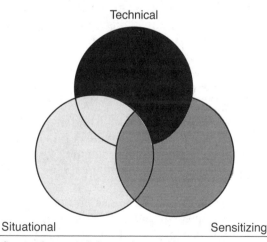

Figure 1.2 Reflective framework for teaching in physical education model: Reflection focus categories.

From S. McCollum, 2000. "The reflective framework for teaching in physical education: A pedagogical tool," *Journal of Physical Education, Recreation & Dance,* 73(6), 39-42.

No matter what category the situation falls in, your task remains the same. According to McCollum (2002), the RFTPE asks you to reflect by doing the following:

- **Describing** an event or a lesson. Simply stated: *What happened?*
- **Justifying** your teaching methods. An action was taken; what was your reaction and the rationale behind it?
- **Critiquing** your actions, analyzing your method, and determining a follow-up procedure.

The RFTPE specifies the goals of all reflective journals, reminding you of the substantive goals of this type of writing. Although the same goals apply to teaching any subject, experts on physical education designed the RFTPE. Its relationship to your subject may help you get started.

There are many more ways to take stock of your own classroom performance. If the journal idea appeals to you but you find writing inconvenient, consider starting an audio diary on tape or on a digital recorder. Listen to the entries regularly. It may help to pull out a pen and paper when you listen and reflect on what you've recorded.

Instead of writing open-ended journal entries, you can try using an observation tool or creating your own to quantify your self-assessments. You can find model forms in several textbooks and journals, including those written by Rink (2005), Tillman and colleagues (1996), and Wuest and Lombardo (1994). Videotape yourself in class, and fill out the form as you watch. Alternatively, you and a colleague can agree to observe one another. Or, in some contexts, you can distribute student evaluations—like the ones you probably filled out as a college student—and find out what students have to say about your teaching. This is especially useful if the problem you are working on would benefit from greater student engagement in class.

REFLECTING OVER TIME

The many frameworks for reflection—open ended or structured, written or recorded—are no more than catalysts for a process that really goes on within you. In designing a method of reflection for yourself, you have many choices. But the first choice, becoming a reflective teacher, is the most important.

As you begin using reflective teaching techniques, remember that you may not see all the changes you need to make immediately. Sometimes you need distance from an experience to interpret it. Richards and Lockhart (1994) note, "What might not have been obvious when written or recorded may later become apparent" (p. 7). Any past experience can become the seed of future reflection.

Over time, your reflective writing will become deeper. Using a journal to describe events, such as those suggested by the earlier questions, is what researchers refer to as stage one reflection (Goethals, Howard, & Sanders, 2004). It's a crucial starting point, but as you use this method more often, you will find yourself devoting more time and space in your journal to the deeper stages of reflection. Stage two involves response to your belief structure about teaching as the result of deeper reflection, incorporating actual classroom experiences and an understanding of student learning and motivation. Stage three, also known as *critical reflection,* is the term for written reflection that demonstrates a true search for answers through the philosophy and practice of teaching (see figure 1.3).

Reaching this level of reflection takes time and dedication. There's no need to solve all your teaching problems in your first journal entries. But starting to reflect early in your career and on a regular basis and maintaining the goal of improving your teaching over the long run by asking critical questions will put you on that path.

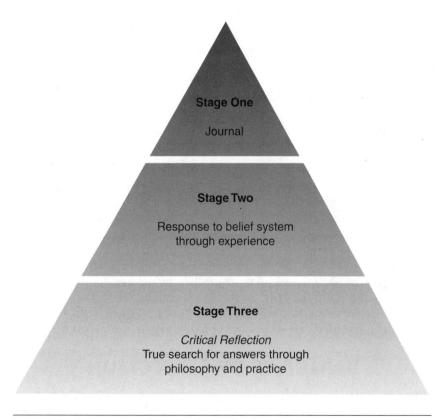

Figure 1.3 Progression to the critical reflection foundation.

USING WHAT YOU HAVE LEARNED

You have learned about ways to begin reflecting on your teaching methods. The next step is to act on your reflections. This is where you begin reaching students because of your ability to teach yourself.

Remember, Outcome 8.1 (NASPE, 2003, p. 17) asks that you not only reflect but that you use your reflections to improve your teaching methods. To reach an acceptable level of reflection, according to the standard, you should do the following:

> Demonstrate a sufficient ability to use a reflective cycle involving description of teaching, justification of the teaching performance, critique of the teaching performance, the setting of teaching goals, and implementation of change, as evidenced by lesson reflections and lesson modifications implemented in subsequent lessons of a comparable nature. (NASPE, 2003, p. 17)

If your goal is to move beyond the acceptable level, reach for the target of Standard 8:

> Consistently demonstrate use of a reflective cycle involving description of teaching, justification of the teaching performance, critique of the teaching performance, the setting of teaching goals, and implementation of change by reflecting in action through the implementation of changes and modifications both during and following instruction in order to impact student learning. (NASPE, 2003, p. 17)

Keep in mind that although you might be able to demonstrate that you know how to use the reflective cycle to enhance your teaching ability, the ultimate goal is for it to become virtually second nature to you. Consistency in this regard is equivalent to constant reflection using various diverse techniques, effecting a positive impact on your students.

Some of the language from these goals outlined in the national standards may sound familiar to you from the RFTPE and other reflective techniques outlined earlier. Description of teaching, justification of the teaching performance, and critique of the teaching performance are all objectives of · journals and other methods of reflection. The missing link in the reflective cycle, then, is action—putting what you've learned into practice.

VARIETIES OF REFLECTION

Looking back on issues and situations you have encountered in the classroom—the types of events you record and write about in a reflective journal—is what researchers call *reflection on action* (Yost, Sentner, &

Forlenza-Bailey, 2000). Solving a problem based on ongoing reflection—changing your teaching methods in the middle of a lesson, for example—is known as *reflection in action*. Finally, *reflection for action* is the academic term for applying reflection to your future—thinking about how you will handle upcoming challenges. All three varieties will become part of your repertoire when you strive to make reflection a part of your career.

It may not always be easy to work out the problems you identify through reflection if doing so involves finding measurable weaknesses in your teaching methods or sensitive issues in your classroom. Stanley (1998) notes that "in going deeper into reflection on one's teaching, it is not unusual to find issues of prejudice or favoritism toward certain students, learning styles, or theories of teaching and learning" (p. 587). This happened to one teacher in an example earlier in the chapter when he noticed himself favoring the better athletes in class. Reflection can also uncover cases of gender discrimination or cultural or political bias. It can be disappointing to catch yourself making the kinds of mistakes teachers and all professionals try hard to avoid. But without reflection, you may never notice yourself making those mistakes.

You may need to step back from these problems in order to solve them. But do not give up on reflective teaching. Reflection is the reason you become aware of your problems, which, again, is the first step to solving them. And do not forget that reflection also provides you with an opportunity to consider those aspects of your teaching that are going well and are having a positive impact on student learning!

REFLECTION IN YOUR PROFESSIONAL PORTFOLIO

Part of the big picture of becoming a reflective teacher in keeping with the goals of Standard 8 is developing a portfolio to showcase your teaching skills, knowledge, and abilities. Fittingly, the reflective work you do can eventually form a part of your portfolio. Actually, your reflections contained in your portfolio, more so than any artifact that you might include, are potentially the most important part of the portfolio. In other words, it is not the event you participated in nor the project you completed, but what you learned from that experience that is most important—and that is what placing reflections in your portfolio has the potential to show. Even though reflection is an internal process, it is so desirable in the teaching profession that you must be able to show others that it is part of your philosophy.

After you have been keeping a record of your reflections for a while, consider adding some of this material to your professional portfolio. Things you have written about yourself—your journey to becoming an effective physical educator—can take their place alongside your teacher evaluations, lesson plans, and written teaching philosophy. Once again, it is not the lesson plan that is most important—it is your reflection about what you learned from doing a lesson plan and how the lesson plan affected your ability to be an effective teacher that is important. Goethals and colleagues (2004) recommend that a portfolio include self-assessment and reflection elements signifying the nature and impact of changes that result in meaningful teaching and learning experiences.

You want to demonstrate real successes that resulted from reflection, so choose to deal with an issue that you have already acted on. Decide on which issue to shine the spotlight. Be prepared to discuss it from start to finish if the potential viewer of the portfolio asks. But also consider the fact that the busy administrator receiving your portfolio may not have time to ask you all the questions he or she wants answered before deciding which of many candidates to invite for an interview. As Drake and McBride (2000) recommend, create a portfolio that tells your entire story. "[I]t is best to imagine this disquieting scenario: that the person who will be reviewing the portfolio knows nothing about its creator, and that its creator will not be available to explain any aspect of the contents," they write (p. 45). You want to be able to show the depth and breadth of your knowledge and skills.

How can you make your reflective work accessible to a potential employer who has never met you? Put your journal entries or self-evaluations in the portfolio. Then supplement them with a written description of how you put your desired change into practice. You might also include other artifacts that show your change in action, such as photos showing how you reorganized your gym or articles from the school newspaper about a new PE program. Of course, it does not hurt to remind potential employers that the reflective materials you submit are part of your effort to meet all of the National Standards for Beginning Physical Education Teachers.

SUMMARY

You may be tempted, as a beginning teacher, to let the days fly by with all their ups and downs. Relieved after a tough day at school, you may not feel inclined to dwell on your setbacks. Faced with the challenge of getting very young students to play with their teammates, demonstrating complex skills, or just getting students to enjoy learning about fitness, you may just want to fall back on the simplest methods, regardless of who gets left behind. Some days you will just long for order and quiet.

But there will always be another day, another lesson, and another group of students. Do not miss out on the chance to prepare. Use the reflective methods outlined in this chapter. Seize those elusive quiet moments and bring out your journal or recorder. Find other teachers who are enthusiastic about their professional development and agree to observe and evaluate one another's performance.

Reflective teaching is your best tool for becoming an adaptable teacher. Adaptability, in the ever-changing world of education, is vital to your effectiveness.

Discussion Questions

1. What are some differences between keeping a personal journal and keeping a reflective-teaching journal?
2. What reflective practices could you use if you are not accustomed to expressing yourself by writing?
3. Give examples of lower-level, or stage one, reflection and of higher-level critical reflection. What happens to reflection if you keep at it for a long time?
4. Think of a situation in your life that you were able to reflect on through writing, discussion with a friend, or another method similar to those used in reflective teaching. How did reflection help you deal with later, similar situations?

Professional Portfolio Contents

1. Using an electronic portfolio, create a digital story (http://electronic portfolios.com/digistory/index.html) about why you wanted to become a physical educator or what it means to be a reflective practitioner, and link it to your introduction page. This will be a powerful "first meeting" between you and the viewer!
2. Include auditory or written reflections that give meaning to the artifacts that you include in your portfolio. Remember, it is not the event or document you are trying to show in the portfolio. Instead, you are trying to show your self-assessment and reflection of that event or document that resulted in a change and the actions and impact these changes contributed to meaningful teaching and learning.

Key Terms

critical reflection—Highest level of reflection involving analytical thought through examining, questioning, and investigating using action research.

reflection for action—Applying reflection to your future; thinking about how you will handle upcoming challenges.

reflection in action—Solving a problem based on ongoing reflection such as changing your teaching methods in the middle of a lesson.

reflection on action—Looking back on issues and situations you've encountered in the classroom.

reflective cycle—A continuum that begins when a teacher plans for change, then acts on this plan, observes the results, and judges the success or failure of the attempt.

reflective framework for teaching in physical education (RFTPE)—A reflective strategy that gives you categories to prompt your writing—technical, situational, and sensitizing.

reflective teaching—The constant self-evaluation that good teachers use to respond to changing classroom conditions.

Resources

Clift, R.T., Houston, W.R., & Pugach, M.C. (Eds.). (1990). *Encouraging reflective practice in education: An analysis of issues and programs.* New York: Teachers College Press.

Pollard, A., & Tann, S. (1987). *Reflective teaching in the primary school.* London: Cassell Educational Limited.

Rink, J.E. (2005). *Teaching physical education for learning* (5th ed.). New York: McGraw-Hill.

Taggart, G.L., & Wilson, A.P. (1998). *Promoting reflective thinking in teachers: 44 action strategies.* Thousand Oaks, CA: Corwin Press.

Tillman, K.G., Voltmer, E.F., Esslinger, A.A., & McCue, B.F. (1996). *The administration of physical education, sport, and leisure programs* (6th ed.). Boston: Allyn & Bacon.

Valli, L. (Ed.). (1992). *Reflective teacher education: Cases and critiques.* Albany, NY: State University of New York Press.

Wuest, D., & Lombardo, D. (1994). *Curriculum and instruction: The secondary school physical education experience* (pp. 247-259). St Louis: Mosby.

References

Drake, F., & McBride, L. (2000, November). The summative teaching portfolio and the reflective practitioner of history. *History Teacher, 34(1),* 41-60.

Goethals, M., Howard, R., & Sanders, M. (2004). *Student teaching: A process approach to reflective practice.* Upper Saddle River, NJ: Prentice Hall.

Langley, D., & Senne, T. (1997). Telling the stories of teaching: Reflective writing for preservice teachers [Electronic version]. *Journal of Physical Education, Recreation & Dance, 68(8)*, 56-59. Retrieved July 19, 2004, from InfoTrac OneFile database.

McCollum, S. (2002). The reflective framework for teaching in physical education: A pedagogical tool. *Journal of Physical Education, Recreation & Dance, 73(6)*, 39-42.

National Association for Sport and Physical Education. (2003). *National standards for beginning physical education teachers* (2nd ed.). Reston, VA: Author.

Reiman, A. (1999). The evolution of the social roletaking and guided reflection framework in teacher education: Recent theory and quantitative synthesis of research. *Teaching and Teacher Education, 15*, 597-612.

Richards, J.C., & Lockhart, C. (1994). *Reflective teaching in second language classrooms* (pp. 6-28). New York: Cambridge University Press.

Rink, J.E. (2005). *Teaching physical education for learning* (5th ed.). New York: McGraw-Hill.

Ross, Dorene D.; Bondy, Elizabeth; Kyle, Diane W. (1993). *Reflective teaching for student empowerment: Elementary* (1st ed.). Upper Saddle River, NJ: Pearson Education, Inc.

Stanley, C. (1998). A framework for teacher reflectivity. *TESOL Quarterly, 32(3)*, 584-590.

Taggart, G.L., & Wilson, A.P. (1998). *Promoting reflective thinking in teachers: 44 action strategies.* Thousand Oaks, CA: Corwin Press.

Tillman, K.G., Voltmer, E.F., Esslinger, A.A., & McCue, B.F. (1996). *The administration of physical education, sport, and leisure programs* (6th ed.). Boston: Allyn & Bacon.

Tsangaridou & O'Sullivan (1994). Using pedagogical reflective strategies to enhance reflection among preservice physical education teachers. *Journal of Teaching in Physical Education, 14*, 13-33.

Wuest, D., & Lombardo, D. (1994). *Curriculum and instruction: The secondary school physical education experience* (pp. 247-259). St Louis: Mosby.

Yost, D., Sentner, A., & Forlenza-Bailey, A. (2000). An examination of the construct of critical reflection: Implications for teacher education programming in the 21st century. *Journal of Teacher Education, 51(1)*, 39-49.

2

Action and Application

STANDARD 8: *Reflection.* Understand the importance of being a reflective practitioner and its contribution to overall professional development and actively seek opportunities to sustain professional growth.

OUTCOME 8.2: Use available resources (e.g., colleagues, literature, professional associations) to develop as a reflective professional.

While teaching students to execute an underhand serve at a learning station during volleyball class, you notice that several students are having difficulty despite numerous demonstrations and one-on-one assistance from you. Comments like "But, I did hit it off my hand" or "I didn't toss it up" are common when you attempt to help the students succeed. Realizing that tossing the ball up is a natural beginner's mistake, and realizing that everyone thinks they are doing a task correctly—even when an experienced eye detects and tries to correct a common and anticipated problem—you decide that a picture is worth a thousand words.

The next day, you set up a video recorder on a tripod at the serving station, and as the students move through the station during the next several class sessions, you record them along with comments about what they do well and how they can improve. During this time, you review each person's segment with him or her, work on correcting problems (or on strengthening the serve for those who executed well from the start), and repeat the taping and review sessions toward the end of the course to show the progress they have made. Later, you share the videos of some of the more markedly improved students at a local workshop for area physical education teachers as an example of a method they might want to try.

Teachers may stand alone in front of a classroom full of students, but they do not labor in solitude. As a physical education teacher, you already expect to be a key player on the team that is your school's faculty. But your professional ties extend beyond your campus. This begins with the fact that you believe physical education is an important part of the development of all children. You have a mission, and this makes you a member of the worldwide community of professional educators. Your formal and informal ties to other teachers place valuable teaching tools at your fingertips. And if you wish to continue to develop as a teacher, it is your responsibility to use them.

Using available resources is the essence of Outcome 8.2 of the National Standards for Beginning Physical Education Teachers, which states that teachers should use the resources available to them through colleagues, literature, and professional associations (NASPE, 2003, p. 17). These three connect you to the collective knowledge of the education community. The standards clearly state that maintaining this connection is vital to becoming a reflective teacher.

In chapter 1, you learned ways to use reflection to turn your everyday teaching experiences into an opportunity for lifelong learning. But reflection also involves looking outward. This chapter discusses ways you can draw on the resources available to you as a member of the professional community of teachers.

Later, standard 10 and chapter 5 will encourage you to become an active participant in the professional community through associations and other formal groups. These activities can enhance your career by making you a leader among your colleagues. For now, however, we will stick to a discussion of the knowledge and networks that these associations create and how you can put these resources to work in your everyday life.

YOUR PERSONAL COACH

The other professional teachers who surround you constitute a natural source for information and knowledge that can help you as you begin your career. You already know from chapter 1 about the benefits you and your colleagues can gain by forming groups to help each other focus on reflection. However, the main purpose of these groups is to prompt you to direct your inward thoughts about your teaching methods and the classroom situations you face. You can also establish relationships that approach your reflective development from a different angle.

Your supervisor is in an ideal position to act as your coach and mentor. You can start developing this kind of relationship with your supervising teacher when you are in a preservice teaching role. When you start your first professional job, an administrator or mentor can act as your coach. The challenges of a new job can be overwhelming, so remember that your success is as important to your mentor as it is to you.

As your supervisor gives you advice and evaluates your performance, engage in open and honest conversations about your progress. If you are not receiving enough feedback, take the initiative and request written evaluations or establish regular meetings with your supervisor. These assessments can help you set specific goals for your career. Take notes as you exchange information with your supervisor about your teaching efforts. You will find that this activity adds another voice to the reflective conversation that takes place within you (Goethals, Howard, & Sanders, 2004).

You can also develop as a professional by working with other teachers on collaborative projects or faculty committees. These activities enhance your professional network and provide an opportunity for you to participate in the life of your school. Harrison and Blakemore (1992) note that "far too often, physical education teachers divorce themselves from the total school environment" (p. 521). You help erase this image by contributing your leadership to schoolwide committees and activities. Even taking your turn as a cafeteria monitor can be an opportunity to reach out to your colleagues—it is perhaps not the best way to take a moment for reflection, but it can be a great way to show that you are a team player. By participating, you will also build respect for your program. Other teachers will come to see physical education as part of the school's unified goal.

CAVEATS

If improving your teaching is what you want out of your collaborative relationships with other teachers, be sure you remain focused on that goal. One study found that in order for collaboration to produce results, all parties must be tuned in to the potential benefits of sharing (Manouchehri, 2001). Collegiality among peers who share experiences produces more effective teachers (Harrison & Blakemore, 1992). This attitude of sharing and increased interdependency is particularly important to the beginning teacher. Insight, humor, and encouragement can serve to calm the nerves of the beginning teacher (Hastie, 2002). Manouchehri (2001) observed pairs of teachers who had agreed to help each other improve by observing each other at work and providing feedback. One pair succeeded, with both team members gleaning ideas for better teaching. But another pair floundered as each team member held to his belief that he alone knew how to work with his students. The pair used what could have been productive, collegial exchanges as chances to socialize instead of reflect. Teachers can collaborate in several ways. Table 2.1 provides a synopsis of collaborative levels and scenarios (Hastie, 2002, p. 342). When you establish a collaborative relationship with another teacher, be open to using the new ideas you will develop as a result of these conversations.

READING: A WAY TO STAY CURRENT

While you are in college training to become a teacher, you have instant access to the latest research about trends and practices in education. It is something your professors and fellow students talk about regularly. You also have regular access to a library and the use of instructional technology. You are also likely to be involved in class discussions and in writing research papers for your coursework. However, research

Table 2.1 Hastie's Levels of Collegiality

Level	Characteristics	Examples
Storytelling and idea scanning	• Are independent teachers. • Contact is opportunistic (e.g., need based). • Contact is sporadic and informal. • Gains information through quick exchange of stories.	• Asks, "May I use the camera?" • Offers information that a certain age group never likes to dress out.
Aiding and assisting	• Mutual aid is readily available. • Helps when asked. • Offers advice but does not interfere. • Rarely asks questions concerned with substantive teaching business.	• Offers rules and protocol explanation to beginning teacher. • Helps order equipment.
Sharing	• Shares materials and methods with open exchange of ideas and opinions. • Reveals how he or she thinks through the materials and ideas shared. • Believes in views toward noninterference or collective experimentation and mutual support.	• Lends teaching tools. • Provides ideas for successful lessons.
Working jointly	• Shares teaching responsibility. • Takes collective action or pursues a single course of action in partnership. • Decides jointly about basic priorities that guide the independent teachers. • Is motivated to work together to the point that each teacher requires the other's contributions for success in his or her own work.	• Interdisciplinary team of teachers (science/PE/health) plans an activity that will offer teaching opportunities in each area. • PE department sets priorities and procedures for evaluating students.

Reprinted from P. Hastie, 2002, *Teaching for a lifetime: Physical activity through quality high school physical education* (Upper Saddle River, NJ: Benjamin Cummings), 342.

may fade into the background when you go from sitting in a classroom to leading a classroom of your own. It will be up to you to go beyond what may be expected of you daily and to keep reading the journals and professional newsletters that you remember seeing in the library during your student years.

Reading academic journals is one way that teachers create a professional network. Reading professional journals becomes your homework as a teacher. Many journals are available online, which makes access even more convenient. Although you are not required to do this homework, making a commitment to it will enhance your teaching skills and advance your career as a teacher. As Rink (2005) points out, "Accountability for staying current comes primarily from a teacher's commitment. Rarely are teachers dismissed because they are not current" (p. 323). As a reflective teacher, you require yourself to do your homework because you believe it will make you a better teacher.

Table 2.2 presents a list of journals most commonly used by physical educators. It also includes the sponsoring agency, a brief publication description, and an agency Web address for obtaining additional information.

No one teacher can independently assess all the changes taking place in education today. Published studies and reports on physical education represent the forefront of knowledge in your field. Some of this information may not be readily applicable, and some studies may be more applicable to your individual teaching situation than others. However, all of them relate to the profession that you have chosen. Over time, your contact with professional literature will become especially important because it will keep your teaching methods fresh and up to date. A teacher who uses exactly the same methods and curricula year after year runs the risk of growing stale and complacent. As Ross, Bondy, and Kyle (1993) point out, teachers should take advantage of the vast amount of ongoing knowledge generated by researchers. Reading journals exposes you to dozens of new ideas from around the world as they emerge. By delving into this body of knowledge, you gain a far wider perspective than if you simply depend on your supervisors and colleagues for help. From your readings, you will glean great ideas that will keep your lessons lively and your students engaged.

Theory-based journal articles written by university researchers far removed from the daily realities of teaching may, at first glance, seem irrelevant to your physical education classroom. But dig further into the theories these works contain and you will find that that is not the case. Don't restrict your reading to practical studies alone. Brookfield (1995) outlines five ways in which keeping up with current theory helps reflective teachers:

Table 2.2 Academic and Professional Journals for Physical Educators

Journal	Agency	Description or focus	Web site
Adapted Physical Activity Quarterly (APAQ)	Human Kinetics	Latest research on physical activity for special populations	www.humankinetics.com/ APAQ/journalAbout.cfm
Journal of Physical Education, Recreation and Dance (JOPERD)	American Alliance for Health, Physical Education, Recreation and Dance (AAHPERD)	AAHPERD's premier journal	www.aahperd.org
Journal of Teaching in Physical Education (JTPE)	Human Kinetics	Teaching process and teacher education in PE	www.humankinetics.com/JTPE/ journalAbout.cfm
Quest	Human Kinetics	Stimulate professional development; higher education	www.humankinetics.com/QUEST/ journalAbout.cfm
Research Quarterly for Exercise and Sport	AAHPERD	Research in the art and science of human movement	www.aahperd.org/aahperd/template. cfm?template=rqes_main.html
Strategies: A Journal for Physical and Sport Educators	National Association for Sport and Physical Education	Professional journal of peer-reviewed research and information	www.aahperd.org/naspe/template. cfm?template=strategies_main.html
Teaching Elementary Physical Education (TEPE)	Human Kinetics	Journal for elementary and middle school PE specialists and teachers (discontinued; last issue December 2006)	www.humankinetics.com/ TEPE/ journalAbout.cfm

- **Theory helps us "name" our practice.** That is, it reminds you that others face the same situations that you do.
- **Theory breaks the circle of familiarity.** It reminds you that things don't always go as you expect them to or as they have in the past. It prepares you to deal with the unexpected.
- **Theory can be a substitute for absent colleagues.** By reading the perspectives of others, you can hold an imaginary conversation with them. You can examine their arguments and evaluate your own. You can take notes on your reading or scribble in the margins of your books, finding out which points get you thinking.
- **Theory prevents groupthink and improves conversation with colleagues.** Even when you are lucky enough to work with a group of people you respect and enjoy, who all share the goals of reflective teaching, it is important to be open to change. You did not become a teacher in order to always follow the crowd. Reading theory helps you bring new ideas to the conversation.
- **Theory locates our practice in a social context.** It reminds you that problems you have are not always specific to your classroom; they may be part of the overall educational system.

These are just a few ways in which reading theory will add to your effort to become a more reflective teacher. Theory has been part of your academic training because it is a valuable tool for teachers in everyday work situations.

As we outlined in the previous chapter, research cannot account for every situation you will encounter as a teacher. Dewey—coined the "father of reflection"—indicated that "the reflective process *begins with an experienced dilemma*" (in Ross et al., 1993, p. 17). Ross and colleagues (1993) define a dilemma as "a problem or problematic situation to which there is no readily identifiable correct answer" (p. 17). Your instincts should still be your first resource for dealing with a dilemma in the moment. But you will find that your reflections become better informed, and you are more able to take a bird's-eye view of problems, if you have been keeping up with the latest research and trends in your field.

In chapter 10, you will learn about using various technologies to facilitate student learning in your classroom, but it is important to mention that professional development opportunities to support your efforts to be a reflective teacher rest at your fingertips via the Internet. Web sites and listservs provide a wealth of current knowledge. A good Internet search engine can link you to these online resources.

PROFESSIONAL ASSOCIATIONS

Joining a professional association instantly makes you a member of a network of concerned educators. Typically, these organizations set standards for their members to implement in their teaching. They also provide access to newsletters and journals, teaching materials, job listings, and other useful resources. A good starting place for physical education teachers is the American Alliance for Health, Physical Education, Recreation and Dance (*AAHPERD*). This group holds national, regional, and state conferences. However, attendance at local workshops and clinics is critical, particularly for the beginning teacher. Surveys indicate that very few beginning teachers attend these valuable meetings (Harrison & Blakemore, 1992). Seeking out these events and attending them could help you find the support you need in your early years in the classroom. The importance of professional associations is discussed in greater detail in chapter 5.

ACTION RESEARCH

Working with supervisors and colleagues, reading journals connected to your field, and joining professional associations will help you build a professional network. You can secure your place in this network by conducting research within your own classroom. Professional educators call this *action research*. As a student, you read research studies conducted in academic environments and designed to contribute to your theoretical understanding of education. Teachers should interpret and act on the results of these studies in their own way as they develop their own teaching style.

Action research, though, involves setting up a structured trial or experiment with your own students and immediately acting on the results yourself. The aim is not to publish the results or make theoretical strides, but to collect information that will help you serve your students better. Richards and Lockhart (1994) say that "action research typically involves small-scale investigative projects in the teacher's own classroom" (p. 12). These projects can be particularly empowering for teachers.

Action research fits directly into the reflective cycle as described in chapter 1: plan, act, observe, and make judgments. In journal writing and other reflective activities, you mainly examine observations of your own behavior. When you begin doing action research, you continue to plan by defining a problem, act by implementing your plan, observe the results, and make judgments about the outcome. But action research is more systematic and project based than personal reflection (Ross et

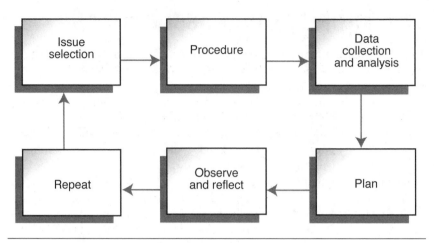

Figure 2.1   Steps for conducting action research.

al., 1993). Action research involves collecting data about your students in particular situations or on your teaching patterns and then using the results to judge how to proceed.

Action research mirrors the steps academic researchers take when setting up a study, only on a smaller and more pragmatic scale. Richards and Lockhart (1994, pp. 12-13) set forth the following steps for an action research project (see figure 2.1):

1. Select an issue or concern to examine in more detail.
2. Select a suitable procedure for collecting information about the topic.
3. Collect the information, analyze it, and decide what changes might be necessary.
4. Develop an action plan to help bring about the change in classroom behavior.
5. Observe the effects of the action plan on teaching behavior and reflect on its significance.
6. Initiate a second action cycle, if necessary.

HOW ACTION RESEARCH HELPS

Some classroom problems lend themselves to immediate reactions and simple adjustments on your part. More involved problems are candidates for the extra efforts that action research involves. Here are some examples:

- You have grouped students to allow more of them to participate in a game. But within the groups, students are losing their focus on the activity. You want to find out why the group structure diverts students' attention.

- A particular class seems apathetic toward physical education. You sense that if they had more of a stake in the lessons, they would be more enthusiastic, but you are not sure what activities will help them change their attitude.

- Your usual technique for correcting student errors seems to be hurting some students' morale. You want to find a way to help students master new skills without causing them to feel like they are failing.

You can search academic literature for case studies of teachers using action research. If you are looking for direction and are unable to find a case that exactly matches the needs of your physical education classroom, you can adopt the methods used by teachers in any subject area. The following is an example from an English Language Learners (ELL) classroom.

Watching the Learners

ELL teachers wanted to understand the learning strategies of students who were learning the language quickly and easily, so they could encourage these strategies in other students (Richards & Lockhart, 1994). They closely observed two outstanding learners in the classroom and then interviewed them about how they used their newly acquired language skills outside of class. The teachers reported that the results did not surprise them—students who were doing well reported that repetition and practice at home were helping them gain a better understanding of the subject. But confirming the value of these activities made the action research project worth it, the teachers said.

Methods of Observation

As with personal reflection, you can choose any of several methods to collect data during an action research project. Taking notes while observing activity is perhaps the simplest method of observation for collecting objective data. However, it is impractical to expect a teacher to take notes or code behaviors while teaching students to make free throws or while refereeing a volleyball game. Audiotaping or videotaping lessons, asking colleagues for help, and asking students for help are alternative ways to collect data during class without interfering with teaching (Rink, 2005). These methods were discussed in chapter 1—when your goal was to monitor your own thoughts and behaviors—and should seem familiar to you. In action research, you review the tapes or another person's collected data on the behaviors and reactions of your students.

Although you can create your own observational tools, and in some cases may need to, many tools have already been developed. Banville and Rikard (2001) offer several useful examples tailored to physical educators in their article in the *Journal of Physical Education, Recreation and Dance*—one of the journals listed earlier as an important resource available to physical educators.

- The Practice Opportunity and Success Rate recording sheet helps analyze students' experience with specific game skills.
- The Student Behavior recording sheet provides a way for you to assess whether students are on task during different parts of the lesson.
- The tally system for teacher feedback helps you categorize student questions and look for patterns.

As you begin an action research project, make your own versions of these observation tools. You can ask a class observer helping with your research to use them during class. Otherwise, you can fill them out as you watch a videotaped lesson.

All of these tools, and variations you gather from other sources, will force you to step back from your initial impressions and analyze the classroom climate more objectively. Perhaps you were tense during class and mistook one student's off-task behavior as a room full of chaos. After reviewing the lesson on video or discussing it with an observer, you might discover that things went more smoothly than you thought. There is a tendency for teachers to be too focused on the activities of the moment to spot patterns that develop. Quantified data makes these patterns stand out instantly.

PUTTING YOUR PLAN INTO ACTION

Research sometimes draws criticism because its academic nature makes it seem distant from real-world practice. Action research is entirely different; it is practical and close to home. Because you design your action research projects and carry them through to completion, you should find that they are closely related to your teaching needs every step of the way. The students you study are the same ones who will benefit from changes you make to your teaching style. The person doing the study—you—is exactly the person empowered to improve his or her physical education experience. In fact, as Watt and Watt (1999) point out, "The results of a study usually include insights into practice, and therefore it is a moral

imperative for an educator entrusted with the lives of children to implement them as soon as they become apparent" (p. 51).

After you have completed your first action research project, putting the
results to work should come naturally. However, if one project does not
provide an obvious answer to the problem you set out to solve, remember that you have other tools in your reflective-teacher's tool belt. If you
have been working alone, ask a colleague to review your action research
results. Search journals and professional newsletters for accounts of other
teachers who have worked on similar issues.

COMBINING PROFESSIONAL NETWORKING AND ACTION RESEARCH

For support during your first foray into action research, consider getting
together with a group of like-minded teachers and helping one another.
Watt and Watt (1999) found that *collaborative research groups* tend to
enhance each member's action research experience. Each member
brings a different set of knowledge and experience skills to the table,
expanding the pool of resources available to the group. Groups can
work together on a single action research project, trade roles in one
another's projects, or simply act as support for a collection of teachers
with similar goals.

ACTION RESEARCH AND PROFESSIONAL SURVIVAL

Often professional development makes the difference between success
and failure in a new job. As a part of the reflective process, action research
can help you develop the self-awareness that will ensure that you can
work independently as a teacher. Rink (2005) tells the story of a physical
education teacher who felt unable to reach her students at a low-income
school during her first year on the job. Classroom difficulties left her con-
vinced that teaching was the wrong career for her. But she remembered
that she was still learning to teach, and she used action research and
other reflective techniques to take stock of her abilities. The exercise
brought her patience and confidence, and she was able to gain control
of the classroom and make a difference in her students' lives.

Action research is a tool that reminds you of your responsibilities to
students and your professional status even as it helps you make specific
improvements to your teaching methods. If you grow comfortable using
action research, you are acknowledging that even veteran teachers never
stop learning.

USING WHAT YOU HAVE LEARNED

You have learned that reaching out to the professional teaching community is a critical part of becoming a reflective teacher. During this ongoing process, your students reap the benefits throughout the lifetime of your teaching experience. Acting on this knowledge is as simple as subscribing to a journal, scheduling a meeting with a colleague, or planning your own action research project.

Outcome 8.2 explains the goal of the National Standards for Beginning Physical Education Teachers for new teachers like you. It says that it is acceptable for a teacher to

> Use several resources such as colleagues, literature, and professional associations to develop as a reflective professional. (NASPE, 2003, p. 17)

The difference between the acceptable level and the target level, which should be your goal, is simply one of degree. The target is

> Use a *wide variety of resources* such as colleagues, literature, and professional associations on a regular basis to remain current and continue to develop as a reflective professional. (NASPE, 2003, p. 17)

There is no mystery behind this standard; it simply requires that you take advantage of the resources available to you as a professional teacher. Habit-forming use of resources becomes the point of emphasis between acceptable and target levels. Action research, in particular, demands a constant focus on self-improvement. Rather than turning to colleagues in crisis situations, or reaching for journals only when your supervisor assigns you some reading, making use of these resources becomes a regular part of your professional practice, as vital to a day at school as unlocking the door to the gymnasium. By staying in touch with the collective body of knowledge of the worldwide community of teachers, you increase your ability to handle the many challenges of teaching.

PROFESSIONAL NETWORKING, COLLABORATION, AND YOUR PORTFOLIO

Through the techniques outlined in this chapter, you should aspire to establish a professional reputation for yourself that will help you as much as anything else when you search for a new teaching position. You can get valuable references from your local liaison to a professional organization or from teachers with whom you have collaborated. Still, just as with reflective journals, you can create documented proof of your commitment to professional development and include it in your teaching portfolio.

Memberships in professional associations belong in your resume, along with references to classes or workshops you have completed through these groups. Keep careful notes on key action research projects you undertake for inclusion in your portfolio. Also include copies of the data you compile and write a brief synopsis of the results. For a microlevel version of the experience of publishing a research study, Watt and Watt (1999) recommend presenting the results of your action research to an audience. If you have formed a collaborative group to support your action research, that could be a natural place to start. You might consider inviting administrators or school board members to see a presentation on a particularly innovative classroom change that you made based on action research. Written documents associated with these presentations will translate easily into material for your portfolio. Or, you could write an article for a professional newsletter explaining your results, adding the article to your portfolio.

Embarking on the adventure of reflective teaching will surely prove beneficial to your students. But, because you will simultaneously embark on the adventure of finding a satisfying career, you should also document the otherwise hard-to-see results of your reflective practices. When you can show written proof of your reflective activities, potential employers will see that you are committed to improving as a teacher and that you have taken the initiative to develop yourself as a professional.

SUMMARY

Part of being a reflective teacher involves taking charge of your professional development. By establishing relationships with other teachers, reading current journals related to physical education, and developing your own action research projects, you demonstrate willingness to change with the times and to mature as a teacher. You have learned to reflect inwardly, using journals and other tools for self-evaluation. When you add the reflective techniques that increase your ties to the professional community of teachers, you begin to reflect outwardly as well.

Discussion Questions

1. What are some of the professional journals or other periodicals that you would put on your personal reading list?
2. Think of coaches you have known and respected. What would you look for in someone who could "coach" you through the early days of your teaching career?

3. Research a professional association on the Internet. What is required to join? What standards does the organization set forth for members?

4. Sketch out a plan for an action research project related to a problem you have encountered in the classroom. If you have not yet completed an internship or other professional experience, select a problem from your college days. Define the problem and list observational tools that you think would help you find a solution if you faced the situation as a teacher.

Professional Portfolio Contents

1. Join AAHPERD and your state affiliate. Include a copy of your membership card and state how joining this association is important to your professional growth.

2. Attend a state, regional, or national conference and include a reflection about what you learned from the experience. A picture of you and your colleagues during a session, a copy of the program cover, or a presentation you made all make great artifacts.

3. Participate in a group action research project with other physical education teachers in your school or district and implement your solution. Present your results at a local or state association workshop and place your research notes and presentation documents in your professional portfolio. Submit an article about your project and its findings to a state or national association newsletter or professional journal for publication. Include the article in your portfolio.

Key Terms

AAHPERD—Acronym for American Alliance for Health, Physical Education, Recreation and Dance, a professional organization for physical education professionals.

action research—Small-scale investigations conducted by a teacher or group of teachers in a classroom environment.

collaborative research group—A group of like-minded teachers who work together on a single action research project.

Resources

Beerens, D.R. (2000). *Evaluating teachers for professional growth.* Thousand Oaks, CA: Corwin Press.

Birmingham, C. (2003). Practicing the virtue of reflection in an unfamiliar cultural context. *Theory Into Practice, 42(3),* 188-194.

Dewey, J. (1993). *How we think: A restatement of the relation of reflective thinking to the educative process.* Chicago: Henry Regnery.

Good, J.M., & Whang, P.A. (2002). Encouraging reflection in preservice teachers through response journals. *Teacher Educator, (37)4,* 254-267.

Goodnough, K. (2001). Teacher development through action research: A case study of an elementary teacher. *Action in Teacher Education, (23)1,* 37-46.

Manouchehri, A. (2001). Collegial interaction and reflective practice. *Action in Teacher Education, (22)4,* 86-97.

References

Banville, D., & Rikard, L. (2001). Observational tools for teacher reflection. *Journal of Physical Education, Recreation & Dance, 72,* 46-49.

Brookfield, S.D. (1995). *Becoming a critically reflective teacher.* San Francisco: Josey-Bass.

Goethals, M., Howard, R., & Sanders, M. (2004). *Student teaching: A process approach to reflective practice* (2nd ed.). Upper Saddle River, NJ: Prentice Hall.

Harrison, J.M., & Blakemore, C.L. (1992). *Instructional strategies for secondary school physical education* (3rd ed.). Dubuque, IA: Brown.

Hastie, P. (2002). *Teaching for a lifetime: Physical activity through quality high school physical education.* San Francisco: Benjamin Cummings.

Manouchehri, A. (2001). Collegial interaction and reflective practice. *Action in Teacher Education, 22(4),* 86-97.

National Association for Sport and Physical Education. (2003). *National standards for beginning physical education teachers* (2nd ed.). Reston, VA: Author.

Richards, J.C., & Lockhart, C. (1994). *Reflective teaching in second language classrooms* (pp. 6-28). New York: Cambridge University Press.

Rink, J.E. (2005). *Teaching physical education for learning* (5th ed.). New York: McGraw-Hill.

Ross, D.D., Bondy, E., & Kyle, D.W. (1993). *Reflective teaching for student empowerment: Elementary curriculum and methods.* New York: Maxwell Macmillan International.

Watt, M.L., & Watt, D.L. (1999). Doing research, taking action, and changing practice with collaborative support. In M.Z. Solomon (Ed.), *The diagnostic teacher: Constructing new approaches to professional development* (pp. 48-73). New York: Teachers College Press.

3

Constructing a Professional Development Plan

STANDARD 8: *Reflection.* Understand the importance of being a reflective practitioner and its contribution to overall professional development and actively seek opportunities to sustain professional growth.

OUTCOME 8.3: Construct a plan for continued professional growth based on the assessment of personal teaching performance.

As a first-year physical education teacher, you begin to think about the career choice you have made. Looking around at the other teachers in the field and in the school in general, you begin to wonder if you will ever measure up . . . there just seems to be so much to learn and do. As a result of this reflection and filled with doubts and concerns, you schedule a meeting with your supervisor to discuss your future as an educator. Your supervisor explains that every teacher experiences the same fears but that the very best teachers develop a plan of action to continue the growth and learning process. Your supervisor suggests that you spend some time thinking about the type of teacher you would like to be and suggests that you set professional goals along a timeline, researching ways to achieve those goals. Offering to help, your supervisor schedules a few meetings to get you started on a professional development plan, helping you to determine and set short- and long-term goals, learn how to periodically evaluate your progress (making changes if needed), and research appropriate organizations and reading materials to enhance your professional growth.

Any veteran teacher knows that a long career will take you in directions you cannot imagine when you are just starting out. But what if some of those surprises are the unpleasant kind?

- After eight years of service to his school, one teacher decided he would like to try for an administrative job. But he needed a master's degree and found that going back to school full time would put his family under extreme financial strain.
- Another teacher stayed at her university to start a master's program immediately after finishing her undergraduate degree. She thought the second diploma would help her earn more money at her first job. But because she lacked experience, she found that the first job offers she got didn't live up to her expectations.

Your career in education will require you to take various steps in professional development, either to work your way toward a promotion or pay raise, or just to keep your skills current. Over time, your goals and interests may change, and life will bring you some surprises. The more you plan to keep your current pursuits in sync with your long-term goals, the less likely it is that you will end up on the wrong path. This is the aim of making a professional development plan: identifying the steps you will need to take to get where you want to go.

Breaking down tasks into small steps helps us tackle problems from paying bills to planning major projects like college applications, job searches, and research studies. The same holds true when you plan your career as a professional physical education teacher. It takes years to get where you want to be. You can stay in control of the process by outlining the steps that will lead you to comprehensive professional development.

You have now learned a variety of techniques for improving your ability to teach. In chapter 1, you learned to reflect on your teaching experience to help you master the techniques and develop the philosophy that will guide you throughout your career. Chapter 2 discussed the importance of strengthening your ties to the professional teaching community. All of the techniques mentioned so far are part of a larger goal. Living up to the National Standards for Beginning Physical Education Teachers means more than just meeting requirements so you can check them off a list. It means bringing your skills in line with those that experts consider vital to the physical education of our youth. It is a way to work toward consistent excellence in physical education across school borders and to help individual teachers feel competent, fulfilled, and successful.

This chapter asks you to synthesize what you have learned about the standards into a comprehensive plan for your own professional development. In doing so, you will meet the third component of Standard 8. You will learn where you stand in your efforts to gain certification by national and state organizations. You will review how looking inward at your own progress and outward at the principles of the teaching community are both important to becoming a successful professional.

WHAT TO EXPECT

No two teachers will follow the same career path. However, researchers have identified a set of stages that describes teachers at different moments in their careers (Lynn, 2002). This set is not a linear progression, even though teachers may move through several of the stages; and although some lead to others, there is no predictable sequence. The stages are as follows:

- Preservice: before embarking on a teaching career for the first time or before starting a different type of job
- Induction: the *socialization* phase, in which a new teacher's colleagues informally educate him on the practices of the school community

- Competency building: a teacher's early years, when she is still feeling new in the profession; the teacher's ability to build confidence is critical to her later success and satisfaction
- Enthusiasm and growth: the teacher is established in his job but pursues learning opportunities to keep his skills fresh and his enthusiasm building
- Career frustration: internal or external pressures cause frustration and mixed emotions; may lead to burnout
- Career stability: teacher remains dedicated and hardworking, but makes less of an effort to enhance her portfolio
- Career wind-down: preparing for retirement or the end of a particular teaching position; the teacher remains excited about the profession but definitely feels that it is time to move on
- Career exit: the teacher leaves the classroom and moves into administration or leaves the profession altogether; may be involuntary

State requirements see to it that all teachers complete a certain level of continuing education. Beyond that, though, teachers in the various phases need different types of professional development. Someone experiencing career frustration may need an intense reexamination of his or her reasons for becoming a teacher or may possibly need a job change in order to continue teaching. But someone in the enthusiasm and growth stage probably could benefit more from professional development work that brings in new ideas to build on past successes.

You are now in the preservice phase, already spending most of your time on training and preparing to teach. The most important professional development activity you can do now is to plan for your future goals.

GETTING STARTED

Get out your notebook and pencil, or fire up your laptop. We encourage you to begin work immediately—as you read—on a written draft of a professional development plan for yourself.

Planning your future strengthens your status as a professional. As Harrison and Blakemore (1992) point out, "Every teacher should develop a personal plan for professional development . . . continuous updating of skills by each teacher should be a matter of professional pride, whether required or not" (p. 64).

Your school or district may very well require you to demonstrate that you have a plan for continuing your education by attending workshops or taking tests. But having a plan of your own puts you in charge. And having a written document to provide evidence of the plan comes with its own advantages. You could use the document in your portfolio. Even if you do not choose to share it with potential employers, it will serve as a constant reminder to you of where you want to take your teaching career. Writing the plan will help solidify all the goals you have set based on reflection, self-assessment, research, collaboration, and professional networking.

For starters, compile the activities you have done based on your reading in the previous chapters. Do you have written self-evaluations? Have you been keeping a reflective journal? Do you have audiotapes or videos of yourself teaching that you have used to observe yourself in action? Have you completed and documented an action research project? Gather your written records of these activities and review them.

Documents such as these provide a record of your past commitment to self-improvement. Your next task is to provide evidence that you will continue this development in the future. Based on your experience and review of your materials, choose a classroom problem you would like to investigate further, a new skill or technology you would like to master, or an action research project you would like to start. It should relate to proving yourself as a talented, committed teacher who can get students excited about learning. Writing down your plan shows that you intend to accomplish something.

If you stick with your professional development plan through the years, you may often work on your own. However, early in your teaching career, try to work on it with a mentor if possible. For starters, a more experienced teacher can reassure you as you work through challenges. As a beginning teacher you will experience both successes and failures on a daily basis because you will be trying new approaches and using recently acquired skills. You will need assistance and guidance in order to provide the best possible educational experience for your students, so do not be afraid to ask for help.

You will also need an outside observer when it comes time to evaluate your progress. You may want to make the person who will evaluate you a partner in the design and creation of your professional development plan.

Goethals, Howard, and Sanders (2004, p. 196) outline a simple framework, explained below, for writing a professional development plan. You can apply this framework to a change you want to make in the classroom or to a teaching skill you would like to learn for yourself. Organize your plan according to the following steps:

1. List one professional development goal for increasing the level of learner expectations that you set for yourself.

    Classroom example: Choose a new activity to incorporate into your classes.

    Skill example: Choose to learn a new technological skill so you can become a more effective teacher.

2. Name the evidence you will use to determine the level of growth made toward reaching the goal.

> **Classroom example:** Begin working the activity into your lesson plans. Define the end goal for the project—the point at which you can demonstrate that you have fully integrated the new activity. Come up with a system to evaluate the students' experience with the new activity.

> **Skill example:** Decide how you will use the new technology once you have learned it. Begin planning lessons that will allow the students to take advantage of your new skill.

3. Determine a timeline you will use for performing these activities.

> **Classroom example:** Make specific plans for using the new activity and conducting assessments. Decide to use the results to plan future lessons.

> **Skill example:** Determine how long it will take you to acquire the new technology skill and decide when you will be able to begin using it in the classroom.

4. Name the external monitors that will provide feedback on progress made toward the professional goals.

> **Classroom example:** Ask a supervisor to monitor your project. Compile written records of the students' progress.

> **Skill example:** Find out if you can take a test or obtain a certification to demonstrate your newly acquired skill. Ask someone with advanced experience to evaluate your progress.

This framework, just one example of how to compose a professional development plan, can help you plan for real progress in your professional life. You direct the entire process by choosing new skills based on your personal experience and setting your own course for learning.

You probably find it easy to get excited about choosing new skills to bring to your classroom. Monitoring your effectiveness, though, is a more ambiguous process. The assessment component of your professional development plan is one area where a mentor or partner can help you. The Florida Department of Education (1995) outlines three goal-setting strategies that clinical educators and new teachers can use together to track progress in a professional development plan.

- Management by objectives: This strategy uses periodic performance reviews between you and your clinical educator or mentor to evaluate progress toward goals the two of you set.

- Top-down goal setting: In this approach, your mentor takes the lead, conducting evaluations, informing you of your strengths and weaknesses, and setting a professional development plan for you.

Inexperienced teachers or those needing specific direction in a new skill may benefit from this approach.

- Self-assessment goal setting: This method calls for you to take the lead, assessing yourself and outlining your own goals and strategies for reaching them. Your mentor remains involved by supervising the process. More experienced or self-motivated teachers may prefer this approach.

Key components of any professional development plan, whether you work alone or with a mentor, are *goals, objectives, a timeline,* and *assessment* (see figure 3.1). You should determine your goals: broad outlines

---

Name: Mark Turner

School: Louise S. McGehee Middle School

Assignment: 7th grade math

Goal: To increase teachers' effectiveness in managing and monitoring student behavior

Objectives	Activities to meet objectives	Resources to meet objectives	Anticipated completion date	Activity assessment
Increase percent of students at task through teacher use of preventive, support, and corrective behaviors from January to May.	1. Attend teacher training.	1. In-service registration		Increased use of effective teaching behavior, including • questions (clarity and level), • follow-up, • distributed response opportunity, and • effective desists.
	2. Attend Assertive Discipline training.	2. Subs for assertive discipline	January–February	
	3. Visit experienced teacher: Kathy Sequino.	3. DH schedule visits, arrange coverage	March	
	4. Audiotape and analyze questions and response patterns.	4. Audiotapes	March	
	5. Engage in four coaching cycles.	5. Coaches: Douglas, Madison	Cycles: 1. January 2. March 3. April 4. June	

Figure 3.1   A sample professional development plan.

of where you want to take your career. To help you reach your goals, you can break them down into objectives: specific, measurable steps that support your goals. To keep yourself accountable, set a timeline for making your goals a reality and conduct assessments that help you decide if your efforts have been effective.

The imperative for planning doesn't just come from your own ideas and ambitions. As you know, teachers must respond to the demands and needs of students, parents, and society at large. Physical education teachers especially face a challenge in today's society to draw attention to the importance of physical education in the curriculum. They must work against the currents of sedentary lifestyles and unhealthy eating habits to help promote lifelong fitness habits among students. You should expect to adapt constantly to changing conditions.

Change happens within the walls of your own school, too. When you were in school, did your gym have a climbing wall? Did teachers consider using computers, VCRs, CD-ROMs, DVD players, digital cameras, and PDAs in physical education class? Did they work with other teachers to plan interdisciplinary experiences for the students? Did schools have specific plans to include students with disabilities?

Years ago, some of these ideas may have seemed unrealistic. Today, they are just a few of the many innovations taking place in school gyms around the world. Don't let them take you by surprise. Through conscious planning, you can ensure that your students have the best, most up-to-date physical education possible, and that you are prepared to lead them to it.

You can also use the framework described earlier to plan for longer-term personal goals. After you have grown comfortable in the classroom, you may want to take your career in new directions. You might like to earn a specialized certificate or a master's degree to enhance your standing at your school. You could learn a new language to help educate your students and reach out to a changing school population. You may have the opportunity to expand your school's athletic program to incorporate new facilities. You could decide to become an advocate for students with disabilities. One day, you might want to begin working toward an administrative position. The framework helps you outline your ambitious, multiyear projects as well as the smaller changes you intend to accomplish within a single term.

USING REFLECTION TO OFFER MORE IN THE CLASSROOM

Looking back at things you have learned while teaching will help you choose the career areas in which you want to grow. Outcome 8.3 of the National Standards for Beginning Physical Education Teachers (NASPE,

2003) states that teachers should begin planning for professional growth *based on the assessment of personal teaching performance.* There should be no surprises for you here; this simply means that the self-assessment methods outlined in the previous chapters belong in the context of long-term professional growth. Self-assessment methods are not only useful for solving your day-to-day problems but also for helping you develop over time. They relate directly to your ability to give your students the best possible physical education.

Here is an example of how your professional plan can make the best use of the other reflective activities you have learned so far. Suppose that you have noticed that students in one of your middle school physical education classes perform as though they get very little physical activity outside of school. You have recognized this problem for some time and have written about it in your journal. But on your own, the only solution you can think of is to talk to the students more often about the importance of developing healthy behaviors for a lifetime. Your own opinions and anecdotes do not seem to be getting through to them, and you are not sure how to encourage them to become active outside of the gym. The problem simmers in the back of your mind until, while catching up on your reading, you notice an article about the same topic. One example comes from the May/June 2003 issue of the *Journal of Physical Education, Recreation and Dance,* in which Smith and Claxton suggest the use of homework in physical education. They describe the positive results of a study in which physical education teachers sent their students home with short assignments for simple activities meant to get them off the couch.

Based on your reading of the professional journal, you decide to try giving homework. You design and conduct a small action research project based on the study from the article. You evaluate the results and find that there are pros and cons to the homework assignment. On the positive side, many students complete the homework and enjoy it. On the negative side, some students tell you they do not have the equipment to practice with at home, and you hear from some parents that their children already struggle to get homework done in their crowded schedules. The results help you narrow your list of possible activities and recommend realistic time commitments. You target the homework program to the students' needs. Over time, the students get more enjoyment and benefit out of your physical education class.

This reflective activity and action research project clearly helped you deliver better results for your students. It could also take you to an even higher level by becoming part of your professional development plan. Suppose the project awakens your interest in teaching lifetime activities in physical education class, where previously you focused on organized team sports and group games? You could write a plan for acquiring more skills in teaching lifetime activities and revamp your physical education curriculum to provide a more equitable environment for all students. In this example, your classroom experience led you directly to a new stage in your professional development. You not only followed a problem through to one possible solution, but you also used the experience as a jumping-off point for future endeavors.

CERTIFICATION

A key goal of your professional development is becoming a certified teacher. Your professional development plan should help you consider your reflective activities as part of the path to *certification* or *recertification*. Your own pursuit of a teaching degree will guide you through the requirements for obtaining a teaching certificate in your own state.

Current education policy places a great deal of value on certification and accreditation procedures. Sometimes they may seem like bureaucratic hurdles, but they are driven by society's demand for skilled, progressive teachers. They also result from the ongoing discussion of bringing greater professionalism to education by setting standards for all teachers. The National Association for Sport and Physical Education (NASPE) sets standards for physical education as part of an effort to make programs more important and more consistent from one school to the next—a goal you probably support.

As Ryan and Cooper (2004) point out, certifications and *continuing-education* requirements relate directly to the concept of teachers as continuous learners. As a reflective teacher, you already share that goal. All that remains is for you to prove to the licensing body that you are a professional teacher, and you will get a stamp of approval for your efforts. The state's approval will allow you to have the job you want.

State tests and standards for professional teachers place a great deal of emphasis on teachers' planning skills. South Carolina's ADEPT standards and Florida's Educator Accomplished Practices (see Resources), which all student teachers must meet in order to have a chance at full-time employment, are an extremely detailed set of expectations for teacher competence. Long- and short-range instructional planning plays a major role in the standards because planning is an inescapable part of teaching. New Jersey and other states encourage professionalism using their own sets of standards.

Assuming that you have a clear plan for what to do with your students, it should be easy for you to transfer those skills to setting expectations for your own professional life. If it helps you get your thoughts on paper, imagine that your professional development plan is nothing more than a large, long-range set of lesson plans for yourself.

NATIONAL CERTIFICATION: PART OF YOUR PLAN?

After you have become an established physical educator, you may wish to pursue a voluntary national certification, such as that offered by the National Board for Professional Teaching Standards (www.nbpts.org). This program requires at least three years of experience, so it's not something to try for—or worry about—immediately. But if it is among your goals, you should begin setting high standards for yourself early in your career, even as soon as your first student-teaching position. Ryan and Cooper (2004) explain that this is a great self-motivation technique, because setting high standards provides focus and direction.

National certification, although designed as a mark of prestige, is a matter of controversy among professional teachers, according to Ryan and Cooper (2004). On the plus side, achieving national certification means that your skills gain nationwide recognition—your "stamp of approval" becomes a passport stamp that helps you cross state borders. However, some see national certification as an insulating mechanism, creating a network of "insiders" and undermining teachers' connections to their students, students' parents, schools, and local communities. Either way, the national certification program is at least causing the education community to reflect on what makes teachers professionals in the same sense as other licensed, skilled workers.

And, no matter what type of license or certification you pursue, you should view the process as a professional activity that can help you improve your teaching, even as you demonstrate your skills to the accrediting body. Thus, seeking certification is more than gaining the approval of others. Going through the process can also help you look inward at your personal progress.

PLANS THAT EXCEL

The National Standards for Beginning Physical Education Teachers set two levels of achievement for Standard 8.3 (NASPE, 2003). Both levels assume you have composed your professional development plan. The difference between the target of this standard and what is merely acceptable is the depth of the self-assessment you use in creating your plan.

To reach the acceptable level, according to the standards, a teacher should

> Effectively assess personal teaching performance and develop a professional development plan based on these data. (NASPE, 2003, p. 17)

Going for the target means a teacher should

> Routinely assess teaching behaviors and relate these data to student outcomes in developing a plan for professional growth. (NASPE, 2003, p. 17)

Assessing your own performance will put you on your way to the target. Getting all of the way there involves, first, engaging in this process regularly. Just as you worked in chapter 1 on integrating reflective activities into your schedule, you should set aside time to add to your professional development plan. As before, you could regularly schedule this type of planning, but don't hesitate to pick up your plan and add to it whenever inspiration strikes.

Even more significant, it involves assessing the way your teaching gets through to your students. This is the highest goal of professional development. You may learn to understand your teaching inside and out, and you may come to enjoy the process of reflecting and fine-tuning your technique. But if you lose focus on student outcomes, you miss the whole point of teacher education, and teaching in general.

Another factor that makes student outcomes vital to your professional development plan is the increasing prevalence of teacher accountability programs in public schools. More and more states are grading teachers based on their students' performance as a way to assure parents that they are placing their children in good hands. You have a responsibility to create a quality experience for your students and to be able to prove it to an audience of outsiders.

Your passion for physical education has already led you to pursue your teaching career. To thrive in it, you will have to live up to these assessments, and that means making sure your teaching makes a difference in students' lives. Keep the standards' emphasis on student outcomes in mind as you write in your reflective journal or plan action research projects designed to assess and improve your skills.

As you may know from your studies of NASPE Standard 7, methods for assessing student performance abound. They generally fall into one of three broad categories, according to Morocco and Solomon (1999): asking questions of students, observing students at work, and examining student results. Within those categories, you will find various tools for gathering data and examining results.

The previous chapters outlined student assessment methods in the context of action research and reflective journaling. It is easy to see how these tools relate to analyzing an individual problem. What you need to remember is that they also relate to your professional development. As Morocco and Solomon (1999) point out,

Assessment tools can play a critical role—by redirecting teachers' focus away from a predetermined pedagogical strategy to an appreciation for what students understand, believe, can and cannot do or for what students may find confusing, interesting, or productively puzzling. (p. 253)

Student assessments turn your attention inward, to your own teaching methods, and outward, to the results of your work. They encourage you to focus on what you are learning as well as what the students have learned.

DON'T GO IT ALONE

Professional development planning is another area in which your colleagues can be vital partners in your success. If you are gathering with other teachers for a reflective-journal group or to share in an action research project or work with others in a professional association, you already know how important it is to work with people who also believe in themselves as professionals. Allow the same collegial spirit to help you plan for future professional growth. Discuss your professional development plans—new skills you want to acquire, new dimensions of classroom activity—with your colleagues, just as you would discuss your work on school business or your efforts to fix a discipline problem. You will share insights that bring your personal goals into focus.

Trends in current research support the value of collegial interaction among teachers. According to Nelson (1999),

Part of the work of teaching, redefined, is to continually question, critique and explore ways to interpret the meaning of what happens in the classroom and to develop the next instructional step. This is best done with colleagues who share the enterprise. (p. 10)

Your partners in professional development need not share your specific experiences. Again, as a physical education teacher, you will often work alone. It is important, though, that they share your interests in reflection and professional growth. You and your colleagues can be there for one another outside the classroom, during moments of constructive reflection. Working with others who share your educational values, if not your specialty, helps you see the common bonds among all teachers, which helps you decide where you want to go as a professional.

The quest for certification is another area in which it is vital that you develop a relationship with a mentor. Your professors and your supervising and cooperating teachers are leading candidates, naturally, but any experienced teacher whom you trust can help you. Look to your mentor regularly as you navigate the often-complex certification process. It helps to have a guide who has been through the same steps before.

YOUR PLAN IN YOUR PORTFOLIO

Written proof of your plans to develop yourself as a professional educator belongs in your teaching portfolio for all potential employers to see. When compiling your portfolio, include a brief written version of your professional development plan, outlining skills you plan to acquire and directions you plan to take in the next few years. This is not the only way to document your professional endeavors, though. Other possibilities, suggested in Drake and McBride (2000), include a list of professional development activities, examples of students' work, evidence of extracurricular and community service activities, and letters from teaching colleagues and supervisors.

SUMMARY

By aspiring to meet the National Standards for Beginning Physical Education Teachers, you have set yourself on the path toward becoming a true professional. You stand a better chance of reaching that goal if you plan for it step-by-step. Planning your professional development and documenting the goals you want to reach and the steps that will take you there enhance the way you present yourself to the community of professional educators. And most important of all, they underscore your commitment to being the best possible teacher for your students.

Teaching is not a job that you can put aside at the end of the day. Without critical reflection, you run the risk of stagnating in your job, leaving yourself jaded and your students deprived of the joy of a good physical education. The same applies to your career. Unless you remain aware of where you want to go and what skills you need to acquire along the way, your professional development will be incremental and haphazard. Planning is the dynamic way to manage your career. You have already found yourself attracted to the teaching profession for its service potential and for the pure enjoyment of working with young learners. As a professional teacher, you have an obligation to keep learning.

Professional development aims at improving your students' experiences and originates from the same source. To summarize Goethals and colleagues (2004), you derive your plans for improving and growing as a teacher from your personal expectations and classroom experiences, particularly the dilemmas you have chosen to solve using your reflective abilities. In effect, the students teach you how to make yourself a better teacher.

Discussion Questions

1. What different steps will help you advance in your career, depending on where you want to end up in the far future? Construct two alternative professional development plans for the next 20 years. What would you do differently if you want to become a school administrator versus continuing as a classroom teacher? What about if you want to become a professor?
2. Research the steps involved in obtaining a national teaching certification. How could they help you develop a framework for writing your professional development plan?
3. Professional educators sometimes disagree about the value of national teacher certification programs. Discuss the pros and cons of these assessments. What is the most important intent of these programs? If you are not interested in obtaining a national board certificate, how else can you demonstrate professionalism?
4. Make a list of professional teaching standards from your state, the National Board for Professional Teaching Standards, and professional associations of your choosing. Organize it in a chart and compare the different sources. What standards seem to be important across the board? What differences do you notice?

Professional Portfolio Contents

1. Include reflections you have written from a variety of practicum classes (elementary, middle, high school, adapted) where you have discussed how you see yourself continuing to improve in a specific area.
2. Include copies of observation instruments that you have used or had a peer use to gather data on a teaching behavior and a reflection on how the information was used in subsequent lessons.
3. Develop a five-year plan of action, reflecting on where you want to be in five years in your teaching career. Include such factors as teaching emphasis, position, and salary as part of setting your goals. Once you have determined where you would like to be professionally in five years, construct a timeline in annual increments showing the tasks you should complete to obtain your goal (like stepping stones) to help you build toward success. For example, your tasks may include research, certifications, continuing education, recertification requirements, and membership in professional associations. Include this in your portfolio and keep your plan and your timeline in a handy, easy-to-review place on your computer or in your day-timer with critical tasks and dates earmarked. Review and act on them regularly.

Key Terms

certification, recertification, and continuing education—An ongoing professional development process by which a trained teacher receives accreditation and meets ongoing professional requirements related directly to the concept of teachers as continuous learners.

professional development plan—A series of steps set along a timeline to achieve specific goals toward developing as a professional teacher.

Resources

Elmore, R.F. (1997). *Investing in teacher learning: Staff development and instructional improvement in community school district #2, New York City.* New York: National Commission on Teaching and America's Future.

Florida Educator Accomplished Practices: www.firn.edu/doe/dpe/publications/preprofessional4-99.pdf

New Jersey Core Curriculum Content Standards: www.state.nj.us/njded/cccs/s2_chpe.htm

South Carolina Department of Education (ADEPT teaching standards): www.scteachers.org/adept/perfdim.cfm

Sparks, D. & Hirsh, S. (1999). *A national plan for improving professional development.* National Staff Development Council. Retrieved June 2, 2005, from www.nsdc.org/library/authors/NSDCPlan.cfm

References

Drake, F., & McBride, L. (2000). The summative teaching portfolio and the reflective practitioner of history. *History Teacher, 34(1),* 41-60.

Florida Department of Education, Division of Human Resource Development. (1995). *PD plans: Design/implementation.* Clinical Educators Training Trainers' Guide. Tallahassee, FL: Florida Department of Education.

Goethals, M., Howard, R., & Sanders, M. (2004). *Student teaching: A process approach to reflective practice* (2nd ed.). Upper Saddle River, NJ: Prentice Hall.

Harrison, J.M, & Blakemore, C.L. (1992). *Instructional strategies for secondary school physical education* (3rd ed.). Dubuque, IA: Brown.

Lynn, S.K. (2002). The winding path: Understanding the career cycle of teachers. *Clearing House, 75(4),* 179-182.

Morocco, C.C., & Solomon, M.Z. (1999). Revitalizing professional development. In M.Z. Solomon (Ed.), *The diagnostic teacher: Constructing new approaches to professional development* (pp. 247-267). New York: Teachers College Press.

National Association for Sport and Physical Education. (2003). *National standards for beginning physical education teachers* (2nd ed.). Reston, VA: Author.

Nelson, B.S. (1999). Reconstructing teaching: Interactions among changing beliefs, subject-matter knowledge, instructional repertoire, and professional culture in the process of transforming one's teaching. In M.Z. Solomon (Ed.), *The diagnostic teacher: Constructing new approaches to professional development* (pp. 1-21). New York: Teachers College Press.

Ryan, K., & Cooper, J. (2004). *Those who can, teach* (10th ed.). New York: Houghton Mifflin.

Smith, M., & Claxton, D. (2003). Using active homework in physical education. *Journal of Physical Education, Recreation & Dance, 74(5),* 28-33.

II

Collaboration

An educator must develop an awareness of and preparation for the collaboration that is necessary for successful, equitable, and diverse education. A physical educator must not only understand how to advocate but must also understand how to collaborate. Advocacy and collaboration are enhanced by clear communication, with the result offering a strengthened teaching and learning environment with new resources, increased community involvement, and valued relationships. Chapter 4 discusses the development of advocacy skills. We are eternal advocates, and embracing that role will enhance our success. Chapter 5 introduces the value of participating in the professional community and personal professional development. We must realize that active participation will produce a wonderful opportunity for idea exchanges and greater understanding of the political climate and the strength gained by collaborative efforts. Chapter 6 encourages the use of community resources. When we reach beyond traditional relationships, we frequently discover new resources, partnerships, and program-enriching experiences. Chapter 7 recognizes the importance of establishing productive relationships in the school with students, faculty, and staff and in the greater school community with parents, administrators, and community members. Acknowledging the reality that the learning experience is not limited to that which takes place within the school walls will contribute to many successful collaborative initiatives.

CHAPTER

4

Developing Advocacy Skills

STANDARD 10: *Collaboration.* Understand the necessity of fostering collaborative relationships with colleagues, parents/guardians, and community agencies to support the development of a physically educated person.

OUTCOME 10.1: Identify strategies to become an advocate in the school and community to promote a variety of physical activity opportunities.

Some of the fourth-grade parents, students, teachers, and the art teacher painted a huge map of the United States on the playground with paint and supplies donated by a local paint company. This was all done in response to the fourth-grade teachers, who indicated that they were having problems helping some of the students learn the names and capitals of the states. They were especially concerned about the students they thought were kinesthetic learners. You developed physical activities using the map to help the students learn about the states. Following this unit of study, the teachers agreed that the map proved to be a great learning aid, not only for the kinesthetic learners but also for other types of learners. It also raised interest among the other students.

The fourth-grade teachers shared the instructions for making the map and the movement activities at their next district teachers' in-service training. A certificate was sent to the owners of the paint company to thank them for helping with the educational activity. This collaborative effort involved parents, students, special-area teachers, and grade-level teachers, as well as a community partner. The project also enhanced the learning process for all fourth graders.

As a teacher, you cannot expect other teachers and community members to advocate for your physical education program if you are not willing to advocate and are not seen as an effective advocate for your own program. Although there is an inherent difference between physical education and physical activity, the two concepts and activities are certainly not mutually exclusive. As an advocate for a variety of physical activity opportunities for your students throughout the community, you will provide children with multiple opportunities to become or stay fit. The more physically active your students are outside of your classroom, the more you can challenge them in your class. Often the community only connects preparedness for grade-level expectations with academic courses and activities such as reading and math. Typically, schools have volunteer classroom assistants, mentors, and PTA activists providing assistance to the core-curricular teachers.

Beginning and experienced physical education teachers must assume responsibility for helping to ensure that every school has a high-quality physical education program. As a beginning teacher, you must be proactive from the moment you teach your first physical education class. First impressions with your students and fellow teachers will define and shape the stature of physical education in your school. Regardless of a situation in your new school where the physical education program does not have a positive reputation, it is essential that you establish yourself as a quintessential professional by implementing exemplary lesson plans and an advocacy program. You must be willing and able to effectively advocate for high-quality physical education in your school. You must advocate for needed equipment, space, classroom assistance, and other issues that will improve the quality of your program. The quality of your advocacy initiatives will be commensurate with the effort that you put into them. Advocacy is the responsibility of all PE teachers. Ask yourself, "If I don't or won't make time to advocate for my own profession and program, how can I expect other teachers and school community members to advocate for my programs and profession?"

By the inclusion of Outcome 10.1 ("identify strategies to become an advocate in the school and community to promote a variety of physical activity opportunities") as part of Standard 10 (Collaboration) in the National Standards for Beginning Physical Education Teachers (NASPE, 2003), the importance of advocacy is codified. As physical educators, we have not traditionally or consistently seen ourselves as advocates for programs beyond our physical education classes. However, this practice can no longer continue. Outcome 10.1 demands that you advocate for physical activity opportunities for students beyond your classroom. Your ability to advocate for additional opportunities depends on your perceived efforts and abilities to advocate for your own program. If you cannot and do not successfully advocate for your own physical education program, you cannot expect members of the community or school to support your advocacy for additional programs.

Successful teachers, in addition to everything they are asked to do, must also successfully market or build support for their programs (Graham, Parker, & Holt-Hale, 2004). Advocating for your own physical education program may seem overwhelming. You are probably thinking, "How can I possibly advocate for additional physical activity opportunities in my school and community?" The good news is that there are many resources to help you identify effective advocacy strategies that can work in your school and community.

WHAT IS ADVOCACY?

Advocacy is communication for the purpose of influencing others about an issue, idea, or concern that is meaningful to you. When you advocate, you seek to influence the attitudes of others in planned and organized ways. Ultimately, you hope to motivate others to action.

Several national, state, and local associations have developed advocacy kits that you can tailor to meet your needs. For example, the National Association for Sport and Physical Education (NASPE) and the National Coalition for Promoting Physical Activity (NCPPA) have produced tools and advocacy kits that can help you as a physical education teacher effectively promote your program (see figure 4.1, p. 69). However, keep in mind that the basis for successful advocacy is having and sustaining an effective physical education program and providing multiple physical activity opportunities for your students. Without an effective program you have nothing for which to advocate.

SIX KEY COMPONENTS OF EFFECTIVE ADVOCACY ACTION

Even though it may seem a bit overwhelming to begin thinking about becoming an advocate for your own program as a beginning teacher, you only need to learn a few basics in order to be prepared to begin designing an advocacy program. This section of the book introduces you to the process, introduces new terms, and provides a sample action plan in table 4.1 (p. 74). The Association of Research Libraries (ARL) (2003) defines advocacy as "organized influence," influencing "the attitudes of others in planned and organized ways" (p. 1). Thus, the following information provides the foundation for your future as an advocate. According to ARL (2003), the following are key to developing an effective advocacy action plan:

1. Clearly define your goals and objectives.
2. Identify your target audience.
3. Gather data for your message.
4. Create a persuasive message.
5. Identify potential action strategies.
6. Review and revise.

Clearly Define Your Goals and Objectives

Goals should be directed toward a vision and be consistent with the mission. Goals are desirable expectations of future accomplishments. Goals are general statements of intent that are usually of a long-term nature and are not stated in measurable terms. For example, physical education instructional goals might include the following:

- Students will demonstrate competency in many movement forms and proficiency in a few movement forms.

- Students will apply movement concepts and principles to the learning and development of motor skills.
- Students will exhibit a physically active lifestyle.

Thus, physical education advocacy goals could include the following:

- My school community (parents, teachers, administrators, and community members) will articulate and support the concept that physical education plays a critical role in educating the whole student.
- An increased number of students will participate in physical education classes and other physical activity opportunities.

An *objective* is a specific measurable result expected within a particular time period, consistent with a goal and strategy. In other words, an objective is a clear "milepost" along the strategically chosen path to a goal. An objective is measurable and should be developed to directly address specific causes of problems identified in the needs assessment data. A measurable objective is sharply defined with no extraneous information, has measurable outcomes (results) rather than processes, and is written to be accomplished within a defined time period. Make sure you develop and utilize SMART objectives in your advocacy endeavor:

Specific—What exactly is supposed to happen to whom?

Measurable—How will I know it happened? (What gets measured gets done, and, typically, what gets measured is valued.)

Attainable—Could this happen in my school and community?

Realistic—Is it possible to make it happen?

Time bound—When will it happen?

The recognition of school physical education's contributions to health led to the inclusion of two objectives related to school physical education in Healthy People 2000, the U.S. Department of Health and Human Services' national health objectives (2001):

Objective 1.8—Increase to at least 50 percent the proportion of children and adolescents in grades 1 through 12 who participate in daily school physical education.

Objective 1.9—Increase to at least 50 percent the proportion of school physical education class time that students spend being physically active, preferably engaged in lifetime physical activities.

These objectives do not meet all of the SMART objectives. They do not identify a time frame by which the objectives should be accomplished. These objectives could easily be revised by adding a time frame in the beginning of the objective. For example, adding "By 2010," to the beginning of Objective 1.8 allows plenty of time to accomplish the objective, yet conveys that the objective is expected to be met in a timely fashion.

As a physical education teacher, you may want to ask yourself questions like these: What do I want to happen as a result of our advocacy program? How can I increase enrollment and ensure the successful completion of students in our school's physical education programs? How can I provide additional opportunities for increased participation in physical activities by our students? How can I increase students' awareness of current physical education and physical activity opportunities? How can I convey the added value of a successful physical education program and increased physical activities for students to my students, parents, school staff, and the community?

Many worthy goals and objectives could frame and drive your advocacy program. However, to create a successful advocacy program it is essential that you prioritize and target critical goals and objectives. It is better to implement a small, targeted advocacy program and accomplish your goals than to implement a broad-based advocacy program where you try to do too much and end up spreading yourself too thin and failing. Keep focused on your advocacy objectives and don't get bogged down in debates on peripheral issues. It is your responsibility as a beginning teacher to get a handle on the political hot buttons in your school. For example, recently there has been debate in many school districts on whether vending machines should contain only healthy items, such as water and dried fruit, a combination of healthy items, or any items as determined by the principal. Although this is an important issue, you need to assess how much of your own political capital and time you can spend on this issue while pursuing your advocacy goals and objectives. This does not mean that you should not be engaged and voice your opinion on the issue; it simply means that you must choose your battles. If you take on every issue, it is likely you will not do justice to any issue.

Identify Your Target Audience

To identify your target audience you need to be able to answer three basic questions: (1) Whom are you trying to influence? (2) Will you focus on one group more than another? and (3) How will your audience shape your advocacy program? Graham and colleagues (2004) identified seven related populations who need to be aware of and supportive of your program: the school administration, especially the principal; other teachers in the school; parents; the school board; the community at large; legislators; and in some instances the students. In addition to these populations, other potential target audiences for your advocacy plan could include community partners such as the YMCA, Big Brothers Big Sisters, local after-school youth programs, and city and county recreation departments.

Work in coalitions and cultivate unconventional alliances, when appropriate, to emphasize the broad, nonpartisan appeal of your issue. Coalitions represent a group of organizations that will support your goals. An organization may support one of your goals but not all of them. Thus, you need to be cognizant of the support you garner for each of your goals. It is totally acceptable for an organization to partner with you on only one of your goals. Think of coalitions as teams that you build to support your goals.

You will need to recruit members of your coalition. Partnerships are formal or informal arrangements to work together. Convince high-profile organizations to take on your issue as a priority or special project. Public–private partnerships have many benefits, including providing additional resources to assist you in the implementation of your advocacy plan. Support from independent groups that consistently demonstrate positive support for your program is critical. Dr. Stephen Cone (2002), past president of AAHPERD, states that, "a partnership or collaboration involves people and their relationship to one another." Another way to view the relationship is an agreement between two or more people who consent to work together to achieve common aims. The partners may share a vision based on mutual needs that result in a joint project or the sharing of resources. For example, one Canadian school has an agreement with the local recreation department whereby the school shares its outdoor facilities with the department, and in exchange the recreation department allows the school's juniors and seniors access to its fitness center for an 11-week unit on physical fitness. This arrangement assists both groups in meeting their budgetary needs (McCrae, 2002).

Gather Data for Your Message

As an advocate for your own program, you need a good sense of your audience. Given your targeted audience, determine which strategies and which messages are likely to have the greatest impact. To do this, you need to establish where your target audience stands on key issues, ascertain their level of knowledge about your program, and identify other issues they have rallied around and supported—know their pulse and stance on similar issues.

Tenoschok and Sanders (1984) stated, "Many parents, students, teachers, and administrators do not know physical education contributes to an individual's growth. The lack of a public relations plan can result in an absence of communication between the physical educator and the public, thereby hampering the growth of the physical education program" (in Graham et al., 2004, p. 683). Thus, it is not difficult to come to the same conclusion as Graham and colleagues (2004)—many people regard physical education as less important than other subjects, such as reading and math. Parents and the community receive much more information about the importance of reading and math than they do about the importance of their child's participation in physical activity, especially from a school system. One can also apply Tenoschok and Sander's (1984) statement to physical activity. Although most people know and believe that physical activity is important, many do not know and cannot communicate why physical activity is important for children.

Given the lack of awareness of the importance and contribution of physical education and physical activity by most parents and community members, the first step in advocacy is to educate these stakeholders. Advocacy is most effective when the message is targeted and refined for each specific target audience. Therefore, it is important that you, as a key advocate for physical education and increased physical activity, know the data. Important national, state, school district, and school data are available and must be used to provide context and urgency for the issue you are advocating. However, the use of complex, complicated, or erroneous data negate any progress you may hope to achieve. Keep your data simple and accurate. The data points must be simple enough that any member of your targeted audience can understand the data and can use it.

Example of Good Data Presented in a Complicated Manner

A *Morbidity and Mortality Weekly Report* released by the Centers for Disease Control and Prevention (CDC) confirmed two significant findings: (1) Physical education can increase student participation in moderate to vigorous physical activity and help high school students gain the knowledge, attitudes, and skills they need to engage in lifelong physical activity, and (2) progress has not been made toward reaching the national health objectives for 2010 related to physical education (U.S. Department of Health and Human Services [HHS], 2004). The CDC analyzed data examining participation in physical education class among high school students in the United States from 1991 to 2003 as a part of the national Youth Risk Behavior Survey (YRBS). According to the recommendations, a coordinated multilevel approach involving schools, communities, and policymakers is needed to increase participation in daily, quality physical education among all students.

This example would be considered complicated by most readers because the data is presented using terms such as "coordinated multilevel approach," the message cites national health objectives and assumes the reader knows what these health objectives are, and the statement, although valid, loses the main points. The statement could be communicated more clearly by stating, "The Centers for Disease Control and Prevention released a report concluding that, although it has been found that physical education can increase student participation in physical activity and provide the foundation for students to participate in lifelong physical activity programs, student participation in physical education programs has not increased over the past few years. Thus, schools, communities, and policymakers must be engaged to advocate for increased participation in daily, high-quality physical education for all students."

Examples of Good Data Presented in Simple Terms

More adolescents, aged 12 to 19, in the United States are overweight than ever before: triple the number who were heavy in 1980—from 5 percent in 1980 to 15 percent in 2000 (HHS, 2004). The following data examples are good because they possess several of the following characteristics: accurate, short, simple, targeted, specific, concise, contain comparative information (comparison of two data points over time), and can be remembered and repeated by a reader. The latest statistics are part of the National Health and Nutrition Examination Survey (NHANES) conducted annually by the Centers for Disease Control and Prevention (Ogden, C., Carroll, M., Curtin, L., McDowell, M., Tabak, C., Flegal, K., 2006; USDHHS, 2006):

- Thirteen percent of children aged 6 to 11 were overweight in 1999, up from 11 percent from 1988 to 1994 and 7 percent in the late 1970s.

- Fourteen percent of adolescents aged 12 to 19 were overweight in 1999, up from 11 percent from 1988 to 1994 and 5 percent in the late 1970s.

- Obesity-related diseases cost the U.S. economy more than $100 billion every year.

- Inactivity and poor diet cause at least 300,000 deaths a year in the United States. Only tobacco causes more preventable deaths.

- Almost half of young people aged 12 to 21 and more than a third of high school students do not participate in regular vigorous physical activity.

- Seventy-two percent of 9th graders participate in regular vigorous physical activity, compared to only 55 percent of 12th graders.

- Children are not as active as they should be. Fewer than one in four children get 20 minutes of vigorous activity every day of the week. Less than one in four report getting at least half an hour of any type of physical activity every day.

- About one in four children do not play on sports teams, either at school or through community programs.

- Physical activity peaks in 10th grade—at 11 hours per week as the median—and then begins a steady decline that is likely to continue into the adult years.

- In all grade levels, girls are significantly less active than boys, yet three-quarters of the girls surveyed felt they got enough exercise.

Participation in Physical Education Class

- Nationwide, 56.1 percent of students were enrolled in a physical education class in 1999. Female students in grade 9 (75.6 percent) were significantly more likely than female students in grades 11 and 12 (36.8 percent and 29.4 percent respectively) to be enrolled in a physical education class, and female students in grade 10 (56.6 percent) were significantly more likely than female students in grade 12 (29.4 percent) to be enrolled in a physical education class.
- Male students in grade 9 (82.3 percent) were significantly more likely than male students in grades 11 and 12 (44.6 percent and 43.8 percent respectively) to be enrolled in a physical education class in 1999.

Daily Participation in Physical Education Class

- Nationwide, 29.1 percent of students attended high school physical education class daily in 1999, down from 42 percent in 1991.
- Among students enrolled in physical education class, 76.3 percent exercised more than 20 minutes during an average physical education class in 1999. Overall, male students (82.1 percent) were significantly more likely than female students (69.6 percent) to have exercised more than 20 minutes during an average physical education class.
- About one in four children surveyed in 1999 did not get any physical education in school. For those who did, 93 percent said they enjoyed physical education classes.

As you can see from these examples, there are many different ways to present supportive data. The power of your data will be diluted if you present it in a complicated manner. A rule of thumb is to present your data points and message in a manner that a ninth-grader can understand and restate back to you. Once you identify several key data points for your objectives, repeat them to anyone and everyone who will listen to you. This is how politicians generally design their campaigns. Politicians select three priority issues and then repeat their messages over and over to different groups.

Effective and Efficient Data Sources

As you search for relevant and accurate data to use to convey your message to your targeted audiences, research national, state, district, and local organizations and associations to learn what data they use. For

Action for Healthy Kids (www.actionforhealthykids.org)

American Alliance for Health, Physical Education, Recreation and Dance (www.aahperd.org)

American Heart Association (www.americanheart.org)

Centers for Disease Control and Prevention: Healthy Youth (www.cdc.gov/healthyyouth/physicalactivity and www.cdc.gov/youthcampaign)

Council of State Governments (www.csg.org)

HealthierUS.Gov (www.healthierus.gov/exercise.html)

National Association for Sport and Physical Education (www.aahperd.org/NASPE)

National Coalition for Promoting Physical Activity (www.ncppa.org)

President's Council on Physical Fitness and Sports (www.fitness.gov)

PE Central (www.PECentral.org)

PE4life (www.pe4life.com)

Robert Wood Johnson Foundation: The Shape We're In (www.rwjf.org/newsroom/featureDetail.jsp?featureID=457&type=3&gsa=1)

U.S. Department of Education (www.ed.gov)

Your state association of AAHERPD: for example, in Florida the state association's Web address (www.fahperd.org)

Your state department of education: for example, in Florida the state department of education (www.fldoe.org)

Figure 4.1 Web-based data resources.

example, the AAHPERD Legislative Action Center provides information and resources you might be able to use that address the health, physical activity, dance, and sport issues debated on Capitol Hill in Washington, DC. Bookmark the resources listed in figure 4.1, and add additional Web sites that you can use as your data library. These should provide data ranging from information about your school all the way to data reflecting national trends. Use this data to identify the top three messages that you wish every single member of your school, school system, and community could repeat and support about physical education and physical activity.

Create a Persuasive Message

The first step in creating a *persuasive message* is to define the problem, situation, or issue in terms that are manageable. For example, if your goal is to increase student participation in your physical education program, simply state your goal. Do not overstate your goal in terms that will seem impossible to achieve. For example, it would not be wise to choose a message stating that all students must participate five times a week, for at least one hour, in a physical education class. Although this is a worthy goal, in most schools it is impossible to attain. State facts and arguments briefly and use bulleted points. One strategy that state and national lobbyists often use is to develop a message they can communicate in less than five minutes. If you cannot communicate your persuasive message in five minutes or less, you probably have not done a good job of developing it.

Avoid inflammatory or empty rhetoric and loaded words at all costs. For example, do not state that *all* children will become obese unless the physical education program is expanded, or that if *all* students participate in physical education programs in your school, your school will have *no* obese students. Exaggeration leads to lost credibility. Once your credibility among your targeted audience is damaged, it very difficult to reestablish.

Hastie (2003) asked a critical question that every physical education teacher must be able to answer: "Can you show me or tell me about ways in which you promote physical activity in general, or physical education, specifically, to the community outside the school?" (p. 337). Graham and colleagues (2004) also stipulate that it is critical that as a physical education teacher you be able to answer the following two questions that a parent may ask: (1) Why should my child take physical education (and participate in physical activity), and (2) what benefits is he or she gaining from participating in your program (or physical activity)? How can you craft a persuasive message that answers these questions? You must be able to communicate the answer in simple terms to your key stakeholder groups.

Examples of Persuasive Messages

Physical activity improves muscular strength and endurance, flexibility, and cardiovascular endurance and serves as a vehicle that helps children establish self-esteem and strive for achievable personal goals. The U.S. surgeon general concludes in the executive summary, *Physical Activity and Health* (HHS, 1996), that regular moderate physical activity can substantially reduce the risk of developing or dying from heart disease, diabetes, colon cancer, and high blood pressure. The American Heart Association (2002) recommends that all children ages 2 years and older should engage in at least 30 minutes of daily physical activity and "should be encouraged to build more physical activity in their lifestyle" (p. 146).

The surgeon general's report calls school-based physical education "the most widely available resource for promoting physical activity among young people in the United States" (HHS, 1996, p. 237) and recommends that "every effort should be made to encourage schools to require daily physical education in each grade and to promote physical activities that can be enjoyed throughout life" (p. 6).

A statement by former U.S. Secretary of Education Rod Paige (U.S. Department of Education, 2004) is a persuasive argument on why physical education should be an integral part of each student's education and is a clear interpretation of the impact of the federal No Child Left Behind education program. He stated,

> While No Child Left Behind (NCLB) puts the focus on academics—where it should be—I am disturbed by reports I hear about schools doing away with recess and sports. NCLB certainly does not encourage these kinds of severe measures. Studies show that dedicating increased time to physical activity during the school day does not detract from academics; on the contrary, it in fact improves academic performance. Physical activity also increases adolescents' self-esteem as well as their physical and mental health. It's also just common sense: children can't learn when they are listless. (p. 1)

This persuasive message defines the problem, situation, or issue in terms that appear manageable. For example, the persuasive message by former Secretary of Education Rod Paige clearly defines the issue: Do not eliminate physical activity opportunities in school as a way to increase student achievement. This strategy may have the opposite effect on increased student achievement. Secretary Paige also stated facts and arguments briefly. Even though bulleted points are not used in this particular example, it is acceptable because the message is very powerful, concise, and targeted.

Identify several other powerful sources with persuasive messages to build from and emulate them to create your own message. Remember, keep it simple and make sure your message is true and based on accurate data. Do not exaggerate; this will do more to harm to your message than any other factor. Additionally, know the data that you use: Research it, learn it, know it.

Identify Potential Action Strategies

Before you make a detailed action plan, identify the major strategies that you will use. How will you communicate your issues? Here are some examples of major strategies. You are encouraged to customize the strategies to meet your needs for an effective advocacy program. Remember that these are only examples of strategies, not necessarily the strategies that you should adopt.

- Work primarily one on one with faculty and administrators.
- Focus on key segments of your stakeholders (e.g., faculty and staff that are physically active, members of your PTA).
- Work with faculty on the departmental or school level by sharing your message in faculty and staff meetings and holding lunch meetings.
- Focus on a particular group of faculty from mixed disciplines.
- Offer small-group instructional sessions.
- Sponsor or cosponsor a symposium with outside speakers.
- Attend a meeting of a group that is already advocating for your issues.
- Establish or join a coalition of interested individuals and organizations, including state and national professional organizations.
- Write a letter to your local or state legislator.
- Invite key stakeholders (parents, other faculty, school administrators, superintendent, school board members, potential community partners) to visit you program.
- Organize an event to tell your story to a wider audience.
- Write an opinion-editorial piece or letter to the local newspaper editor.
- Volunteer to provide seminars at local community events.
- Set up a booth at local events with information that presents your issues clearly and concisely.
- Send information directly to parents.
- Raise funds for things such as brochures and travel that will support your advocacy efforts.
- Contact your principal and the school district personnel in charge of staff development to determine if there is an opportunity to provide a class or seminar in physical education to fellow employees.
- Write an article for your school's newsletter.
- Post information about your program on your school's Web site.

Review and Revise

When your advocacy program has been up and running for a few months, take time for assessment. Review your program objectives, intended audience, program plan, and actions. What is working? What is not working? Should you drop any part of the program or add activities? Should you change your approach? An advocacy program is very much a practical endeavor: Keep what is working and discard what isn't. At the same time, remember that advocacy needs time to gather momentum. A strategy should not be dropped just because an anticipated result is not happening as quickly as you would like. Measure and celebrate your success. Success is often directly related to the scope and focus of your desired outcome. Those who understand and care most passionately about an issue are the most successful advocates.

CREATING AN ADVOCACY ACTION PLAN

You can use a variety of styles and formats to develop an advocacy action plan. Creating an advocacy action plan is similar to creating a lesson plan. When you develop your lesson plans, you have a general goal in mind for the lesson, you know what you want to accomplish with the lesson, you know the needs of your students, you plan strategies to teach your lesson, you assess whether your lesson plan was effective, you determine whether you need professional development to enhance the delivery of your lesson plan, and you know how much the lesson plan will cost to implement in your class. An action plan has the same elements (see table 4.1).

Table 4.1 Sample Physical Education Advocacy Action Plan

Goal	To increase student participation
Goal statement	Increase the number of students who successfully complete physical education classes and programs
Needs assessment (gather data)	• Determine the number and percentage of students enrolled in physical education classes or programs at your school. • Determine the number and percentage of students who successfully completed a physical education program or course over the past five semesters (establish a baseline to measure improvement) in your school. • Conduct a student survey to determine why students select physical education classes as electives or do not participate in physical education classes as electives. (Keep it simple: Create a postcard that students can complete and drop off in your office; enter completed surveys in a raffle and award prizes for completed surveys. Make sure the students identify their grade level on the anonymous postcard survey. Make sure you ask and identify solutions. What classes would students like your program to offer?) • Identify issues that may preclude your school from offering additional classes (e.g., budget, facilities, personnel).

(continued)

Table 4.1 *(continued)*

Goal	To increase student participation
Objective	Increase the number of students in each grade level who successfully complete physical education programs or courses by 5% in the following school year.
Action strategies	• Create a marketing campaign directed toward students and parents to help them make more-informed decisions about the benefits of physical education programs and classes (target your intended audience). • Offer programs and courses that students identified in their survey responses. • Communicate via the school newspaper and e-mails to parents about new courses and the added value of student participation in physical education programs (persuasive message). • Use horizontal and vertical team-teaching strategies to link physical education instruction between grades in physical education courses and across disciplines. • Use community and business partnerships to secure additional funds that may be needed for equipment. • Organize an informal assessment of the physical education program among the physical educators in the school: What needs to be improved? What is working well? Identify components of an effective physical education program and courses and determine where improvements can be made to the program. • Provide data to the school administration, faculty, staff, and parents on participation rates. Use context to present your data. What does the data mean?
Evaluation (review and revise)	Conduct a mini-assessment of each strategy used to determine which strategies are most effective and cost efficient in increasing the number of students who successfully complete a physical education program or course.
Research-based program	Identify research that supports the basis for your goal. Use the research to frame your persuasive message and to validate the importance of your goal statement.
Professional development	Determine whether physical education teachers need additional training to offer courses that will entice increased student participation.
Budget	• Issues to address • Needs (e.g., equipment, personnel cost, facility costs) • Funding source • Total funds available • Unmet funding needs

Now, you have the tools that you will need to assist your development and implementation of a successful advocacy action plan. Be bold, be progressive, and be your own advocate for your programs and profession.

SUMMARY

Physical educators must learn to be advocates for their own programs. Key components of advocacy include setting clearly defined and measurable goals and objectives (using SMART principles), identifying your targeted audiences, collecting data to create and support the message you want to convey, creating a convincing persuasive message, identifying potential action strategies for implementation, and assessing your program's progress. Developing an advocacy plan can help physical educators develop the skills necessary to become successful advocates.

Discussion Questions

1. As a physical education teacher, what strategies could you use to advocate and promote a variety of physical activity opportunities for your students?
2. Why is it important that you create a persuasive message?
3. What are the critical elements of an objective?
4. Identify a national, state, and local advocacy message.
5. Why is it important that you, as a physical education teacher, become an advocate to promote a variety of physical activity opportunities for your students?

Professional Portfolio Contents

1. Design your own physical education advocacy action plan using the model found in table 4.1.
2. Determine the specific action you want to emphasize and develop the plan using the steps provided.
3. Attend a legislative day, promoting physical activity to your lawmakers. You could include in your portfolio pictures of the event, legislative members that you met, or a speech that you gave.

Key Terms

advocacy—Organized influence; communication for the purpose of influencing the attitudes of others about an issue, idea, or concern that is meaningful to you in planned, organized ways.

objective—A specific measurable result expected within a particular time period, consistent with a goal and strategy.

persuasive message—A specific message designed to persuade a targeted audience to support a specific goal or strategy.

Resources

American Heart Association (physical education advocacy information): www.americanheart.org/presenter.jhtml?identifier=3023536 or 727-570-8809

National Association for Sport and Physical Education (physical education advocacy information): www.aahperd.org/naspe/template.cfm?template=advocacyTips.html

National Coalition for Promoting Physical Acitivity (NCPPA): www.ncppa.org

National Health and Nutrition Examination Survey (NHANES): www.cdc.gov/nchs/nhanes.htm

References

American Heart Association. (2002). Cardiovascular health in childhood. *Circulation, 106,* 143-160.

Association of Research Libraries. (2003). Advocacy kit: Introduction and links to tools. *Create Change.* Retrieved October 23, 2004, from www.createchange.org/archive/librarians/advocacy/intro.html.

Cone, S. (2002). *The strength of many.* Paper presented at the American Alliance for Health, Physical Education, Recreation and Dance National Student Leadership Conference, Jackson Gap, AL.

Graham, G.M., Parker, M., & Holt-Hale, S.A. (2004). *Children moving: A reflective approach to teaching physical education* (6th ed.) (pp. 683-693). New York: McGraw-Hill Education.

Hastie, P. (2002). *Teaching for a lifetime: Physical activity through quality high school physical education* (pp. 333-348). San Francisco: Benjamin Cummings.

McCrae, J. (2002, January). *Erasing the chalk line! School and community make connections to keep kids healthy & active.* Ontario Physical and Health Education Association (OPHEA). Retrieved March 4, 2005, from www.ophea.net/opheaSearch.cfm?startrow=56&area=Articles&Value=erasing%20the%20chalk%20201inc&KeyType=N&hans=A&MaxRow=5.

National Association for Sport and Physical Education. (2003). *National standards for beginning physical education teachers* (2nd ed.). Reston, VA: Author.

Ogden, C., Carroll, M., Curtin, L., McDowell, M., Tabak, C., Flegal, K. (2006). Prevalence of overweight and obesity in the United States, 1999-2004 [Electronic version]. *Journal of the American Medical Association, 295 (13)*, 1549-1555. Retrieved September 15, 2006, from http://jama.ama-assn.org/cgi/reprint/295/13/1549.

Tenoschok, M., & Sanders, S. (1984). Planning an effective public relations program. *Journal of Physical Education, Recreation & Dance, 55,* 48-49.

U.S. Department of Education. (2004, March 12). Statement by U.S. Secretary of Education Rod Paige on controlling obesity in children and adolescents. Press Release. Retrieved October 30, 2004, from www.ed.gov/news/press releases/2004/03/03122004.html.

U.S. Department of Health and Human Services, Centers for Disease Control and Prevention. (1996). *Physical activity and health: A report of the surgeon general executive summary.* Retrieved March 17, 2005, from www.cdc.gov/nccdphp/sgr/pdf/execsumm.pdf.

U.S. Department of Health and Human Services, Centers for Disease Control and Prevention. (2004, September 17). Participation in high school physical education—United States, 1991-2003. *Morbidity and Mortality Weekly Report, 53(36),* 844-847. Retrieved February 23, 2005, from www.cdc.gov/mmwr/preview/mmwrhtml/mm5336a5.htm.

U.S. Department of Health and Human Services, Centers for Disease Control and Prevention. (2006, April 14). Obesity still a major problem. Retrieved September 15, 2006, from www.cdc.gov/nchs/pressroom/06facts/obesity03_04.htm.

U.S. Department of Health and Human Services, National Center for Health Services. (2001). *Healthy People 2000 Final Review.* Hyattsville, MD: Public Health Service. Retrieved September 2, 2006, from www.cdc.gov/nchs/data/hp2000/hp2k01.pdf.

5

Personal Professional Development

STANDARD 10: *Collaboration.* Understand the necessity of fostering collaborative relationships with colleagues, parents/guardians, and community agencies to support the development of a physically educated person.

OUTCOME 10.2: Actively participate in the professional physical education community (e.g., local, state, district, and national) and within the broader field of education.

It's your first week on the job as a physical education teacher, and already you've been encouraged to get involved in a professional organization by your principal and asked to attend a beginning-of-the-year district workshop by a couple of your colleagues. With so much else to think about as a new teacher, you wonder when you would possibly have the time to take on outside activities and why you should even have to consider it at all. *Of course* you want to be the best teacher you can be. *Sure* you have some great ideas that you could share, and you are excited about getting started. But aren't professional organizations designed for "seasoned" teachers or for those with political or administrative aspirations? And aren't workshops boring? After all, they are called *work*shops. You're just getting started, and managing five classes and lesson plans a day is about all you can handle for now. Who knows where you'll be in five years or, with the way teachers come and go, if you'll even be around then? Why be bothered now with the future, particularly when there's so much else to do?

A s with anything in life, planning a course of action is important for success. We all want something—to own a home, a bigger paycheck, respect and recognition for what we do—to validate our lives. Planning a career path is particularly important to obtaining these broad-based goals. In chapters 2 and 3, you learned about ways to develop professionally and how to construct a professional development plan as part of the reflective cycle. For those who have chosen teaching, the first step in the professional development plan has been taken—getting an education. Completion of this step leads to certification in a chosen field, confirming that you are on your way down the career path. But obtaining a degree and certification doesn't mark the end of professional learning. Rather, it is the beginning of your lifelong learning process. Whether you want to become a leader in a national professional organization or simply want to spend your days teaching in the small community in which you grew up, affecting the children of your friends and their children, each day will be a learning experience. That experience requires a plan, a commitment, and an attitude toward *personal* professional development.

WHY PROFESSIONAL DEVELOPMENT?

Imagine that you have just graduated and have your degree in hand. You may question the need for professional development—after all, you have just completed rigorous training in your chosen field and are armed and ready to tackle the world of education. Research indicates that improved teacher knowledge and skills raise student performance (Sparks & Hirsh, 1999). The National Center for Education Statistics (NCES) has conducted surveys and prepared statistics showing that teachers who teach using standards-based methods shown to increase student achievement are more likely the same teachers who attend and participate in standards-based personal development activities (Sparks & Hirsh, 1999). However, as a 2000 NCES survey of 5,253 full- and part-time elementary, middle, and high school teachers indicates (figure 5.1), most public school teachers spent just one to eight hours on professional development activities in a 12-month period in 2000 (U.S. Department of Education [USDOE], 2001). The good news is that of those who spent more than eight hours participating in professional development activities, more were likely to report that participation greatly improved their teaching.

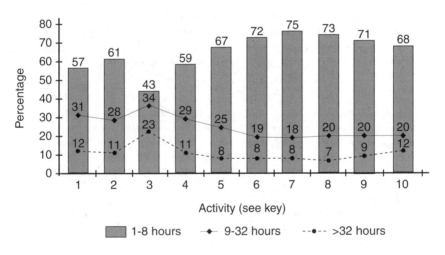

1-8 hours   9-32 hours   >32 hours

Activity Key

1. State or district curriculum and performance standards
2. Integration of educational technology in the grade or subject taught
3. In-depth study in the area of main teaching assignment
4. New methods of teaching (e.g., cooperative learning)
5. Student performance assessment (e.g., methods of testing, applying results to modify instruction)
6. Addressing the needs of children with disabilities
7. Encouraging parent and community involvement
8. Classroom management, including student discipline
9. Addressing the needs of students from diverse cultural backgrounds
10. Addressing the needs of students with limited English proficiency

Figure 5.1   Professional development participation by hour, 2000.

As figure 5.2 shows, the activity that teachers were likely to devote the most amount of time to was in-depth study in the subject area of the main teaching assignment. Slightly more than one-third reported devoting more than 32 hours (less than one week) to in-depth subject-area study. Interestingly, 75 percent of the teachers in the study reported spending only 1 to 8 hours (one day or less) in a 12-month period participating in professional development activities focused on encouraging parent and community involvement in education.

Most teachers (80 percent) reported participating in professional activities focusing on state or district curriculum and performance standards. Almost three-quarters of those surveyed reported participating in grade- or subject-specific educational technology integration programs (74 percent), in-depth subject-area study (72 percent), and new methods implementation (72 percent). The responsibility of education reform does not solely rest on the shoulders of the teachers, however:

> [U]ltimately improvements come down to how well teachers understand the standards and instructional techniques to reach all students. If states want teachers to radically change their results to get all students achieving, they must give teachers the tools, support, and training to radically change their practice. America cannot climb past its current achievement plateau without educating teachers, administrators, and other educators on what they need to do to reach the higher levels. (Sparks & Hirsh, 1999, p. 2)

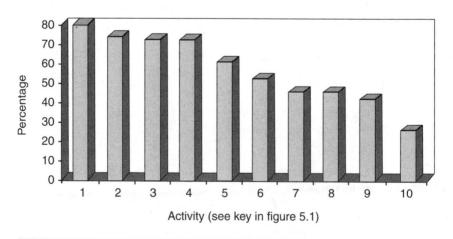

Figure 5.2   Participation by professional development activity, 2000.

PROFESSIONAL COMMITMENT

By choosing a course of study and completing all of the requirements over several semesters, the student physical educator has indicated a sincere desire to actively participate in the teaching profession. But what does it *truly* mean to be a "professional" physical educator? One word— commitment (Harrison & Blakemore, 1992; Rink, 2005, Ryan & Cooper, 2004); commitment to the student by striving toward optimal development, to the public by promoting a positive image, and to the profession (Harrison & Blakemore, 1992). Further, and by way of definition, a "professional person is one who is dedicated to providing a service to other people. Educators should strive to provide a service that is highly esteemed . . . . Physical educators should never lose sight of the fact that they are educators and that the purpose of all programs in the school is to educate students" (Harrison & Blakemore, 1992, pp. 62-63). Additionally, according to Rink (2005, p. 334), this commitment to "state-of-the-art service" is to be maintained for the lifetime of your career.

Harrison and Blakemore (1992) also remind us that the professional checks and balances are not in place in the same manner as they are for doctors and lawyers or other service providers. We choose who we want to take care of or represent us. Students usually do not have that same luxury, and tenure laws often protect teachers who are incompetent. The professional physical educator also has "an obligation to preserve and develop public trust by doing a good job" (Rink, 2005, p. 334). Therefore, it becomes imperative for educators to set and expect high standards.

BEST PRACTICES

According to Rink (2005), "[P]rofessionals should be prepared at the start of their careers to provide best practice" (p. 334). This book has focused on the standards set by the National Association for Sport and Physical Education (NASPE) (2003), and those standards dictate that, although the outcome is to "[a]ctively participate in the professional physical education community," the target goal is to "[p]articipate in the professional physical education community *on numerous levels*" (p. 18). NASPE set their guidelines and expectations for best practice in 1996, and it becomes the duty of the student who grows into a professional to also make a corresponding shift to his or her commitment: from an *other-directed* to a *self-directed* commitment. In other words, to shift from being told what to do to meet an outcome (e.g., meeting requirements for obtaining an academic degree) to setting your own career goals, keeping the concept of professionalism at the forefront (Rink, 2005; Rock & Levin,

2002). Professionalism manifests itself in a variety of ways and through an assortment of practices: reflection (as discussed in previous chapters); communication with students, colleagues, and family members; advocacy; accurate record-keeping; participation in school and district activities; action research; and professional growth (Goodnough, 2001; Rock & Levin, 2002; Ryan & Cooper, 2004).

Working together as teachers (or collaborating with other professionals in the field) to develop a professional dialogue and to "construct new knowledge" is another important best practice for teachers (Mazurkiewicz, 2003; Rock & Levin, 2002). Teachers tend to communicate and interact with one another about grades, students, parents, administrators, and other day-to-day topics, but they are alone when they are educating. "Why do teachers talk about grades, individual students, school absences, the choice of a principal, or financial issues and not about how they teach and how best to educate students?" (Mazurkiewicz, 2003, p. 169). According to Mazurkiewicz, teachers face many barriers to teaching that are difficult to discuss—fear of burnout, a sense of isolation, and in some cases, the tough job of answering the question of "Why am I teaching?" Although not an easy task, Mazurkiewicz (2003) asserts that developing a professional dialogue between teachers about best education practices is essential to any type of education reform and to helping alleviate teachers' fears by allowing them to recognize that others face the same issues.

DEVELOPING A PROFESSIONAL ATTITUDE

"Human capital is developed through education, and the effectiveness of a child's education depends on the quality of his or her classroom teachers" (Schacter, 2003, p. 101). Developing an appropriate attitude toward professional development becomes vital to the process. Michael Fullan (in Ryan & Cooper, 2004, p. 380) puts forth four attitudes of teachers seeking to improve themselves (see table 5.1).

Table 5.1 Four Attitudes Conducive to Professional Self-Improvement

Attitude	Characteristic
1. Accepting	Accepts that it is possible to improve
2. Self-critical	Is willing to be self-critical
3. Humble	Recognizes that practices exist that are better than their own
4. Willing	Ready to learn and to do what has to be done

Adapted from L. Horine and D. Stotlar, 2003, *Administration of physical education and sports programs,* 5th ed. (New York: McGraw-Hill Companies), 75-93.

Developing an attitude of humility during the first year of teaching is also an important step toward professionalism. Beginning teachers are not expected to know everything there is to know about teaching, but oftentimes, some act as though they do, perhaps in an effort to convey confidence. Ryan and Cooper (2004) suggest instead that the beginning teacher should develop a humble attitude of "alertness and quiet observation of your new context" (p. 449), fostering an apprentice type of attitude. They caution that there is a distinct difference between humility and submissiveness.

As an "apprentice" teacher, locating a mentor becomes a means by which to build collegiality while developing professionally under the guidance of someone who "knows the ropes" and can show them to you. According to Ryan and Cooper (2004), "[S]eventy percent of teachers who have been mentored claim that the experience significantly improved their teaching" (p. 449).

LEVELS OF PROFESSIONALISM

Ryan and Cooper (2004, pp. 465-466) define three levels of professionalism (see table 5.2). Level one is robotic and substandard. It is characterized by the desire to simply get students through the requirements and can be found in teachers who "teach to the test" or who use "teacher-proof materials," materials that provide rigid, step-by-step instructions for teaching the materials. Obviously, level three is the desired achievement level of the true teaching professional—a creative, self-directed approach to learning and to meeting the students' individual needs. According to Ryan and Cooper (2004), many teachers enter the field at level two. The

Table 5.2   Levels of Professionalism

Level	Characteristic
Level one—imitative maintenance	Mechanically imitates prescribed teaching methods; concerned with maintaining discipline and keeping students busy
Level two—meditative	Reflects within narrow range; goes beyond rigid guidelines, but adaptations are few; varies teaching patterns, but is not innovative
Level three—generative and creative	Focuses on individual students; has wide knowledge view; uses instructional guidelines as launching pads rather than targets; as a diagnostician, seeks the best ways to engage students; creates student desire and self-directed classroom environments

road to professionalism for the beginning teacher means working toward the highest level.

The National Board for Professional Teaching Standards (NBPTS) was developed in 1987 in support of experienced teachers with baccalaureate or advanced degrees and in response to the President's Commission on Excellence in Education's report *A Nation at Risk: The Imperative for Educational Reform* (1983), which sounded the alarm for the nation to raise teaching expectations and standards. As an organization, NBPTS leads the way in recognizing and providing support to superior teachers (Ryan & Cooper, 2004). The NBPTS offers five core propositions, board certification guidelines, and its distinguishing characteristics on the NBPTS Web site at www.nbpts.org.

Another organization, the Council of Chief State School Officers (CCSSO), provides information for prospective teachers about attaining state teaching licenses. Details about CCSSO and useful publications are available on the Internet.

CHARACTERISTICS OF EFFECTIVE PROFESSIONAL DEVELOPMENT

We have learned that it is important to continue to develop as a professional teacher throughout your teaching career. Not only does this practice lead to better teaching but also to developing competencies related to interests, which creates increased job satisfaction (Schacter, 2003). But how do you determine if you are engaging in *effective* professional development? Ryan and Cooper (2004, p. 379) provide a comprehensive, yet handy, checklist of effective professional development (see figure 5.3).

TYPES OF PROFESSIONAL DEVELOPMENT TRAINING: CONTINUOUS LEARNING

So, you have decided that being a level one teacher is unacceptable, and you refuse to settle for level two. How do you work toward becoming a level three, or truly professional, teacher? Fortunately, there are several ways to work toward achieving the goal. The best approach is perhaps a well-rounded and balanced one using continuous learning, which includes keeping abreast of current theory and conducting research or writing articles and books, participating in locally based workshops and professional committees, pursuing a graduate degree, and joining and getting involved in state and national associations (Harrison & Blakemore, 1992; Ryan & Cooper, 2004). Ryan and Cooper (2004) offer several ways in which a teacher can continue to learn while in the field: independent, group,

- Focuses on teachers as central to student learning, yet includes all members of the school community
- Focuses on individual, collegial, and organizational improvement
- Respects and nurtures the intellectual and leadership capacity of teachers, principals, and others in the school community
- Reflects the best available research and practices in teaching, learning, and leadership
- Enables teachers to develop further expertise in subject content, teaching strategies, uses of technologies, and other essential elements of teaching to high standards
- Promotes continuous inquiry and improvement of schools
- Is planned collaboratively by those who will participate in and facilitate that development
- Requires substantial time and resources
- Is driven by a coherent long-term plan
- Is evaluated ultimately on the basis of its effects on teacher instruction and student learning and uses this assessment to guide subsequent professional development efforts

Figure 5.3   Ryan and Cooper's characteristics of effective professional development. Kevin Ryan and James M. Cooper, *Those who can, teach,* Tenth Edition. Copyright © 2004 by Houghton Mifflin Company. Used with permission.

and graduate study; supervision and mentoring; in-service programs; and systematic reflection on practice.

Independent, Group, and Graduate Study

Continuous learning is important to educators and students alike. Research indicates that improvement in student achievement is correlated with improvements in teacher knowledge and skill (McCarthy & Young, 2001; Sparks, 2002; Sparks & Hirsh, 1999). Personal and professional growth can be achieved by continuing coursework beyond graduation (Rink, 2005; Ryan & Cooper, 2004). Independent study is a means for a teacher to independently research a specific interest area—perhaps something directly related to a teaching experience that piques the educator's interest. A study group (or group study) typically starts as committee work to address a specific problem with a direction toward resolution (Ryan & Cooper, 2004). Graduate study involves structured college coursework toward an advanced degree. Courses can be taken on a college campus or at home through distance learning.

Supervision and Mentoring

Supervision, or basically one-on-one help, is typically offered to the beginning teacher in the form of observation and feedback sessions performed by a department head or other school official. These sessions offer insight into practices, although at times they may seem intimidating to a new teacher. It is important to understand that supervision is an opportunity to receive constructive criticism and assistance in an effort to improve overall performance that will benefit the students. A newer, modified approach to supervision and mentoring that bears mentioning is *coaching*—experienced teachers are brought into a school with the goal of improving instruction, particularly in lower-performance schools (Poglinco & Bach, 2004). Coaches provide professional opportunities by leading a variety of group-focused staff activities and study groups as well as offering in-class support.

Mentoring might well be considered an expanded form of supervision in the sense that mentors also observe and offer feedback to the beginning teacher, but the focus is primarily on providing guidance over a stretch of time. "Master and mentor teachers in various disciplines and grade levels are instructional leaders who infuse and distribute their expertise across the staff" (Schacter, 2003, p. 103). New teachers report frustration at not being able to implement the strategies they learned in their coursework and feel that they are not supported during their transition process (Nugent & Faucette, 2004). In this regard, mentoring becomes an important learning tool for the new teacher. By definition, a *mentor* is "an experienced teacher who is willing to act as a guide and confidant" (Ryan & Cooper, 2004, p. 449). Essentially, a mentoring program is one that assigns experienced teachers to assist beginning teachers, although seasoned teachers frequently seek those more experienced in their field to continue the mentoring process. Mentoring is particularly important to the beginning teacher, where the mentor serves as a type of interpreter-guide. So, ask your mentor to support your efforts to use your learned strategies and give you constructive feedback for future implementation.

As mentioned earlier, 70 percent of those who have been mentored report improved teaching; however, only one in five teachers reports being mentored (Ryan & Cooper, 2004). Mentoring decreases the five-year teacher dropout rate from 50 to 15 percent; but unfortunately, the practice of mentoring is not widespread (Scherer, 2003). Benefits to mentors may include special training, salary increases, and a reduction in teaching responsibilities (Ryan & Cooper, 2004).

In-Service Programs

"Professionals are identified not only by their specialized learning but also by their socialization into membership organizations and their affiliation with colleagues who are the source of new knowledge and lifelong learning" (Morocco & Solomon, 1999, p. 247). According to Morocco and Solomon, by associating with like-minded individuals, standards of excellence are set, affording communities of practitioners the ability to attain higher levels of skill through peer mentoring and monitoring, building on the skills and competencies of community members. Locally, these colleagues can develop school or district workshops and training sessions that are particularly beneficial to the beginning teacher. Unfortunately, few take advantage of opportunities to build a professional community, living instead in isolated, self-contained classroom environments with minimal emphasis on their own learning (Morocco & Solomon, 1999). Sparks and Hirsh (1999) recommend, as part of the National Staff Development Council's (NSDC) guidelines, that "at least 25 percent of teachers' time be devoted to their own learning" (p. 6).

In-service training is essential to building a community or cooperative team of teachers within a school, promoting enthusiastic creativity and communication (Bucher & Krotee, 2002). During the "competency building" stage of a teacher's career cycle, "the teacher strives to improve teaching skills and abilities by seeking out new materials, methods, and strategies," and teachers "are receptive to new ideas, attend workshops and conferences willingly, and enroll in graduate programs through their own initiative" (Lynn, 2002, p. 180). In-service training may include such staff development activities as current trend workshops, orientations, and study groups; retreats and training seminars that include consultants who are experts in the field; developing a professional library with the latest print and electronic resource materials; staff meetings to discuss relative and pertinent issues and coping techniques for handling job-related stress; arranging for monetary subsidies for attendance at professional meetings and conferences; encouraging sabbaticals; fostering action research; and other research activities and peer coaching (Bucher & Krotee, 2002; Desimone, Porter, Birman, Garet, & Yoon, 2002). School districts play key roles in communicating the importance of in-service training and the implications of local and state professional development standards to administrators, teachers, and professional development providers (Desimone et al., 2002).

The NSDC recommends the creation of a National Center on Professional Development overseen by the U.S. Department of Education and funded by states, corporations, and foundations whose purpose is to strengthen the responsibility that has formerly been left primarily to state and local governments in the areas of funding for compensatory programs, protecting the rights of various groups, serving as an adviser to states, and conducting research (Sparks & Hirsh, 1999). This proposed national center would conduct research tracking the relationship between teacher professional development and student learning improvement, publishing and sharing the results with states and districts in an effort to "use staff development successfully to achieve the vision of a standards-based reform agenda" (p. 7).

Systematic Reflection on Practice

The classroom is more than a place to impart learning to students—it is also the perfect place to learn. As discussed in previous chapters, daily reflection is important to the developing teacher. However, daily systematic reflection about what takes place in the classroom is important for both new *and* experienced teachers—it is an ongoing process of asking what worked and did not work in class and how to enhance the teaching and learning experience, whether through researching engaging activities or through materials and resources (Ryan & Cooper, 2004).

TYPES OF PROFESSIONAL DEVELOPMENT TRAINING: ORGANIZATIONS

As a beginning teacher, you may wonder why you should bother joining a national association, because you will clearly have your hands full at the local level in the classroom. Keep in mind that Outcome 10.2 of the NASPE standards clearly stipulates that you should "actively participate in the *professional* physical education community (e.g., local, state, district, and national) and within the broader field of education" (NASPE, 2003, p. 19). Membership in professional organizations will help you achieve this desired outcome. "Professional organizations exist to help members of a given profession work together to achieve common goals" (Harrison & Blakemore, 1992).

Membership in a national association comes with many benefits, and many organizations have state and regional chapters. National organizations and associations sponsor conferences and workshops dedicated to professional improvement, and they also serve as advocates for teachers, often having an impact on decisions affecting teacher salaries (Ryan & Cooper, 2004). National organizations give teachers a political voice during policy creation that affects you and your students, educate the public about the teaching profession, and are committed to providing members with "best practice" resources through journals, conventions, workshops, and newsletters (Rink, 2005). Some offer worker training programs, published job openings and career opportunities, and programs to facilitate worker–management communication and to reduce staff turnover. Some members of organizations may receive higher salaries than nonmembers. Members share ideas through convention speakers and journal articles and by attending conventions, serving on committees, and holding offices (Harrison & Blakemore, 1992). Several organizations are geared toward advancement of the physical education professional. The following section highlights those and other teaching-related associations.

American Alliance for Health, Physical Education, Recreation and Dance (AAHPERD)

The American Alliance for Health, Physical Education, Recreation and Dance (www.aahperd.org) is a nonprofit alliance of five national and six district associations and a research consortium. It is the national affiliate for the physical education profession, and it offers memberships at the state, regional, and national levels. AAHPERD provides ongoing research resources through the publication of four journals: *Journal of Physical Education, Recreation and Dance; Strategies; American Journal of Health Education;* and *Research Quarterly for Exercise and Sport.* The *Journal of Physical Education, Recreation & Dance (JOPERD)* is purported by the Web site to be the "cornerstone journal of AAHPERD, reaching 25,000 members." Other services include a newsletter; career services; awards; research grants; scholarships; reduced rates for health, auto, and liability insurance; leadership and volunteer opportunities; and an online store. AAHPERD also offers undergraduate and graduate student membership rates, so you might want to get a jump on the job scene by joining. The alliance is composed of the following organizations, which have links on the main AAHPERD Web site:

- American Association for Health Education (AAHE)
- American Association for Physical Activity and Recreation (AAPAR)
- National Association for Girls and Women in Sports (NAGWS)
- National Association for Sport and Physical Education (NASPE)
- National Dance Association (NDA)

National Association for Sport and Physical Education (NASPE)

The National Association for Sport and Physical Education (www.aahperd.org/naspe/template.cfm) is worthy of distinct mention because it is the association that sets the professional standards for physical educators, which is the primary focus of this book. In addition to setting industry standards, NASPE Professional Services offers workshops and consultants in K-12 education, college and university physical education teacher education programs, coaching education, and physical activity programs for children. Information about these and other programs can be found on the Web site.

Education Associations

Other education associations worthy of mention to beginning teachers are the National Education Association (NEA), the American Federation of Teachers (AFT), and the Association for Supervision and Curriculum Development (ASCD). The NEA (www.nea.org) operates at local, state, and national levels and represents roughly 2.6 million teachers, administrators, support personnel, retired teachers, and college students preparing to teach (Ryan & Cooper, 2004). Membership benefits include research and publications; insurance, investment, book, and travel programs; and a UniServ program of field professionals whose purpose it is to assist local teachers with collective bargaining issues. Education reform emphasizing class-size reduction, improved working conditions and salaries, updated resources and technology, and the quality of education programs can be effectively addressed through a collective bargaining political voice (Ryan & Cooper, 2004). Additional information about the NEA and other similar teacher-oriented organizations can be found on the Internet.

Perhaps Ryan and Cooper (2004) state the teacher's professional development quest best:

> Becoming a teacher may be compared with sculpting a work of art from a piece of stone. The difference is that the teacher is both the sculptor and the stone. The teacher begins with a vision of what he or she wants to be and then sets to work transforming the vision into a reality. . . . To be a teacher, particularly a teacher who is continuously moving forward, is a lifelong commitment to be an artist (p. 482).

SUMMARY

Involvement in professional development is important to helping you achieve your career and teaching goals. Immediate involvement will start you well on your way to becoming a level three teacher and toward accomplishing the edicts of Outcome 10.2. Keep in mind that at the very least, individuals committed to professional development tend to be better teachers (NCES, 2001), and that should be the first focus of each teacher. Beyond that, professional development can assist you with learning the ins and outs of your job and provide an avenue for advancing your career, taking it in the direction you want to go. As we have outlined in this chapter, numerous local-, state-, and national-level involvement and training opportunities exist for the beginning as well as the most advanced teacher. The rest is up to you.

Discussion Questions

1. List three qualities you consider to be important in a teacher. Describe how professional development can aid in developing those qualities.
2. Describe the advantages of collaboration between colleagues. What types of things can you learn?
3. Do you see value in joining a professional organization? Do you think a national or local association is a better fit for you? Why?

Professional Portfolio Contents

1. Put together a personal development plan of action. You can start right away by joining the student arm of a national organization (such as AAHPERD). Set and write down specific, achievable personal professional development goals, such as attending local workshops; performing an action research project and writing an article or paper to share the results; holding weekly journal readings; or taking a continuing education, postbaccalaureate, or graduate class. Keep records (certificates, documentation of attendance at professional meetings and conferences) of your accomplishments and notes on your readings (books and journal articles) and the workshops or conferences you attend.
2. Provide a reflection describing how these activities have facilitated your professional development.

Key Terms

mentor—An experienced teacher who is willing to act as a guide and confidant.

professionalism—Dedication to providing high-quality service to other people.

self-directedness—A personal commitment to setting and obtaining personal career goals.

Resources

Association of Teacher Educators (www.ate1.org/pubs/home.cfm)

American Association of Colleges for Teacher Education (www.aacte.org)

American Educational Research Association (www.aera.net)

Association for Supervision and Curriculum Development (www.ascd.org)

Council of Chief State School Officers (www.ccsso.org)

Miles, K.H. (2001). Rethinking school resources. *District Issues Brief.* New American Schools: Retrieved March 10, 2005, from www.naschools.org/uploadedfiles/rethinking-resources.pdf.

President's Commission on Excellence in Education. (1983). *A nation at risk: The imperative for educational reform.* Retrieved March 10, 2005, from www.ed.gov/pubs/NatAtRisk/risk.html.

Sparks, D. (2004). Professional development apartheid. *Results.* National Staff Development Council. Retrieved March 10, 2005, from www.nsdc.org/library/publications/results/res4-04spar.cfm.

References

Bucher, C., & Krotee, M. (2002). *Management of physical education and sport* (12th ed.). New York: McGraw-Hill.

Desimone, L., Porter, A.C., Birman, B.F., Garet, M.S., & Yoon, K.S. (2002). How do district management and implementation strategies relate to the quality of the professional development that districts provide to teachers? *Teachers College Record, 104(7),* 1265-1312. Retrieved March 7, 2005, from www.blackwell-synergy.com/links/doi/10.1111/1467-9620.00204/abs/.

Goodnough, K. (2001). Teacher development through action research: A case study of an elementary teacher. *Action in Teacher Education, 23(1),* 37-46.

Harrison, J.M, & Blakemore, C.L. (1992). *Instructional strategies for secondary school physical education* (3rd ed.). Dubuque, IA: Brown.

Lynn, S.K. (2002). The winding path: Understanding the career cycle of teachers. *Clearing House, 75(4),* 179-182.

Mazurkiewicz, G. (2003). How professional dialogue prevents burnout. In M. Scherer (Ed.), *Keeping good teachers* (pp. 169-175). Alexandria, VA: Association for Supervision and Curriculum Development.

McCarthy, J., & Young, M.W. (2001). The seamless web: The role of graduate teacher education programs in continuous teacher development. *Action in Teacher Education, 23(2),* 9-17.

Morocco, C.C., & Solomon, M.Z. (1999). Revitalizing professional development. In M.Z. Solomon (Ed.), *The diagnostic teacher: Constructing new approaches to professional development* (pp. 247-267). New York: Teachers College Press.

National Association for Sport and Physical Education. (2003). *National standards for beginning physical education teachers* (2nd ed.). Reston, VA: Author.

Nugent, P., & Faucette, N. (2004). Developing beginning teachers through an interactive induction and internship program. *Action in Teacher Education, 26(1),* 53-63.

Poglinco, S.M., & Bach, A.J. (2004). The heart of the matter: Coaching as a vehicle for professional development. *Phi Delta Kappan, 85(5),* 398-400.

Rink, J.E. (2005). *Teaching physical education for learning* (4th ed.). New York: McGraw-Hill.

Rock, T.C., & Levin, B.B. (2002). Collaborative action research projects: Enhancing preservice teacher development in professional development schools. *Teacher Education Quarterly, Winter,* 7-21.

Ryan, K., & Cooper, J. (2004). *Those who can, teach* (10th ed.). New York: Houghton Mifflin.

Schacter, J. (2003). How career paths improve job satisfaction. In M. Scherer (Ed.), *Keeping good teachers* (pp. 101-117). Alexandria, VA: Association for Supervision and Curriculum Development.

Scherer, M. (2003). Improving the quality of the teaching force: A conversation with David C. Berliner. In M. Scherer (Ed.), *Keeping good teachers* (pp. 14-21). Alexandria, VA: Association for Supervision and Curriculum Development.

Sparks, D. (2002, September). Conversations that make the case for professional learning. *Results.* National Staff Development Council. Retrieved March 15, 2005, from www.nsdc.org/library/publications/results/res9-02spar.cfm.

Sparks, D., & Hirsh, S. (1999). *A national plan for improving professional development.* Oxford, OH: National Staff Development Council. Retrieved April 26, 2005, from www.nsdc.org/library/authors/NSDCPlan.cfm.

U.S. Department of Education, National Center for Education Statistics. (2001). Teacher preparation and professional development: 2000. Retrieved April 26, 2005, from http://nces.ed.gov/surveys/frss/publications/2001088.

6

Using Community Resources

STANDARD 10: *Collaboration.* Understand the necessity of fostering collaborative relationships with colleagues, parents/guardians, and community agencies to support the development of a physically educated person.

OUTCOME 10.3: Identify and seek community resources to enhance physical activity opportunities.

Your school sponsors a one-day districtwide fitness fair, working together in a partnership with other physical educators, health and fitness experts, businesses, community recreation departments, state parks, and civic and government organizations to educate your community about the value of physical activity and fitness for all ages and abilities. Information booths, health indicator stations, and equipment demonstrations are set up throughout your gym or a centralized large facility borrowed from the local recreation department or college or university.

Information from various organizations is provided about the effects of inactivity on young and old alike and the importance of physical activity and fitness in combating obesity and various diseases. Offerings of fitness opportunities through community recreation departments or various church and civic groups, state park biking and hiking trails, fitness clubs, and myriad other community-oriented activities are promoted from a wide range of community vendors. And, not to be left out, you also have a booth—and encourage other physical educators in your district to do likewise—providing information on your school's physical education program, highlighting and recognizing the accomplishments of your students.

As society has become more health conscious, physical education has moved away from the traditional "throw out a ball and let 'em play" mentality and toward an inclusive philosophy based on activity for life. Through the initiation of a thorough public relations campaign that promotes a solid physical education program, it is possible to convey the message of the physical, psychological, and social merits of physical education for students to an assortment of publics concerned with their well-being (Tillman, Voltmer, Esslinger, & McCue, 1996). However, promoting the goal of lifetime physical fitness achievement for "students" of all ages and abilities is a monumental task for schools to undertake alone. Such training should begin early in life (Helm & Boos, 1996) and expand until one's golden years if it is to be a serious undertaking. Given the enormity of the task, the challenge becomes one of identifying resources and opportunities for all, distinguishing factors that might pose limitations to reaching the goal, and seeking ways to overcome those limitations through *collaboration* with like-minded professionals and community leaders. School and community programs provide children with opportunities to develop lifelong fitness and activity habits from an early age.

According to the American School Health Association (ASHA) (1997), schools and communities working hand in hand to coordinate efforts toward the best use of available facilities offer the best potential for improving students' health and for developing lifelong physical activity practices. Because they reach most children, high-quality school physical education programs go far toward meeting these goals by providing physical activity instruction led by qualified teachers teaching appropriate content and following appropriate instructional practices, and by providing related services and programs (ASHA, 1997; Patrick, Spear, Holt, & Sofka, 2001). For many children, in-school physical education programs may be their only preparation for developing lifetime physical activity habits.

According to ASHA (1997), a quality program involves a coordinated effort between physical education, health education and services, counseling and social services, nutrition services, the psychosocial and biophysical environment, and faculty and staff health promotion to support "optimal physical, emotional, social, and educational development of students" (p. 8). This approach has been called a coordinated school health program.

Opportunities should also extend beyond school physical education classes (Patrick et al., 2001). Extracurricular and after-school programs offering at least 30 minutes of activity geared toward children's needs and interests and staffed with positive instructors are excellent ways to meet that need. Programs so designed lead to increased physical capability and self-efficacy (Patrick et al., 2001). Valuable because they offer care while productively occupying students' time, after-school programs have increased dramatically in recent years, in part because of the 21st Century Community Learning Centers component of the No Child Left Behind Act (Dustin, Hibbler, McKenney, & Blitzer, 2004).

However, school recreation facilities tend to be underused. Open from 8 a.m. until 5 p.m. (given that an after-school program is operating), school recreational facilities are underutilized and could be more community friendly because taxpayer dollars fund most public school facilities (Dustin et al., 2004). Bringing recreation professionals into the school after hours and into the evening to operate programs using school tracks, courts, fields, and other facilities is a way to provide family activity in a safe, familiar environment while making the best use of available facilities (Dustin et al., 2004).

SUCCESSFUL COLLABORATION: PUBLIC RELATIONS OF PHYSICAL EDUCATION

As strange as it may seem, successful physical educators must also be salespeople, "selling" the value of what they do. Consumers of this "value-added" component called physical education are not just the students who want to take the classes. They also include required-credit students, teachers who view physical education as "play time," administrators faced with budget and program cuts, and parents who may not fully recognize the benefits of a physical education program. These people may or may not have had negative personal experiences with physical education. Using a variety of publicity tools, physical educators should send out a consistent, clear message about the positive physical, social, and emotional contributions of a program. Included in the message should be the program's objectives and means of meeting those objectives (Tillman, et al., 1996).

Principles of public relations are important to a successful physical education program both inside and outside of the school environment, even though a physical education program is not a commercial enterprise. In stressing the importance of public relations to school physical education and athletic programs, Horine and Stotlar (2003) contend that "[t]he bottom line is not to sell a product, but rather to build an efficient program based on policies, regulations, and laws. The public must be kept informed of how the programs are meeting these objectives" (p. 76). In their discussion on how to perform a PR audit—how to gauge the feelings and knowledge of various constituencies toward or about a program—they delineate four categories: (1) identifying relevant *publics* (constituents), (2) determining what these publics think about the program, (3) measuring what the relevant publics believe are important issues, and (4) evaluating the importance and power of these publics. To accomplish these tasks, they outline eight principles of effective public relations (see table 6.1).

WHO GETS THE MESSAGE?

We discussed the importance of communicating a consistent, clear message about the benefits of a good physical education program. But, who should get that message? Who is the collaborative base, or public, important to your program? Once the target groups have been identified, a variety of steps can be taken to determine how important they are to your program and what they think (Horine & Stotlar, 2003). Collaboration and support from a variety of sources are especially important to a physical education program for two reasons: (1) physical education is not viewed by most to be as important as other subjects, and (2) a physical

Table 6.1 Horine and Stotlar's Principles of Public Relations

Principle	Summary
1. The foundation of a successful PR program is an excellent product.	Provide great service—your first job is to serve the public.
2. PR must be based on the truth and the premise that the public has a right to be informed.	Avoid misrepresentations and ignoring problems.
3. PR programs must be continuous.	Adopt a long-term plan of year-round communication with the public.
4. The PR program is an advocate or spokesperson, representing the physical education or athletic program to the public.	Educate the public about the positive values of the program (sportsmanship, increasing the quality of life, quest for excellence).
5. The PR program must be based on two-way communication.	Avoid the "silver bullet" method of just sending out information. Adopt a reciprocal attitude of listening to ideas and suggestions from others who may not be in your field.
6. The PR program must explore the use of all forms of media and communication avenues.	Use typical media (print, TV, radio), but also be creative and use other avenues (bulletin boards, open houses, demonstrations, newsletters, fairs).
7. Positive human relationships must be developed for a PR program to be successful over the long term.	Report negatives as well as positives even if it means "taking heat," involve a variety of people in planning, and develop personal visibility with others.
8. Define the particular public groups whose opinions affect the program, and structure the PR program to reach them.	The immediate public (administrators, students) directly affects the program. The active public (parents, boosters) pays close attention to the program. The casual public (other teachers and staff) follows the program, but not closely. The public at large are people who have never been interested and have no current interest in the progress of the program.

Adapted from L. Horine and D. Stotlar, 2003, *Administration of physical education and sports programs,* 5th ed. (New York: McGraw-Hill College), 75-93.

education program is expensive compared to other programs because of the equipment needed (Graham, Parker, & Holt-Hale, 2004). Figure 6.1 depicts seven related publics, as referred to by Horine and Stotlar (2003) and defined by Graham and colleagues (2004), that are significant to the success of a physical education program.

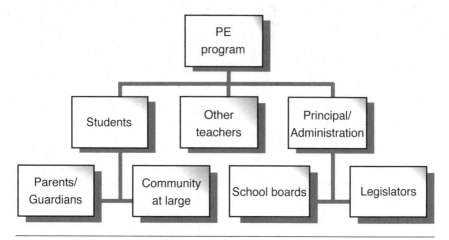

Figure 6.1 Identifying publics affecting PE programs.

From G. M. Graham, 2004, "Building support for your program." In *Children moving* (New York: McGraw-Hill), 684.

School Boards and Legislators

These are the entities at the top of the decision-making line. School boards and legislators appropriate educational funds and resources, making financial and staffing decisions that can significantly affect a program. Paying attention to current issues affecting children (e.g., No Child Left Behind, the CDC fight against childhood obesity trends, state and local education-related issues) and communicating the value of solid physical education programs toward achieving goals can go a long way toward keeping a program from the financial chopping block.

Administrators and Colleagues

Effective teachers communicate with one another as colleagues about their activities and students, share ideas, develop an attitude of cooperation, and nurture support for their program for the benefit of their students and to build a successful program (Graham et al., 2004; Hastie, 2003; Ryan & Cooper, 2004; Tillman et al., 1996). They seek to collaborate with administrators, school board members, legislators, other governmental representatives and social agencies, and others in authority in an effort to gain resources for their students in an environment of communication and understanding, balancing the needs of the student against available resources (Hastie, 2003; Ryan & Cooper, 2004; Tillman et al., 1996).

Developing a sense of collegiality is especially important for new teachers because it fosters an encouraging and supportive environment for those just getting started (Hastie, 2003; Ryan & Cooper, 2004). Graham and colleagues (2004) offer several ideas for developing a collegial program.

- Invite the principal to your class or to another school to observe a program that may have aspects critical to the development of your own.
- Attend school board meetings and try to get to know the school board members and invite them to special programs.
- Contact your legislator about an important bill that may affect your program.
- Involve the entire school or a certain grade level in an idea or theme.
- Work with a classroom teacher on a project (e.g., incorporating activities such as expressive dance to enhance creative writing skills).
- Work with a teacher to allow students to work on a physical education activity log as part of their class assignment.
- Arrange for younger classes to view a video of an older class to show how the older students have progressed.
- Arrange for the principal to view a video of other teachers or programs that outlines critical aspects of your program needs.
- Invite the classroom teacher to a PE class demonstration at the end of a unit as a way of sharing how the students have progressed.
- Spend time with other teachers outside of the classroom (e.g., eating lunch) to build rapport.

Students and Parents

As important as peers and administrators are to the success of a physical education program, they are not the only ones who count—and in some respect, they may not be the most important. Rather, they are a piece of a larger pie of "publics" with whom the physical educator must work in a collaborative effort toward success. Students of a program are likely the most important public in developing a successful program (Graham et al., 2004; Tillman et al., 1996). After all, they are the primary consumers of the "product" you are putting forth—a path to lifelong physical activity and fitness. They offer daily reports about the program to their peers and family members, and they are the future publics to be satisfied (Tillman et al., 1996). Gaining the support of others for your program becomes difficult if students are not advocates of your program or have been adversely affected through humiliation, neglect, or mistreatment (Graham et al., 2004; Tillman et al., 1996). Students will spread the word about a poor program—probably more quickly than about a good one if the old adage, "Bad news travels fast," holds true. And the first to hear the news is likely to be their parents—either through complaints or through expressions of how much they enjoyed a particular activity.

Let us not underestimate the influence parents have on developing their child's attitude toward physical activity. Parental support and sibling participation positively influence participation (ASHA, 1997). Whether through simple role modeling or through a combination of encouragement, support, and beliefs, parents who value physical activity and have high expectations for it can more effectively influence their children toward physically active behavior (Welk, 1999).

Parental support can be very helpful to a successful program, particularly when funds are needed for equipment or facilities (Graham et al., 2004; Horine & Stotlar, 2003). Hardly any parent can resist hearing positive reports about his or her child's activities, and these should be reported regularly (Tillman et al., 1996). Communication to the parents about the program is a crucial component for success. Newsletters, parent letters, open houses, presentations, bulletin boards, phone calls, e-mails, parent hotlines, parent work nights (or days), attendance at PTO and booster club meetings, parent workshops, and invitations to parents with special skills to speak to a class are just some of the ways teachers can communicate with parents about their program (Graham et al., 2004; Ryan & Cooper, 2004; Tillman et al., 1996).

Community at Large

Building good relationships with social agencies, such as scouting organizations and 4-H clubs, community and neighborhood centers, boys' and girls' clubs, the YMCA and YWCA, and local recreation departments, is imperative to a successful program when it comes to obtaining facilities, equipment, and support for a program (Tillman et al., 1996). The various agencies, the support they can offer, and suggestions for community-based activities will be discussed in greater detail later in this chapter.

As community leaders and business owners, parents also offer valuable input. When it comes to locating facilities or raising funds for equipment, sometimes the old adage, "It's not what you know, but who you know," rings true. However, the community at large is generally the least interested in your particular program. Thus, it becomes important to be creative in attempting to reach them. Working with booster clubs and seeking business sponsorships or partnerships are effective ways to promote a program outside of the school environment (Horine & Stotlar, 2003).

Performing demonstrations at malls or during breaks in school sporting events; developing a speaker's bureau; hosting a community fitness fair, field day, or promotional event; and using creative advertising are examples of ways to reach the community at large (Graham et al., 2004; Horine & Stotlar, 2003).

Another important public worthy of consideration, yet not expressly included by Graham and colleagues (2004) as a major public affecting physical education programs, is the media. Print, radio, and television reports about a program, its staff, and activities keep the public informed while highlighting the success and progress of the students within the program (Tillman et al., 1996). Building good relationships with the local newspaper and radio and television stations takes advantage of powerful tools that influence public opinion and reach sizeable numbers of the community at large (Tillman et al., 1996). Other media suggested by Tillman and colleagues (1996) include videos, graphics, bulletin boards, public addresses and demonstrations, school publications, and annual reports.

IDENTIFYING COMMUNITY RESOURCES AND ACTIVITIES

Having identified the various constituencies that are important to developing a successful physical education program in and out of the school setting, we can turn to involving the community in assisting with the program. According to the National Association for Sport and Physical Education (NASPE) (n.d.), assigning students out-of-school activities for learning support and practice is one element of the standard of the NASPE guidelines for appropriate instruction.

Obviously, for any activity to be successful and meaningful, students should have a desire to participate, and teachers should find ways to encourage and foster that desire. Teachers can accomplish this task by identifying agencies and businesses within the community that provide and support physical activities and fitness through programs, facilities, and funding and offering a wide range of activities to pique students' interest in participation. The National Center for Chronic Disease Prevention and Health Promotion, a division of the CDC, offers a state-based physical activity program directory on their Web site at http://apps.nccd. cdc.gov/DNPAProg/StateV.asp. The directory can be searched by state or by keyword to view available programs and services geared toward physical activity and to identify partnering agencies.

Agencies

Most communities, including those in rural areas, have agencies that offer some type of lifetime physical fitness activity (see table 6.2). One obvious starting point is the community recreation department. Recreation departments traditionally offer various types of team sports (e.g., basketball, baseball and softball, football, soccer, tennis) at all age levels. Sometimes equipment, uniform, and facility costs are involved in participation, but these are usually minimal, and some support agencies and businesses offer individual scholarships or agree to sponsor a team.

Table 6.2   Identifying and Locating Community Resource Agencies

Agency	Resources offered	Suggestions for locating agency
Community and faith-based recreation programs	Facilities, equipment, uniforms, variety of team sports, aquatics, tennis, and so on	Local government offices, churches, and church schools
YMCA and YWCA	Same as community and faith-based programs, but with emphasis on family participation, also programs for people with disabilities	YMCA: www.ymca.net YWCA: www.ywca.org
Boys & Girls Clubs of America	Facilities, team and individual sports, uniforms, equipment, instruction	www.bgca.org
Boy Scouts of America Girl Scouts of the USA	Outdoor wilderness and adventure activities, aquatics, horseback riding, health, fitness, and nutrition instruction	Boy Scouts: www.scouting.org Girl Scouts: www.girlscouts.org
Amateur Athletic Union (nonprofit volunteer sports organization)	Sponsorship of Junior Olympics, traditional and nontraditional sporting opportunities	www.aausports.org
National Center for Chronic Disease Prevention and Health Promotion	State-based physical activity program directory (searchable by state or keyword)	http://apps.nccd.cdc.gov/DNPAProg/StateV.asp

Agency	Resources offered	Suggestions for locating agency
Women's Sports Foundation	Support of activities for girls, grant funding, and scholarships	www.womenssportsfoundation.org
Special Olympics	Activities for people with intellectual disabilities	www.specialolympics.org
International Paralympic Committee	Activities for people with physical disabilities	www.paralympic.org
American Heart Association	Exercise and nutrition guidelines for children, fitness campaigns	www.americanheart.org
Club sports	Sport opportunities for children and adolescents who desire more competition (some can be costly)	
U.S. Tennis Assoc. Tennis & Education Foundation	Tennis opportunities for people of diverse socioeconomic, cultural, ethnic, and physical backgrounds	www.usta.com/communitytennis/fullstory.sps?iNewsid=14574
Pop Warner Little Scholars	Organization of football and cheerleading leagues and instruction	www.popwarner.com
Amateur Softball Assoc., National Softball Assoc.	Organization of softball leagues and instruction	ASA: www.softball.org NSA: www.playnsa.com
Volleyball World Wide & U.S. Youth Volleyball League	Organization of volleyball leagues and instruction	VWW: www.volleyball.org USYVL: www.volleyball.org/usyvl
Babe Ruth League & Little League	Organization of baseball and softball leagues and instruction	Babe Ruth: www.baberuthleague.org Little League: www.littleleague.org
American Youth Soccer Organization	Organization of soccer leagues and instruction	http://soccer.org
Youth Basketball of America	Organization of basketball leagues and instruction	www.yboa.org
U.S. Bowling Congress Youth	Organization of bowling leagues and instruction	www.bowl.com/youth

Students who enjoy a particular team sport may choose to get involved in the various "club" sports. These are geared toward developing higher skill levels in a sport and offer higher levels of competition, frequently through traveling to other communities to compete or through some type of tournament play. Club team involvement can be costly, even with sponsorship, and may be prohibitive to many students. However, many teams hold fund-raising functions to offset the cost of participation. These functions teach team members the value of and responsibility for equipment, facilities, and transportation when earned through hard work. Sports clinics and camps can be located and researched through sports-related Web sites.

Other agencies include state and federal parks and trails, universities, and community colleges. Civic organizations (such as the Jaycees, Kiwanis, Rotary, and other business-oriented clubs) and fraternities and sororities are not only great sources of volunteer instructors and coaches, but many will conduct fund-raisers for school programs or offer sponsorships to meet equipment, facility, and uniform needs.

Partnering

Partnerships are mutually beneficial arrangements among businesses, communities, agencies, or other organizations (Merenda, 2000). *Partnering* involves joining businesses with schools to promote the education and training skills needed in the business community. According to Ryan and Cooper (2004), "[M]ore than 100,000 business–school partnerships have been formed since 1983, and business has donated hundreds of millions of dollars to improve elementary and secondary schools." They cite that "the education market represents potential revenue of $600 billion for corporate interests" as incentive for business involvement in education (p. 343). Nike, Apple, IBM, Procter & Gamble, and Coca-Cola are examples of large corporations involved in partnering (Ryan & Cooper, 2004).

Businesses use many strategies to help improve our nation's public schools and to cultivate future customers. Businesses typically participate in fund-raising activities (e.g., discount coupon cards), donate supplies and equipment, and post school-event fliers in their buildings. Business–school partnerships are a win–win for students and the business, as is evident from the potential buying power of students now and in the future.

Partnering with local businesses and organizations can be beneficial to classroom instruction as well. For instance, partnering with a hospital can provide instructors in the areas of health, nutrition, and diet for a weight-management course, or access to physicians and physical therapists to teach units on basic anatomy and physiology, stress management, and anger management through exercise, and so on. Universities and local community colleges provide tremendous opportunities for all types of classroom and practical instruction, as well as facility space. Private businesses may offer space for activities as well as sponsorship dollars. The possibilities are endless. Here are just a few ideas of local businesses to contact for assistance with your physical education programs:

- Hospitals
- Physical and occupational therapy clinics (particularly for students with disabilities)
- Universities and community colleges
- Professional sport teams
- Fitness clubs
- Golf courses
- Bowling alleys
- Aquatic centers
- Skating rinks
- Martial arts centers

Activities

Keeping in mind that the ultimate goal of getting students involved in physical activity is to develop habits to last a lifetime, the focus should be on activities that interest students and that they find enjoyable (Patrick et al., 2001). Many children find familiar traditional team and individual sports, such as soccer, basketball, softball, baseball, tennis, football, volleyball, golf, dance, swimming, and gymnastics to be enjoyable and interesting. An estimated 44 million children ages 7 to 17 participated in some type of sports activity during 2002 (U.S. Census Bureau, 2004).

However, not every child enjoys participating in traditional team sports, and many are not considered lifetime sports (Rivera, 2003). Today's popular culture fosters a different take on "sports" through participation in nontraditional physical activities. Often dubbed "extreme sports," a new "wide world of sports" has emerged featuring roller-blading, rock climbing, skate- and snow-boarding, break and line dancing, yoga, in-line skating, Frisbee, mountain biking, and extreme running as the lifetime sporting activities of today's youth and as excellent vehicles for physical educators to encourage youth activity (Rivera, 2003). Thinking outside the box about the actual local community environment and culture in which your students reside can lead to interesting activity ideas. For example, a rural farming community could turn to rodeo-based activities, including rodeo clown training, as a way to encourage kids to get involved, using skills learned in daily life for fun.

Adventure education is another avenue to explore. Rope courses, white-water rafting, scuba diving, hiking and backpacking, cave exploring (spelunking), and orienteering are challenging activities that can lead to building confidence through problem solving, team building, social interaction, and perceived sense of risk taking (Slentz & Chase, 2003).

There are an infinite number of community-based activities that youth can enjoy—many with parents, siblings, and friends and many at little or no cost. Pedometers, fairly inexpensive and even occasionally offered as promotional items, are popular among kids today and promote something as simple as counting steps daily with a goal of increasing the number of steps taken each day (Rivera, 2003). Other activity ideas include the following:

- Par course training, track and field, biathlon, duathlon, and triathlon
- Spinning classes, cycling, speed skating
- Weight training, aerobic classes, Pilates
- Skiing (water, cross-country, downhill), swimming, canoeing, surfing, rowing, sailing
- Hunting, fishing, shooting, archery
- Martial arts, boxing, kick boxing, judo, wrestling
- Dance, gymnastics, cheerleading, and circus training classes
- Handball, racquetball, table tennis, badminton
- Horseback riding, bowling

Service Learning

Defined as "a teaching method that provides opportunities for students to acquire academic, career, social, and personal skills through community service projects," *service learning* is another way for PE programs to work hand in hand with the community for the benefit of the student (Cutforth, 2000, p. 39). Bridging the gap between school and the real world, service learning differs from volunteerism because of the reflective experience that students gain through training, service, reflection, and recognition (Cucina, 2001; Cutforth, 2000).

Many states have or are considering making community service hours a graduation requirement (Ryan & Cooper, 2004). Planning, engineering, and implementing a structured community service activity centered on meeting the sport and recreational needs of a community builds positive relationships between the community and school while building the student's skills on several levels. Some activities can generate funding for school physical education programs as well as other worthwhile causes. The following are examples of community-based service learning:

- Organize a walk-a-thon, fun run, or bike-a-thon to raise funds for a worthy cause
- Plan or build a student-run community fitness center
- Run a weight-management program
- Participate in a mentoring program for students designed to train sports officials, coaches, and future instructors

NO CHILD LEFT BEHIND

Until now, our primary focus has been on the mainstream K-12 student and on students who may have an increased interest in physical education, athletics, and other extracurricular physical activity. However, we would be remiss in overlooking children who may have physical or intellectual disabilities or who have chronic illnesses, yet who would still enjoy and benefit from physical activity (ASHA, 1997; McAvoy & Lais, 2003; Special Olympics, n.d.a).

Children with Disabilities

Obesity-related disability rates among people ages 18 to 59 are on the rise (AAHPERD, 2004), and special education needs for children with disabilities are also increasing (Helm & Boos, 1996). However, even though research indicates that children with disabilities experience many of the same benefits of physical activities as those without disabilities, leisure time is often spent watching television or in some other sedentary activity (Sayers, Shapiro, & Webster, 2003).

Obese children, children with chronic health conditions, and those with physical or cognitive disabilities are deliberately or inadvertently overlooked or discouraged when it comes to physical activity and often excused from physical education classes, even though they may have a distinctive need for them (ASHA, 1997). Modifying physical education programs by enlisting the aid of physical and occupational therapists, therapeutic recreational therapists, and other health care service providers and community recreation resources, such as fitness or aquatic centers, to meet the needs of these students not only helps them physically but also mentally and socially (ASHA, 1997; Sayers, Shapiro, & Webster, 2003). Many local Ys; scouting programs; and parks, recreation, and community sports programs offer activities for children with disabilities, integrating them into their regular activities and offering therapeutic recreation services such as special camps and classes staffed with trained professionals. Students with disabilities can enjoy outdoor wilderness activities, such as camping, horseback riding, canoeing, swimming, and kayaking. Wilderness Inquiry is an integrated, community-based wilderness education organization that sponsors wilderness adventure trips for "people of all ages, backgrounds, and abilities" (McAvoy & Lais, 2003).

Special Olympics and Paralympics are international organizations recognized by the International Olympic Committee. Special Olympics offers free year-round Olympic-type sports training and competition to people with intellectual disabilities. Paralympics focuses on people with physical disabilities rather than intellectual disabilities (Special Olympics, n.d.b).

Home-Schooled Children

For obvious reasons, home-schooled children do not have the same in-school exposure to physical education classes; however, most can participate in community-based extracurricular recreation activities much the same as children who go to traditional schools. One developing option for home-schooled children who would like to include physical education credits in their curriculum is online PE classes (Gussow, 2002). The Florida Virtual School is an example of technology meeting physical education, resulting in activity. Students are given physical activity assignments and are required to maintain workout logs signed by their parents for the teacher.

SUMMARY

Collaboration among physical educators and a variety of vested publics is important to the success of a physical education program. Physical educators should offer consistent and clear messages about the benefits of their program to students, parents, other teachers, administrators, school boards, and legislators. Myriad agencies and businesses offer support to programs. Physical educators should work together with agencies and partner with businesses within their communities to build resources for their programs. School- and community-conscious collaboration provides children with increased opportunities to develop positive attitudes toward lifelong physical fitness.

Discussion Questions

1. Are public relations important to a physical education program? Why or why not? Are they more or less important to a school or nonschool program and why?

2. What are other factors that adversely affect participation in community-based physical activities, and how might they be overcome?

3. What role should parents, other teachers, and administrators play in discussions about developing either a community-based physical activity program or a school-sponsored after-school program?

4. How would you go about setting up a partnership with a local business?

5. Identify potential funding resources for a community-based or extracurricular program or activity.

Professional Portfolio Contents

1. Include a list of community resources to enhance physical activity opportunities. Search local newspapers, telephone yellow pages, and the Internet to get an idea of agencies, clubs, and programs that support community-based physical activity programs and for businesses and churches that might have facilities to loan.

2. Participate with others to organize and conduct a fitness fair like the one described in the vignette in the beginning of this chapter. Include a description of the event, pictures, letters you write to community sponsors, thank you letters, or other items to showcase the event.

3. Invite a scholar to your school or physical education majors club to speak. Include copies of the program, pictures of participants, or evaluation materials that reflect how the program enhanced others' understanding of physical education.

Key Terms

collaboration—To work together, especially in a joint intellectual effort.

organized physical activity—Physical activity with an organized group that has a coach, instructor, or leader.

partnering—Forming partnerships by joining businesses and civic organizations with schools to develop strategies and programs to enhance education.

publics—Constituencies; people who play an important role in the development of an idea or program.

service learning—A teaching method providing opportunities to acquire academic, career, social, and personal skills through community service projects.

Resources

Austin, K. (n.d.). Extracurricular activities: Get your child involved. *Children Today*. Retrieved February 20, 2005, from http://childrentoday.com/resources/articles/extraactivity.htm.

Kidscamp.com: www.kidscamps.com

Florida Virtual School: www.flvs.net

Lawson, H.A. (2005, March). Empowering people, facilitating community development, and contributing to sustainable development: The social work of sport, exercise, and physical education programs. *Sport, Education, & Society, 10(1)*, 135-160.

National Center for Chronic Disease Prevention and Health Promotion: http://apps.nccd.cdc.gov/DNPAProg/StateV.asp.

Walsh, D.S. (2002). Emerging strategies in the search for effective university-community collaborations. *Journal of Physical Education, Recreation & Dance, 73(1)*, 50-53. Retrieved January 26, 2005, from InfoTrac OneFile database.

WebSportsCoach: www.websportscoach.com

Women's Sports Foundation (community action programs): www.womenssportsfoundation.org/cgi-bin/iowa/comm/index.html

References

American Alliance for Health, Physical Education, Recreation and Dance. (2004). Disability rates rising among the young [Electronic version]. *Journal of Physical Education, Recreation & Dance 75(6)*, 10. Retrieved February 11, 2005, from InfoTrac OneFile database.

American School Health Association. (1997). Guidelines for school and community programs to promote lifelong physical activity among young people. Report by National Center for Chronic Disease Prevention and Health Promotion and the Centers for Disease Control and Prevention. *Journal of School Health, 67(6)*, 202-220, August 1997. Retrieved January 26, 2005, from InfoTrac OneFile database.

Cucina, I.M. (2001). A student-created community-service project for higher education [Electronic version]. *Journal of Physical Education, Recreation & Dance, 72(9)*, 47. Retrieved February 11, 2005, from InfoTrac OneFile database.

Cutforth, N.J. (2000). Connecting school physical education to the community through service learning [Electronic version]. *Journal of Physical Education, Recreation & Dance, 71(2)*, 39. Retrieved January 26, 2005, from InfoTrac OneFile database.

Dustin, D., Hibbler, D., McKenney, A., & Blitzer, L. (2004). Thinking outside the box: Placing park and recreational professionals in K-12 schools [Electronic version]. *Journal of Physical Education, Recreation & Dance, 75(1)*, 51. Retrieved February 11, 2005, from InfoTrac OneFile database.

Graham, G.M., Parker, M., & Holt-Hale, S.A. (2004). *Children moving* (6th ed.) (pp. 683-693). New York: McGraw-Hill Education.

Gussow, J. (2002, August 5). Online PE class is more than mouse clicks. *St. Petersburg Times.* Retrieved January 26, 2005, from www.sptimes.com/2002/08/05/news_pf/Technology/Online_PE_class_is_mo.shtml.

Hastie, P. (2003). *Teaching for lifetime physical activity through quality high school physical education* (pp. 333-348). San Francisco: Benjamin Cummings.

Helm, J.H., & Boos, S. (1996). Increasing the physical educator's impact: Consulting, collaborating, and teacher training in early childhood programs [Electronic version]. *Journal of Physical Education, Recreation & Dance, 67(3),* 26-27. Retrieved January 26, 2005, from InfoTrac OneFile database.

Horine, L., & Stotlar, D. (2003). *Administration of physical education and sports programs* (5th ed.) (pp. 75-93). New York: McGraw-Hill College.

McAvoy, L., & Lais, G. (2003). Wilderness, hope, and renewal: Programs that include persons with disabilities [Electronic version]. *Journal of Physical Education, Recreation & Dance, 74(7),* 25-28. Retrieved February 11, 2005, from InfoTrac OneFile database.

Merenda, D. (2000, November 7). Guest viewpoint: School–business partnerships; essential to student success. *School Board News,* 1-2. Retrieved November 4, 2005, from www.nsba.org/site/doc_sbn.asp?TrackID=&STD=1&DID=7779&CID=338&VID=58.

National Association for Sport and Physical Education. (2003). *National standards for beginning physical education teachers* (2nd ed.). Reston, VA: Author.

National Association for Sport and Physical Education. (n.d.). *What constitutes a quality physical education program?* Retrieved January 26, 2005, from www.aahperd.org/naspe/template.cfm?template=qualityPePrograms.html.

Patrick, K., Spear, B., Holt, K., & Sofka, D. (Eds.). (2001). *Bright futures in practice: Physical activity.* Arlington, VA: National Center for Education in Maternal and Child Health. Retrieved February 23, 2005, from www.brightfutures.org/physicalactivity/tools/d.html.

Rivera, E. (2003, December 20). New PE goal: Activities good for a lifetime. *The Washington Post,* p.b. 01.

Ryan, K., & Cooper, J. (2004). *Those who can, teach* (10th ed.). Boston: Houghton Mifflin.

Sayers, L.K., Shapiro, D.R., & Webster, G. (2003). Community-based physical activities for elementary students [Electronic version]. *Journal of Physical Education, Recreation & Dance, 74(4),* 49-54. Retrieved January 26, 2005, from InfoTrac OneFile database.

Slentz, T.C., & Chase, M.A. (2003). Climbing Mount Everest: A new challenge for physical education adventure education students [Electronic version]. *Journal of Physical Education, Recreation & Dance, 74(4),* 41-44. Retrieved February 11, 2005, from InfoTrac OneFile database.

Special Olympics. (n.d.a). *About us.* Retrieved February 23, 2005, from www.specialolympics.org/Special+Olympics+Public+Website/English/About_Us/default.htm.

Special Olympics. (n.d.b). *Differences between Special Olympics and Paralympics.* Retrieved February 23, 2005, from www.specialolympics.org/Special+Olympics+Public+Website/English/About_Us/Differences+from+Paralympics.htm.

Tillman, K.G., Voltmer, E.F., Esslinger, A.A., & McCue, B.F. (1996). *The administration of physical education, sport, and leisure programs* (6th ed.) (pp. 90-117). Boston: Allyn & Bacon.

U.S. Census Bureau. (2004, December 8). *Statistical abstract of the United States, 2004-2005* [Electronic version], (p. 774). Washington, DC: U.S. Government Printing Office. Retrieved February 25, 2005, from www.census.gov/prod/www/statistical-abstract.html.

Welk, G. (1999). *Promoting physical activity in children: Parental influences.* U.S. Department of Education, Office of Educational Research and Improvement (ERIC). Washington, DC: ERIC Clearinghouse on Teaching and Teacher Education. Retrieved February 23, 2005, from www.vtaide.com/png/ERIC/Physical-Activity.htm.

7

Establishing Productive Relationships

STANDARD 10: *Collaboration.* Understand the necessity of fostering collaborative relationships with colleagues, parents/guardians, and community agencies to support the development of a physically educated person.

OUTCOME 10.4: Establish productive relationships with parents/guardians and school colleagues to support student growth and well-being.

You have been given the responsibility of planning a schoolwide Olympics traditionally held each fall in your school that includes events for students in all grades. With the backing of teachers and the principal, you have selected this year's event theme: Family Fun Day. This event has been scheduled for a Saturday so that parents and teachers can help set up and run various competitive, fun events. To further involve the parents, several events are scheduled as child–parent events. These events will also include accommodations for those with differing physical abilities.

A parent and child run–walk event will kick off the Family Fun Day. Other events include stations focusing on individual and team efforts. You have invited some of the local fitness-related businesses to staff booths to exhibit their products and to offer discounts to their fitness centers. Volunteer parents and children who practice yoga, tai chi, and some of the martial arts will give demonstrations and presentations about their organizations. The PTO will have a kid-friendly concession stand stocked with healthy foods and drinks. They will also host a silent auction of a variety of fitness- and sports-related equipment along with team paraphernalia donated by the local college football and volleyball teams. A short volleyball tournament between teachers and parents will round out the day's events—sure to provide a laugh or two for the kids. Student volunteers have been designated to referee the match. Proceeds from the Family Fun Day will be used to buy needed equipment to help students meet their fitness goals.

The Family Fun Day will help to meet your goal to increase parent and guardian understanding of the importance of physical education for their children's growth and well-being by encouraging exercise and healthy eating while enjoying and promoting exercise as a family tradition.

As a physical educator, you certainly recognize the growing need to improve student physical well-being. Because of growing national attention on the increasing problem of childhood obesity, the general public is beginning to share concern for the problems that result from things such as lack of physical activity (see figure 7.1) and poor eating habits (Dietz & Gortmaker, 2001; U.S. Department of Health and Human Services [HHS], 2004, 2005). Even McDonald's, the fast-food chain that received criticism for contributing to child obesity through its menu of

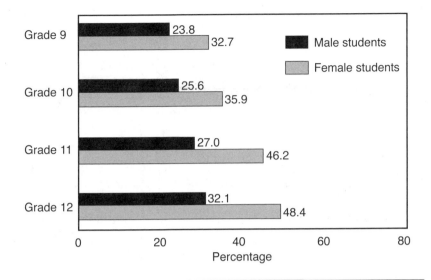

Figure 7.1   High school students not engaging in recommended amounts of physical activity (neither moderate nor vigorous) by grade and sex in the United States, 2003.

From CDC, National Center for Health Statistics. *Health, United States, 2004.* Accessed September 14, 2005. Available at www.cdc.gov/nchs/data/hus/hus04.pdf.

foods high in fat content, has launched a program announced in *USA Today* to support school physical education programs and has begun offering healthy choices on its menu (Hellmich, 2005). However, despite increased public awareness of the problems, many parents, teachers, and administrators do not know exactly how physical education contributes to a person's overall health and how it increases a child's ability to learn in the classroom and beyond (Graham, Holt-Hale, & Parker, 2004; Tenoschok & Sanders, 1984). It is imperative for physical educators to help others view physical education as an educational basic—rather than a frill—and to work collaboratively to improve children's well-being.

FINDING SUPPORT

As discussed in chapter 6, physical educators need support from many people, or "publics," to garner the funding needed to develop the type of high-quality programs desired for children and adolescents (Graham et al., 2004; Horine & Stotlar, 2003). Outside of students, three important publics affecting physical education programs, identified by Horine and Stotlar (2003), that are also clearly targeted in Outcome 10.4 are parents and guardians, other teachers, and administrators (see figure 7.2).

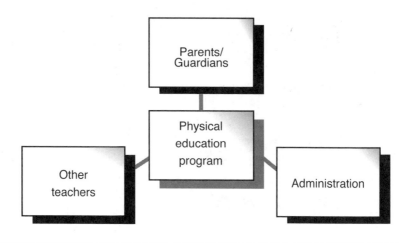

Figure 7.2   Primary nonstudent publics affecting PE programs daily.

Unlike legislators, school board members, and the at-large community who rarely visit your classroom, these parents, other teachers, and administrators are the primary publics with whom you interact daily and who have the greatest potential to directly affect your program. As a physical educator, it is important to build support and productive relationships in the form of partnerships with those who could prove to be your strongest allies as you work to improve your program (Graham et al., 2004; Hastie, 2003; Ryan & Cooper, 2004; Tillman, Voltmer, Esslinger, & McCue, 1996).

COMMUNICATION: THE KEY TO SUCCESSFUL RELATIONSHIPS

Effective teachers communicate (Graham et al., 2004; Tillman et al., 1996). As you learned previously, there are several advantages to collaborating with colleagues and the many other publics affecting your program. You gain support, ideas, and mentoring opportunities from colleagues and administrators, and insight about your students and support for your program from parents. One of the chief reasons that collaboration fails is that those involved do not communicate effectively or follow through on their responsibilities (Younger, 2004). NASPE (2003) Standard 5 addresses the importance of positive communication. Effective communication is a critical skill for the physical educator who is building a positive learning environment, not only with students but also with those who affect the program. By using the communication skills and methods addressed in NASPE (2003) Standard 5, you learn to build a collegial relationship with the most important *stakeholders:* teachers and staff, administrators, and parents. Successful partnerships require a relationship that involves closeness, sharing, and mutual trust.

Another important part of finding positive solutions together is to develop a feeling of ownership of the problem by all stakeholders. Little (1990) wrote that schoolteachers have been a group of entrepreneurial individuals whose autonomy is grounded in their expectations and desires for privacy to do their work. This autonomy has been sustained by the traditional systematic organization of schools and teaching. Little (1990) also noted that as the shift to collaboration began, teachers were pushed, invited, and cajoled into collaborative ventures; yet the organization of their daily work often gave them little reason to do so.

Progress in collaboration has been made since Little's (1990) observations. Educational researchers and change agents indicate that it has become increasingly clear from various sources that professional learning communities can improve schools as places to learn and grow (Hastie, 2003; Ryan & Cooper, 2004; Sparks, 2003). Today, greater numbers of educators support the idea of working in collaboration. They have learned that talking with one another and other stakeholders about their curriculum, class projects, and teaching materials allows them an opportunity to give and receive ideas to improve learning in their own classes. Simply stated, teachers and leaders can accomplish more in learning communities by consistently focusing on increasing students' knowledge, skills, and abilities. You must develop and share common goals and clear learner objectives for the most effective learning to occur. Unless there is unity and support for the program from parents, you and other teachers, and administrators, little may be gained in initiating such a program or attempting to sustain an established learning community. And, because student success is the ultimate focus of your program, effective communication and relationships with your students are also necessary for creating a true learning community.

ADMINISTRATORS AS COLLEAGUES

In large organizations such as schools, teachers, parents, and students turn to the school principal or other administrators to guide and support their efforts to build a viable education program. With the administrator's guidance, you and the other stakeholders can develop a plan to build and improve the *learning community.* You can be the initiator, as well, to bring attention and credibility to your program.

Getting Administrators Involved

You can help your administrators to learn or to maintain the belief that physical education is vital to student learning within and beyond physical education classes. By asking the principal for time on the staff meeting agenda to share information about your subject area and your professional development activities, you gain the administrator's attention for your program while showing how seriously you value what you do. Another way to garner attention from administrators is to invite them into your classroom more often than just the yearly evaluation, particularly if you are aware of previous or current sports involvement. You might ask an administrator who has collegiate or professional sport experience to demonstrate a skill or talk about the positive role physical education played in his or her advancement in athletics. Or you could invite the principal to come to an intraclass game or for a special class time in which students demonstrate and celebrate their improved skills during a grading period. Students typically react positively to special visits, particularly when the visitor participates in the classroom activity. This is conducive to a fun learning community and serves double duty by providing the administrator with a kinesthetic, stress-reducing experience. Through this collaborative effort, teachers and administrators alike can develop a greater appreciation for different subject areas and overcome prejudice toward a program area, such as physical education (Ryan & Cooper, 2004; Tillman et al., 1996).

Other ideas that draw the administration's attention to your program include displaying charts showing each student's skill progression and taking pictures of students practicing their skills and posting them on a centrally located school bulletin board. Bulletin boards that provide useful information about the mind–body connection or the food–body connection lend credibility to your activities and curriculum.

Building Administrative Trust

The administrator plays an important leadership role in a positive learning community (Southeastern Educational Development Laboratory, 1997). In learning communities with outstanding physical education programs, the administration trusts its teachers, encourages professional development, and supports teachers' decisions and programs. You have an important role as well. You must be the one to prove your trustworthiness, seek professional development opportunities, develop programs, and make decisions worthy of support.

To earn the administration's trust, you should follow some simple, commonsense rules: complete assignments in a timely manner, ask for help long before a difficulty turns into a significant problem, avoid becoming part of gossip, and always ask—do not assume—if you have questions. Seek your administrator's support to attend or create professional development opportunities that will help fill your learning gap and help you reach your professional goals. The following are examples:

- If you need to learn more about student discipline, attend a workshop on the topic or observe the classes of teachers your administrator says provide good class environments.
- If you want to learn more about the mind–body connection, contact physical education and nonphysical education organizations that provide seminars or conferences about these topics and accelerative learning.
- If you want to be a college coach, see if you can get experience at the nearest university or community college or go to coaches' clinics.
- If you are interested in a future administrative position, seek your administrator's guidance in creating opportunities to learn about building and leading an effective school.

Fostering a Safe School Environment

The overall school environment is another area where the principal's assistance can be important. The learning community must provide a safe and comfortable atmosphere for learning to occur. If students (and teachers) feel unsafe and experience hostility, positive learning and growth seldom occur (Ryan & Cooper, 2004). It is difficult for us to think clearly when we are under stress because our "thinking caps," the neocortex of the brain where information sorting and problem solving occur, will not properly function (Hannaford, 1995). You need to take responsibility for constructing an assuring and safe school environment and help students take responsibility for maintaining this atmosphere. The administrator can collaborate with you (and other stakeholders as needed) to determine approaches for creating such an environment. Administrators have the advantage of most easily viewing the entire school milieu and can support teacher (and student) efforts for change and can cheer positive elements on a continuous basis.

As presented in NASPE (2003) Standard 5 regarding communication, treating each other with respect and enthusiastically encouraging each other to reach personal and academic goals are important aspects of a constructive educational setting. According to a joint study conducted by the National Center for Education Statistics and the Bureau of Justice Statistics, in 2003, 7 percent of middle and high school students (aged 12 to 18) reported being bullied at school; 33 percent of high school students (grades 9 through 12) reported being in a physical fight, and 9 percent reported being threatened or injured with a weapon on school property during the previous 12 months (National Center for Education Statistics [NCES], 2004). These are frightening statistics, and combating them requires joint efforts from teachers and administrators. Such efforts may include helping students apologize after arguing or bullying one another, promoting sportsmanship and respect, and working together with the administration to provide schoolwide treatments, such as introducing a peer-to-peer mediation board. Because your survival and acceptance by colleagues may be tied to your ability to control your classes and keep students on task (Hastie, 2003), the principal's support can help you develop a positive learning community for all.

Evaluation Effort

Evaluation is a critical element for improving learning. Although state and local education departments and boards use a growing number of statewide testing requirements to measure learning gains, physical education as a subject area is often not evaluated or, if evaluated, not widely reported. Yet, if physical education is to be recognized to be as important as reading, writing, and mathematics, the quality of the program must be demonstrated. A principal can further show support for the physical education program by supporting your efforts.

You must have a clear plan of action for meeting current evaluation requirements. Be receptive to peer evaluations so that you understand how colleagues in other fields view the activities and worth of physical education classes. Peer evaluations can deter inaccurate perceptions and negative stereotypes about the field of physical education.

Initiation of evaluative research by the physical educator goes beyond required and peer evaluations, and the results can do much to illustrate the worth of physical education classes. The results of well-designed and well-executed research can help you prove that student learning is taking place and serve as a vehicle to share best practices. Here are examples of research topics you may want to consider:

- Determine if there is a relationship between sport involvement and grade point average by comparing students involved in sports with those who are not.
- Is there a relationship between scores on physical fitness tests and statewide reading and math tests?
- Does the percentage of students who are within the recommended range on the body mass index change as students get older?

Again, beyond helping students measure and celebrate their own improvement, you can use the evaluation results to show others the importance of physical education. Administrators like and need statistical data to support funding positions that could be critical to your program. These facts and figures may be as significant as students' positive feelings about physical education. Research provides you the opportunity to extol the benefits of the program and to change aspects of the program to get the results you desire.

PARENTS AS COLLEAGUES

Research clearly indicates that most students will not succeed without effective parental involvement in the schools (National Education Association [NEA], n.d.; Redd, Brooks, & McGarvey, 2002; Ryan & Cooper, 2004). In a national survey of school superintendents, 68 percent identified a lack of parental involvement as the biggest obstacle to student progress (Ryan & Cooper, 2004). Parents need to be key players on the learning team, as partners with the professional staff, helping their children achieve academic success. Furthermore, parents can be important colleagues by encouraging their children to develop the skills that promote lifetime fitness and health that are being taught in physical education.

Family patterns and parent or guardian work patterns have changed over the years. These changes often affect the parent or guardian's ability to engage in the educational process in traditional ways. If parents are divorced, one parent may not live in the area and may be unable to attend events. Single parents may need to stay home with other children or to work instead of attending evening or weekend school events, PTO meetings, or even parent conferences. The physical educator must work to keep parents informed and communication channels open.

Keeping Parents Informed

You can obtain the support of parents and guardians by providing an excellent program that contributes to the health, fitness, skill development, social adjustment, and recreational competencies of the children. Nothing is as powerful as a child arriving home every day talking excitedly about what he or she is learning in physical education class. For parents who are already interested in the content of their children's physical education classes and the value that each activity has for them, it is important to keep them informed about the curriculum and their child's progress (Tillman et al., 1996). This is also important in order to develop interest for otherwise uninterested or distracted parents. There are many ways to do this (Hastie, 2003; Horine & Stotlar, 2003; Wuest & Lombardo, 1994):

- Send a letter home at the beginning of the year telling parents about your general program, curriculum goals, and the general rules the students will be expected to follow.
- Include a letter with report cards at the end of each grading period talking about the curriculum, goals, and learner objectives for the upcoming grading period. This keeps parents on track and updated and shows that you are following the plan and goals described at the beginning of the year.
- Attend PTO meetings regularly, even if you are not required to do so, taking this opportunity to meet some of the parents.
- At elementary and middle schools, have students demonstrate newly learned skills at the PTO meetings. It will provide you with another chance to meet the parents who attend and to speak directly with them about the importance of physical education.
- Ask a supportive parent to speak at a PTO meeting about the value of the program.
- Ask to place an article or health facts or tips in each school newsletter.
- Send home a note or certificate telling of individual student accomplishments in class.
- Phone or e-mail parents to let them know how their child is doing in class and to answer questions or listen to ideas they might have. Set a goal to personally contact a certain number of parents each week, making sure at the beginning of the year that they know how to reach you. The effect of a positive call or note on a parent's attitude toward physical education is immeasurable.
- Post information on a bulletin board in an area frequented by parents.
- Create a Web site for your physical education program and be sure to provide the address to your students' parents.

Keeping Parents Involved

Another way to build positive relationships is to identify ways parents can be involved in the physical education program. Seek assistance from parents who can help you accomplish your program goals and objectives. These opportunities serve two purposes. First, parent involvement is a great help to you; and second, the exposure can be great publicity for your program. Parents see firsthand what is happening in your program and what needs you may have to ensure success. Parents can help you build or even donate class equipment. You may have parents or grandparents with expertise in some of the skill and knowledge areas you want to teach. For example, a parent or grandparent might be a golf or tennis professional, a dance instructor, a current or retired professional baseball player, or a health professional who can extol the virtues of lifetime physical fitness. These people can bring a wealth of knowledge to your program. You may even want to invite them to team-teach with you for a week.

You can invite parents to your class to assist you, even if they are not content experts. Follow the example set by core-subject teachers and ask parents to help with the following tasks:

- Grading papers or inputting grades to a computer
- Working with a small group at a station, or providing remediation for a student who is having difficulty with a task
- Completing an equipment inventory
- Putting up a bulletin board
- Creating a video to be shown at a PTA or PTO meeting
- Painting targets on a wall or floor
- Assisting with fitness or skill assessment
- Putting together a newsletter
- Assisting with a running or walking club

Parents can also help with Olympic Day or other play days by refereeing, bringing refreshments, or serving as a base coach during a teacher–student softball game (Wuest & Lombardo, 1994).

Developing an occasional "parent and student night" is another way to involve parents and to benefit all members of the family (Harrison & Blakemore, 1992). Work with local businesses, such as the local skating rink, swimming pool, or bowling alley, to secure group discounts. You might want to plan to have the parent-and-student night during the week rather than the weekend for a couple of reasons. The recreational businesses you might approach often have fewer customers during the week and would be more inclined to offer deals to attract your business— particularly if these activities lead to families coming back on their own at other times. Weekends are often busy for families, so an event during the week works well for many families. Therefore, scheduling occasional weeknight outings provides a win–win situation for both businesses and families—businesses attract more customers and families get family time and exercise at discounted prices.

If many of the parents of your students work two jobs and have neither weekends nor evenings free, you can recruit adult partners from local service organizations, local college and civic service organizations (e.g., sororities and fraternities, Jaycees), and businesses or churches to attend and participate with the students. Volunteer parents can help you line up these partners, too. Additionally, local businesses may be willing to help pay the costs for students who would otherwise be unable to attend.

OUT-OF-FIELD TEACHERS AND STAFF AS COLLEAGUES

Although little is known about the effects of teacher collaboration on student productivity and enjoyment, specific evidence shows that educators' collaborative relationships can positively affect classroom climate, which, in turn, affects student achievement (Cusick, 1980). Far too often, physical education teachers detach themselves from the total school environment. Many times this happens because they are physically located away from the other teachers and may have different schedules. As a new teacher, you must be viewed as a positive addition to the educational environment, proving yourself in the workforce in order to garner collegial acceptance (Hastie, 2003). Although it makes perfect sense to associate with other professional physical educators, it is imperative that you make an extra effort to connect with other teachers outside the field of physical education if you want to successfully gain respect for your program (Irwin & Irwin, 2004; Markos, Walker, & Colvin, 1998). Effective teachers in true learning communities make the effort to emerge from the gymnasium and outdoor fields to share experiences with the rest of the faculty (Harrison & Blakemore, 1992). The following are examples:

- Attend faculty meetings and schoolwide events.
- Volunteer to serve on faculty committees.
- Regularly eat lunch with colleagues or seek opportunities to strike up conversations.

These interactions help you gain new ideas about your learning community and can have a positive effect on your program.

Integrating with Other Subject Areas

Research conducted during the last two decades has produced a growing number of findings that confirm that the whole body is involved in the learning process (Hannaford, 1995; McPhee, 1996). Child development experts have shown that children have different learning styles, are concrete learners, and learn actively by doing. You need to be able to take information that is often abstract and present it in a practical hands-on manner (Cone, Werner, Cone, & Woods, 1998). For example, students can act out such things as the concept of machines. Have students actually work with full-size pulleys, levers, and fulcrums to allow students to experience and physically feel how these items can make work easier. Physical educators are the likely candidates to share this information with their colleagues. They need to keep abreast of the research, not only through physical education literature but also through searches of research in other areas such as physiology, kinesiology, brain-based research, or multiple intelligences.

You should watch for opportunities to integrate physical education concepts with other subject areas in the curriculum (Cone et al., 1998; Markos et al., 1998; McPhee, 1996). Table 7.1 offers examples of integrative techniques you can apply. You can help classroom teachers understand how to use movement in their classrooms to facilitate student learning and learn about the methods they use to help students learn.

Other teachers may share information with you about individual students who are experiencing problems, such as inability to focus and sit still. These and other student difficulties and challenges can have physical solutions. You can help teachers work with these students, using kinesthetic and stress-reduction work to teach students how to learn to focus and to integrate their thinking (Hannaford, 1995; McPhee, 1996). Sharing information and ideas on how to help these students builds collegial relationships with other teachers while helping the students.

Sometimes a student's difficulties or challenges require the attention of the school counselor or other specialized staff. Because of your background in anatomy, physiology, and kinesiology and knowledge of how the body works, you can offer assistance to counselors and school health staff. Music and art teachers can use the therapies their specialties offer as well, integrated with physical education, to assist students

**Table 7.1 Ideas for Integrating Physical Education
With Other Subject Areas**

Subject area and topic	Integration activity
Science—respiratory system	Use a dance unit to learn teach how the respiratory system works.
Geography—United States	Draw a map on the playground or gym floor and develop a quiz game that requires students to move from one state to another.
Math—addition	Take students bowling and have them bring their scorecards back to score in math class—or better yet, invite the math teacher along!

who are having difficulty learning in other areas (McPhee, 1996; Ryan & Cooper, 2004).

Integrating Through Health-Related Initiatives

Another way to integrate physical education throughout the school environment is to be a positive influence on the personal development of faculty colleagues. Stress has become a health concern, and teacher and staff stress is no exception (Harrison & Blakemore, 1992). As part of the learning community, you can offer after-school aerobics, running and walking clubs, or yoga. In addition to the health benefits, these opportunities provide an important time for socializing and getting to know your colleagues. This could also be used as an opportunity to bring in a parent who can teach a yoga class, offer dietetic advice, or provide other forms of stress relief.

TEACHING AND MENTORING STUDENTS

Physical education involves teaching more than just physical skills. Just as the mathematics teacher and English teacher hope to instill the knowledge, skills, and abilities they cover in their classes as life skills, you should be doing the same. Beyond teaching physical skills that can be used throughout life, it is essential that students gain the attitudes and abilities that allow them to want to learn more about well-being in combination with the newly learned physical skills. You have the chance to develop positive relationships with students that go beyond simple communication (Ryan & Cooper, 2004). This may be even more critical for students who may be neglected or mistreated at home. School may be the key place that these students are accepted for who they are and still challenged to be the best person they can be.

Building Rapport and Mentoring

Through your attitude and regular encouragement, you communicate to students your belief that they will achieve the goals of the instructional program while building a positive rapport with your students (Ryan & Cooper, 2004). In effect, you get across to students a "can-do" attitude about learning. You should also feel and exhibit genuine concern about students' well-being and recognize students' accomplishments (Wuest & Lombardo, 1994). This includes honoring students who may have different skills. Howard Gardner's work on multiple intelligences points out the importance of acknowledging diverse abilities (McPhee, 1996).

Your efforts are important for helping to create a favorable impression of physical education in students' minds. Moreover, through your mentoring and emphasis on the importance of developing the whole person, you are more likely to instill lifelong habits. If students sense that you genuinely care about them while under your charge, they may be more likely as adults to choose physical activity and other healthful activities for themselves and their own families.

Your Growth as a Student

Another way for you to connect with students and enhance the students' learning is to continue to build your own professional and personal knowledge and skills. According to Mortimer Adler (1997), teachers who fail to continue to learn hinder students who are developing their learning habits. Gaining new information about emerging and changing topics related to physical education (e.g., cardio exercise, eating habits, and stress-reduction techniques) and sharing it with students not only helps to educate students but also increases your knowledge base and keeps you up to date on current trends in the field. By pointing out the sources of new information and giving students assignments that require them to explore and report on research findings themselves, you instill in students the idea of lifelong learning, as you learn.

COACHING STUDENTS

Many of you will coach one of your school's sport teams. Coaches serve as the premier role models in the sporting world. Your conduct and personal characteristics can influence the population's opinion about the worth of athletics (Tillman et al., 1996). In addition, a team that plays to its potential and follows the principles of good sporting behavior represents the school and community well.

The primary role of a coach is to develop athletes and help them succeed, but also to accept the responsibility for educating their parents. Parents should learn how best to support their children's sport participation and the importance of appropriate behavior in the youth sport environment (NASPE, 2003). Parents, along with coaches, are vital role models for their student-athletes and, like the students, represent the school and community through their behavior. Therefore, the National Association of Sport and Physical Education (NASPE) urges coaches to hold a formal meeting with the coaching staff, athletes, and the parents before the start of a season. Agenda topics should include coaching philosophy and style, typical practice session routines, expectations for the athletes, and athlete risk and safety issues. The NASPE position paper (2003) also urges coaches to cover expectations for the parents, communication procedures, officiating, and sportsmanship and to hold a question-and-answer period. Covering the information carefully and addressing all questions up front can prevent problems later in the season.

CONTENT IMPROVEMENT

As addressed throughout this chapter, collegiality is a responsibility for all within the school and for parents as well. Collegial relationships are necessary for building schools of excellence. Educational reform expert Michael Fullan wrote, "The single factor common to successful change is that relationships improve. If relationships improve, schools get better. If relationships remain the same or get worse, ground is lost" (Sparks, 2003, p. 3). Part of building an atmosphere of collegiality is the constant effort by stakeholders to improve themselves and the school. The Japanese have a name for such improvement: *kaizen*. Kaizen is the concept of constantly improving little by little. In a world where we often feel overwhelmed by the demands from all around, you can learn to enjoy the results brought by constant steps of improvement.

Michael Fullan (Sparks, 2003) believes that teachers seeking to improve themselves are characterized by four attitudes: (1) They accept that improvement is possible, (2) they are ready to self-evaluate to define their learning gap, (3) they seek practices better than their own, and (4) they recognize the importance of continued learning. This applies to the other stakeholders besides the teacher (Deming, 1986). Everyone needs to be aware of their role within this charge and be willing to put in the time and effort needed to reach the positive results desired. As a leader and colleague, you will need to take whatever steps you can to achieve your learning community's goals.

SUMMARY

As you enter the teaching world, your primary focus will be providing the best physical education program that you can for your students—your number one public. This chapter explored several ways to develop your program through the other publics who are also important for success—your professional colleagues, administrators, and parents. Each is a stakeholder, and much can be learned and accomplished through collaborations with people who desire similar results as you. Cultivating relationships and garnering support can be accomplished in a variety of ways, but each method begins with effectively communicating your goals, needs, activities, progress, and accomplishments to those who can positively affect your program.

Collaboration through administrative mentoring, exchanging ideas with teachers, integrating lessons with other subject areas, coaching and mentoring your students, seeking personal learning opportunities, and keeping parents involved in their child's progress are all important to your professional and personal growth and are imperative keys to the success of your program.

Discussion Questions

1. Why are positive relationships with parents important?
2. Why are positive relationships with colleagues important?
3. Name four actions you could take to build positive relationships with your colleagues at your school.
4. How can technology help you improve relationships with other stakeholders?

Professional Portfolio Contents

You can begin to collect these artifacts as a preservice student and continue when you begin teaching.

1. Include reports on parent–teacher conferences attended and reflect on your growth with respect to this area of teacher responsibility.
2. Provide copies of form letters, certificates, newsletters, and so on used to communicate with parents and guardians, students, and the community.
3. Document school and community service and describe how these experiences contributed to your professional growth.
4. Include or describe videos you used to help students learn or to provide information for parents and the community. If you videotaped student performance, describe your use of these tapes to provide student feedback.
5. Include copies of newsletters with physical education articles and information.
6. Include photos of bulletin boards used to communicate with others about the program, curriculum, student achievement, and special programs.

Key Terms

kaizen—A concept of constantly improving little by little.

learning community—A school in which all stakeholders create a positive environment where students can enjoy learning and achieve their learning potential.

stakeholder—Individual or group with a vested interest in an outcome.

Resources

Education World: www.educationworld.com

Fischer, M. (2002). What I've learned about cultivating parent involvement: National Education Association. Retrieved September 1, 2006 from www.nea.org/classmanagement/ifc021029.html

Teacher-to-Teacher Collaboration: http://teachnet.edb.utexas.edu/~lynda_abbot/teacher2teacher.html#A

References

Adler, M.J. (1977). *Reforming education: The schooling of a people and their education beyond schooling.* G. Van Doren (Ed.). New York: Macmillan.

Cone, T.P., Werner, P., Cone, S.L., & Woods, A.M. (1998). *Interdisciplinary teaching through physical education.* Champaign, IL: Human Kinetics.

Cusick, P.A. (1980). *A study of networks among professional staffs of two new secondary schools.* East Lansing, MI: Michigan State University.

Deming, W.E. (1986). *Out of the crisis.* Cambridge, MA: Massachusetts Institute of Technology.

Graham, G., Parker, M., & Holt-Hale, S. (2004). *Children moving: A reflective approach to teaching PE.* New York: McGraw-Hill.

Dietz, W.H., & Gortmaker, S.L. (2001). Preventing obesity in children and adolescents. *Annual Review of Public Health, 22,* 337-353. Retrieved August 24, 2005, from http://arjournals.annualreviews.org/doi/abs/10.1146/annurev.publhealth.22.1.337.

Hannaford, C. (1995). *Smart moves: Why learning is not all in your head.* Arlington, VA: Great Ocean.

Harrison, J., & Blakemore, C. (1992). *Instructional strategies for secondary school physical education* (3rd ed.). Dubuque, IA: W.C. Brown.

Hastie, P. (2003). *Teaching for a lifetime: Physical activity through quality high school physical education.* San Francisco: Benjamin Cummings.

Hellmich, N. (2005, September 14). McDonald's kicks off school PE program. USA Today. Retrieved September 14, 2005, from www.usatoday.com/news/health/2005-09-12-mcdonalds-pe_x.htm.

Horine, L., & Stotlar, D. (2003). *Administration of physical education and sports programs* (5th ed.). New York: McGraw-Hill College.

Irwin, C.C., & Irwin, R.L. (2004). Public relations for physical education. *Strategies, 18(2),* 25-34.

Little, J. (1990). The persistence of privacy: Autonomy and initiative in teachers' professional relations. *Teachers College Record, 91,* 509-536.

Markos, N.J., Walker, P.J., & Colvin, A.V. (1998, March/April). Elementary "Think Tank." *Strategies, 11(4),* 7-8.

McPhee, D. (1996). *Limitless learning: Making powerful learning an everyday event.* Tucson, AZ: Zephyr Press.

National Association for Sport and Physical Education. (2003). *National standards for beginning physical education teachers* (2nd. ed.). Reston, VA: Author.

National Center for Education Statistics, Bureau of Justice Statistics. (2004). *Indicators of school crime and safety: 2004.* Retrieved October 6, 2005, from www.ojp.usdoj.gov/bjs/pub/pdf/iscs04.pdf.

National Education Association. (n.d.). *What the research says: Parent involvement helps students succeed in school and in life.* Retrieved September 4, 2006, from www.nea.org/parents/research-parents.html.

Redd, Z., Brooks, J., & McGarvey, A.M. (2002, August). Educating America's youth: What makes a difference. *Child Trends Research Brief.* Washington, D.C.: Child Trends. Retrieved October 17, 2005, from www.childtrends.org/Files/K4Brief.pdf.

Ryan, K., & Cooper, J. (2004). *Those who can, teach* (10th ed.). Boston: Houghton Mifflin.

Southeastern Educational Development Laboratory. (1997). *Professional learning communities: What are they and why are they important?* Retrieved September 1, 2006, from www.sedl.org/change/issues/issues61.html.

Sparks, D. (2003). Interview with Michael Fullan: Change agent. *Journal of Staff Development, 24(1).* Retrieved from www.nsdc.org/library/publications/jsd/fullan241.pdf.

Tenoschok, M., & Sanders, S. (1984). Planning an effective public relations program. *Journal of Physical Education, Recreation & Dance, 55,* 48-49.

Tillman, K., Voltmer, E., Esslinger, A., & McCue, B.F. (1996). *The administration of physical education, sport, and leisure programs* (6th ed.). Needham Heights, MA: Allyn & Bacon.

U.S. Department of Health and Human Services, National Center for Health Statistics, Centers for Disease Control and Prevention. (2004). *Health, United States, 2004.* Retrieved September 14, 2005, from www.cdc.gov/nchs/data/hus/hus04.pdf.

U.S. Department of Health and Human Services, National Center for Health Statistics, Centers for Disease Control and Prevention. (2005, February 8). *Health E-Stats: Prevalence of overweight among children and adolescents: United States, 1999-2002.* Retrieved February 18, 2005, from www.cdc.gov/nchs/products/pubs/pubd/hestats/overwght99.htm.

Wuest, D., & Lombardo, B. (1994). *Curriculum and instruction: The secondary school physical education experience.* New York: McGraw-Hill.

Younger, L. (2004). Partnerships 101. *Project for Public Spaces. Urban Parks online.* Retrieved September 14, 2005, from www.pps.org/topics/pubpriv/roles/Younger_Ptnrs.

III

Curricular Implementation

One purpose of this book is to address content that has traditionally been taught in organization and administration courses. Teaching in a litigious society, managing resources effectively, using technology appropriately, documenting personal growth, and identifying future opportunities are the focus of this section. Chapter 8 recognizes the importance of reducing liability and risk. The content addresses topics such as legal issues, implementation of federal guidelines, addressing individual needs, and constant improvement approaches. Chapter 9 places the content in a school context, examines teacher decision making, and addresses appropriate use of resources. An educator's success is frequently measured by the initial goal, the process involved in addressing that goal, and the ultimate outcome assessment. This chapter explains the progression and points out opportunities for future success. Chapter 10 addresses technology use in the physical education program. Appropriate technology use can facilitate communication, increase available resources, strengthen student learning, and place the physical educator in a leadership position. Chapter 11 presents professionalism and professional growth as essential components in a physical educator's career. Getting off to a good start by developing a philosophy, embracing an employment strategy, committing maximum effort in the induction year, and embracing the continuous reflection and self-evaluation process will facilitate personal and professional growth and development and will enhance your chances for success. Chapter 12 guides the educator through the process of creating a professional portfolio that is purposeful and provides value. You will explore format and content that will provide evidence of your growth and development.

CHAPTER

8

Reducing Liability and Risk

STANDARD 4: *Management and Motivation.* Use and have an understanding of individual and group motivation and behavior to create a safe learning environment that encourages positive social interaction, active engagement in learning, and self-motivation.

OUTCOME 4.2: Organize, allocate, and manage resources (e.g., students, time, space, equipment, activities, and teacher attention) to provide active and equitable learning experiences.

It is the last day of a seven-week soccer unit, and you decide to give in to the students' request to participate in one large soccer game, unlike the small-sided games you usually organize. Following a unit cognitive test, you post a list of two teams of 11 players on the wall. Students organize themselves into the teams for one large soccer game for the last 20 minutes of class. You serve as the referee and begin the game. After 10 minutes of game play, two students, running straight at one another, accidentally lock ankles while going after the ball. Both students go to the ground in serious pain. You stop the game, and as you get closer to the students, you realize that one student has broken his ankle. Immediately, you direct two students to get the nurse. You tell two more students to get the athletic trainer (who happens to be the other physical education teacher). You also instruct all of the students to pick up the equipment and to sit on the bench at the edge of the soccer field. Realizing the severity of the situation, all of the students quickly comply with the requests. Within 30 minutes, an ambulance has transported the student to the hospital, the student's parents have been contacted, and an accident report has been filed in the principal's office. That night you contact the parents to check on the health status of your student. One week later, you are called to the principal's office and notified that the school district, the principal, and you have been named in a lawsuit submitted by the parents of the injured student. After meeting with a teacher's union representative, the school district's lawyer, and the principal, it is internally determined that your actions comply with the district policies and procedures and that there is no evidence of negligence. Because effective management, safety techniques, and enactment of the district emergency plan are evidenced, the lawsuit is eventually dropped.

Physical activity settings are highly litigated areas in the courts today. Sport and learning are associated with physical and psychological risk and *liability*. The vignette illustrates a scenario that could have taken place at any high school in the United States. The context and outcome of this situation reiterate the importance of classroom management. In this case, the organization, allocation, management of resources (e.g., students, time, space, equipment, activities, teacher attention), and adherence to educational policy contributed to the creation of active and equitable learning experiences. Teachers and coaches often first think of injuries when considering risk and liability related to physical activity. It is important to keep in mind that discrimination and unfair treatment are also common reasons for *litigation*. This chapter will provide an overview on how to create safe learning environments that encourage positive social interaction, active engagement, and self-motivation. However, this is not a comprehensive reference for sports law; it is merely a springboard for discussion related to issues of risk and liability. The authors encourage the readers to take preventive action.

We live in a litigious society. In general, we believe that when accidents occur that someone is to blame. Parents no longer simply accept injuries or psychological harm to their children as accidents. A *tort* is a "civil wrong which does not involve a contractual relationship" (Wong, 1994, p. 782). A tort signifies wrongdoings and potential reward of damage resulting from someone's actions. There are two types of torts: intentional and unintentional. Much of the risk and liability associated with physical education is unintentional. Teachers do not teach gymnastics with the intent to hurt their students; however, injury is sometimes an unwelcome outcome. Teachers who do not exercise *due care* are considered negligent, even if the outcome was unintended.

Negligence is the failure to act reasonably or to exercise due care under the circumstance of the situation (Hart & Ritson, 1993; Wong, 1994). Negligence addresses issues related to those who have been harmed by the carelessness of others. The determination of the appropriateness of someone's actions or judgments is often a difficult process. Negligence depends on the existence of four essential elements: "(1) the *duty* or obligation recognized by the law, requiring the actor to conform to a certain standard of conduct, for the protection of others against unreasonable harm, (2) a *failure on his part to conform* to the standard required, (3) a reasonably *close causal connection* between the conduct and resulting injury, and (4) an *actual loss or damage* resulting from the interests of another" (Conn, 2004, p. 9). It only takes the absence of one of these elements for the injured party to recover damages. It is important to realize that negligence is considered an unintentional tort, meaning the teacher did not intentionally or purposefully plan to hurt the student; the injury simply happened under his or her supervision.

In the case of *Smith v. Vernon Parish School Board* (1983), the physical education teacher had properly instructed her students in technique and adequately practiced and enforced classroom rules (performing her duty), yet she still had to go to court when a student was injured during her class. Because of inclement weather, the physical education teacher gave the students the choice of sitting in the bleachers or using the trampoline. Smith had received more than four years of instruction in the use of trampolines. The teacher told the students that only two people were allowed on the trampoline at a time. At the end of gym, the teacher left the stage where the trampoline was located and went to talk to the other physical education teacher. After sending a friend to make sure the curtains were closed on the stage so that the physical education teacher could not see them, Smith and four other girls started to play on the trampoline. After one jump, Smith fell off of the trampoline and broke her wrist. The Court of Appeals of Louisiana determined that the teacher had exercised reasonable care, had properly instructed her students, and was not negligent.

LEGISLATION

Three federal acts of legislation govern educational policy: (a) Title IX (1972), (b) the Americans with Disabilities Act (1990), and (c) the Safe School Act (Act 26 of 1995 and Act 30 of 1997). Unlike federal law, "state constitutional and statutory provisions vary from state to state and often jurisdiction to jurisdiction" (Conn, 2004, p. i). Although state laws are not specifically discussed in this chapter, teachers must be aware of the local and state laws governing their school district.

Title IX (1972)

Signed into law by President Richard Nixon on June 23, 1972, Title IX of the Educational Amendments was a landmark decision banning sex discrimination in schools.

> No person in the U.S. shall, on the basis of sex be excluded from participation in, or denied the benefits, or be subject to discrimination under any educational program or activity receiving federal aid. (U.S. Department of Labor, 2004)

Title IX is easily identifiable because of its association with equality in sports participation, athletic scholarship opportunities, and general benefits. General benefits require equality between males and females in facilities, equipment, health services, and other remuneration stemming from athletic team participation. With regard to Title IX, we are most familiar with intercollegiate athletic cases such as *Cohen v. Brown University* (1993). Despite the fact that two men's teams had simultaneously been downgraded to club status, the judge still ruled that there were inequities in the finances extended to athletic programs for men and women at Brown University. The court ordered Brown University to reinstate women's volleyball and gymnastics, which had been eliminated in a cost-cutting move. Few coeducational universities offer equal opportunities for males and females; however, many institutions offer opportunities comparable to the percentage of females in attendance at the university. It is often debated that the high cost of football prevents a dollar-for-dollar equity among the genders.

Although most commonly linked to athletics, Title IX applies to all educational programming. "The law prohibits sex discrimination in all aspects of education, including career and vocational programs, admissions and employment policies, standardized testing, and treatment of pregnant and parenting teens" (U.S. Department of Labor, 2004). Additionally, Title IX prohibits single-sex classes, including physical education, in coeducational schools. Single-sex classes are permitted only during physical education instruction involving contact sports, such as wrestling or football. Sex should be considered when assigning ability groups or matching students. Students can be grouped by gender in physical education if objective standards of performance are applied. For example, to participate in an advanced swimming class, students must complete basic Red Cross swimming competencies. If Red Cross swim testing results in all-male or all-female classes separated on the basis of ability, this is an acceptable practice under the guidelines of Title IX. However, if a single standard of measure of skill or progress (e.g., lifting 100 pounds [45 kilograms]) in physical education class has an adverse effect on members of one sex, schools must alter their practice. For example, a public assessment of strength, as a criterion for participation in a weight training class, is unacceptable because application of this standard may exclude girls.

Title IX attempts to address issues related to inequities in all educational settings, including the student–teacher interactions. Teachers are often unaware of their actions toward students. Gender bias can be found in student–teacher interactions, instruction, and curriculum. Although teachers believe that they treat males and females the same, they frequently do not (Brophy, 1985). Male students actually receive more attention than females (Hulley, 2001). Unknowingly, teachers provide more instructive, corrective feedback to male students (Hulley, 2001), perhaps resulting from males' strategies to ensure teacher attention (French & French, 1984). Both the student and teacher contribute to the gender bias as a teacher react to the attention-getting strategies employed by the male students.

The type of activities selected for the curriculum could also lend itself to gender bias. If a teacher were to provide opportunities for participation only through traditional team sport activities, it could be considered gender bias if he or she does not provide equity between male and female sports. Strategies must be employed so that unintentional gender bias can be identified by teachers. Expression of the same expectations for males and females, equal reinforcement of rules, focus on all learners, and individual as well as small-group practice are ways a teacher can minimize gender bias.

One way to evaluate potential gender bias in your teaching is to video-tape yourself teaching and review its contents. You can evaluate the quantity and quality of your interactions with male and female students by using a coding sheet (see figure 8.1).

Males and females should have equal access to activities, equipment, and teacher attention, and both should receive equal support to promote success. Future initiatives falling under Title IX include a decrease in sexual assaults and threats in the high school setting, more involvement of girls and women in technology and science, increased equality in high school varsity sports, increased equality in athletic scholarships, and equal wages for males and females. A recent trend has held school

Instructions: Record the time and date of the observation. When a teacher-to-student or student-to-teacher interaction occurs, circle the type of interaction that transpired. Total the number of interactions with both male and female students and write a one-page reflection about your findings.

Observer's name: _____   Date:_____

Time lesson began: _____   Time lesson ended: _____

Time	Male interaction			Female interaction		
	Positive	Corrective	Negative	Positive	Corrective	Negative
	Positive	Corrective	Negative	Positive	Corrective	Negative
	Positive	Corrective	Negative	Positive	Corrective	Negative
	Positive	Corrective	Negative	Positive	Corrective	Negative
	Positive	Corrective	Negative	Positive	Corrective	Negative
	Positive	Corrective	Negative	Positive	Corrective	Negative
	Positive	Corrective	Negative	Positive	Corrective	Negative
	Positive	Corrective	Negative	Positive	Corrective	Negative
	Positive	Corrective	Negative	Positive	Corrective	Negative

Total number of male interactions: _____

Total number of female interactions: _____

Figure 8.1   Sample coding sheet for male and female student interactions.

districts legally liable for student-to-student harassment. Title IX influences physical education through teacher–student interactions, student–student interactions, ability grouping, single-sex classes, curriculum, and instruction. Similar to Title IX legislation, the Americans with Disabilities Act addresses discrimination issues.

Americans with Disabilities Act of 1990 (ADA)

Forty-three million Americans have one or more physical or mental disabilities. The Americans with Disabilities Act of 1990 (ADA) prohibits discrimination based on disability. This legislation stemmed from the Individuals with Disabilities Education Act (formerly called Education of All Handicapped Children Act), which required public schools to make available to all eligible children with disabilities a free public education in the least restrictive environment appropriate to their individual needs. IDEA serves four purposes: (1) to assure that children have a free appropriate public education, (2) to assure the rights of children and their parents, (3) to assist states in providing an education to children with disabilities, and (4) to assess and assure the effectiveness of efforts to educate all children with disabilities (U.S. Department of Education, Office of Civil Rights, 2002). It is easily forgotten how few opportunities for individuals with disabilities existed before 1975, now that the majority of children with disabilities are educated in public schools with their peers.

Section 504 of the Rehabilitation Act of 1973 specifically addressed participation issues:

> No otherwise qualified individual with a disability in the United States shall, solely by reason of her or his disability, be excluded from the participation in, be denied the benefits of, or be subjected to discrimination under any program or activity receiving Federal financial assistance. (U.S. Department of Education, Office of Civil Rights, 2002)

Section 504 (originally of the Rehabilitation Act of 1973) specifies that physical education is a required educational service. More specifically, physical education is "the development of physical and motor fitness; fundamental motor skills and patterns; and skills in aquatics, dance, and individual and group games and sports, including intramural and lifetime sports" (U.S. Department of Education, Office of Civil Rights, 2002). Physical education services must be made available to every child with a disability. Each child must be afforded the opportunity to participate in regular physical education unless the child is a full-time student at another school or the child has an individualized education program that requires modifications to his or her physical education class.

An individualized education program (IEP) is documentation defining the least restrictive environment, goals, and objectives for the student. The IEP should identify the goals and objectives for physical education; however, few physical education teachers participate in the writing of these goals. In many instances, the least restrictive environment is defined as full inclusion in a regularly scheduled physical education class. Modifications to regular physical education should be prescribed in the child's IEP. If special physical education is not available in the school directly, then arrangements must be made to provide these services. It is recommended that special physical education be delivered by qualified personnel, such as those identified as certified adapted physical educators (CAPE). (See www.cortland.edu/apens for more information about becoming a CAPE.)

An adapted or special physical education teacher is a direct-service provider, not a related-service provider, because special education is a federally mandated component of special education services. This means that physical education needs to be provided to the student with a disability as part of the child's special education. This is contrasted with physical therapy and occupational therapy, which are related services.

Physical education teachers should get to know all of the students at their school and be involved in writing goals and objectives for IEPs. School districts, many times, will not want to include physical education modifications within an IEP because then the service must be provided. Providing said services might mean that the physical education teacher would be unavailable during a specific class period because the teacher is working directly with one or two students with disabilities, or an entire adapted physical education class may need to be created.

To ensure success for all, students should be observed and assessed in the environment in which they will be most successful. Obesity, although not considered a disability, falls under Section 504, "other health impairment." If an obese child is not receiving special education services but is, however, having a difficult time being successful in regular physical education class, the pupil may qualify for special physical education under Section 504. If the teacher involved in the case of *Landers v. School District No. 203* (1978) had used the legislation related to Section 504, the lawsuit may never have been initiated. In this case, an obese student was directed to practice a backward somersault without supervision. The student was untrained in the backward roll and was afraid to perform the task because she was obese. The student was awarded $77,000 for the serious neck injury she sustained performing the backward roll. Children who cannot keep pace within a regular physical education class are at greater risk of injury or psychological harm than their peers. A proactive teacher can identify the least restrictive environment (LRE) for students with disabilities, thereby creating a safe environment and thus more effectively manage risk and liability.

The LRE is the "educational setting in which the individual can most adequately function and meet their potential" (Kelly, 1995, p. 11). This could mean a student might be fully included in all aspects of physical education. Other students may have a cognitive disability, in which participation in physical education would look the same as it does for all other participants; however, the student might receive assistance with test taking. Still other students may need substantial modifications to the physical education curriculum and may require additional staff for support or participation in a self-contained adapted physical education class. Regardless of the level of modifications required for the student to be the most successful, it is the physical education teacher's and school district's responsibility to physically educate in the LRE.

Safe School Act

Enactment of the Safe School Act varies from state to state. The mandate is intended to provide a safe learning environment within the school setting. State safe-school policy can include legislation relating to weapons, CPR training, student conduct codes, drug-free schools, classroom management, and conflict resolution. The primary focus of the Safe School Act has been to secure the school grounds. Guidelines for supervision; the use of school resource officers; the visibility of administration; the monitoring of the facilities and students; the identification of visitors; and the purchase of security technology, such as metal detectors, protective lighting, and surveillance equipment, are all examples of how local school districts have attempted to make school grounds safe from violent crimes. The Safe School Act affects teachers because it is their duty to create a safe environment for students.

As identified in other legislation, such as Title IX and ADA, a safe environment can be created by teachers providing equitable learning experiences for all individuals. The teacher's role in creating safe schools is different according to state legislation and local interpretation of that legislation. For example, in Missouri, it is recommended that the schools develop and implement a program to train the students in the administration of cardiopulmonary resuscitation and other lifesaving methods. It further suggests that successful completion of the CPR program be a requirement for graduation. As a teacher, you may be required to deliver some of this content within the physical education setting.

Another example might be the promotion of specific conflict-resolution strategies. A school, especially a middle school, may have an established protocol for peer mediation. Teachers may have the responsibility for facilitating the methodology. Presenting content related to drug use and abuse is another example of how a teacher may have to integrate safe-school content into the curriculum. After all, it is the physical education teacher's responsibility to promote healthy decisions, such as those related to physical activity and nutrition.

An alternative avenue for preventing violence on school grounds involves students identifying and reporting the actions of their classmates. Teachers can be resources for students who have observed unsafe behaviors or threats. In 1999, the United States Supreme Court concluded that students may recover monetary *damages* from a school district when student-to-student harassment is evident (*Davis v. Monroe County Board of Education*, 1999). For statements or actions to be considered harassment, they must be severe or objectively offensive and have impeded educational opportunities. The school district must exhibit "deliberate indifference to the harassment" (*Davis v. Monroe County Board of Education*, 1999). Teachers and administrators must take seriously a student's report of harassment or threats and must be concerned with resolving these issues.

Steps to ensure a safe environment within schools have required collaborative efforts from administration, teachers, school staff, students, parents, and community members. Safe schools are created and maintained, they do not just happen. Through prevention strategies, the implementation of policy, and management of risk, schools become a safe place for learning. The physical education teacher has a duty to facilitate this environment.

PREVENTION AND RISK MANAGEMENT

Many lawsuits could be prevented through proactive decision making on the behalf of the teacher or coach. There are several actions that a physical education teacher can take to help increase the likelihood of physical and psychological safety. Planning, proper monitoring and supervision of students, care of equipment, care of facilities, and documentation of incidents are all prevention mechanisms. Not necessarily considered prevention, but more of protection, insurance is another consideration for physical education teachers. Each mode of prevention will be discussed further.

Planning and Instruction

When planning physical education lessons, a teacher must consider (a) the inherent danger of an activity, (b) the purpose of the activity, (c) student abilities and readiness, (d) class rules and policies warning of risk, and (e) method of instruction (Gray, 1995). The inherent danger of an activity should be considered before inclusion in a lesson. Activities that are deemed unsafe should be replaced by safer ones. Most teachers do consider possible injury before selecting an activity (Gray, 1992), but fewer consider the legitimacy of those activities or the potential psychological harm.

Determining if a drill or activity has a legitimate purpose or learning objective is a key part of identifying negligence. Physical education teachers should ensure that each activity relates to the national, state, or local physical education content standards. Punitive activities or drills that unfairly single out individuals, such as running laps around the gym while other students continue with the lesson, must be avoided. Likewise, activities that have little or no value, such as those involving human targets, should not be included in lesson plans. For instance, a student suffering multiple facial fractures as a result of a game of bombardment (dodgeball) filed a lawsuit contending that bombardment was an inappropriate game for inclusion in the physical education curriculum (*Fosselman v. Waterloo Community School District,* 1975). Although the jury returned a verdict in favor of the teacher and a judge dismissed the charges against the school district, this lawsuit still raises concerns regarding the legitimacy of inclusion of specific games. The case dismissal related more to the lack of factual detail than it did to the legitimacy of the activity. An activity should be judged to determine whether it is in the students' best interest to participate in it. Simply put, if the risk (physical or psychological) outweighs the learning potential, then the activity should be modified or eliminated. Effective teachers minimize the amount of time spent on activities that do not contribute to lesson objectives (Rink, 2005).

Physical educators must modify activities in order to promote success among younger and less-skilled students. Such modifications include size of the playing area, number of players, and size of the ball or target (Rink, 2005). In most cases, students will profit from equipment or practice modifications, and safety will be increased. Reducing the complexity of practice conditions can ensure student success and safety, simultaneously. For example, when girls were allowed to use a smaller basketball and a lower basketball hoop (eight feet [2.4 meters]), self-efficacy and shooting performance increased (Chase, Ewing, Lirgg, & George, 1994). Game or drill modifications are a prudent method of caring for the students and are an expectation of physical education teachers.

Proper instructional techniques must not only be planned but also enacted by the teacher. On the first day of a track and field unit, a student was injured while long jumping at full speed. He claimed in a lawsuit that the physical education teacher was negligent when he failed to properly instruct the student on the technique of long jumping. The judge awarded $207,000 in damages because the court found that the coach failed to properly prepare and instruct the student and this contributed to the injuries (*Scott v. Rapides Parish School Board,* 1999). In a similar case, *Dibortolo v. Metropolitan School District of Washington Township* (1982), a sixth-grade student broke a permanent tooth when she hit the wall, attempting the vertical jump during physical education. Although the lawsuit was dismissed, the *plaintiff* claimed that one demonstration on the vertical jump was not enough instruction to prevent injury. The instructional methodology selected by a teacher must provide simple to complex demonstrations, practice, and feedback on performance. Absence of or poor instruction constitutes negligent teaching behavior. The selection of an instructional style alone does not prevent injury. For example, the guided-discovery teaching style (a style of instruction that indirectly facilitates learning) should only be implemented in an educational gymnastics unit if a worklike environment has been previously created by the teacher (Werner, 2004).

How students are matched for participation in class activities is another component of a safe learning environment. Matching students merely because they are in the same grade or are the same age is not enough. To appropriately match students, teachers must consider ability, gender, maturation, physical characteristics, and experience. A student must exhibit physical and psychological readiness before participating in the activity. Physical education teachers should not leave the pairing of students to chance; they should instead analyze their lesson plans for potential mismatches. Pairs or groups of students should be teacher selected and systematically organized by specific characteristics for a given activity. This of course requires knowing the skill and experience level of each student. For beginning teachers, this can be difficult because their own inexperience may limit their knowledge of a specific population or individual. Teachers must assess student ability and get to know each student's maturity level. Once assessment has been completed and documented, activities in which a child or adolescent will be physically or mentally unsuccessful should be eliminated from lessons.

Mismatches will occur; however, it is the recognition and reassignment of partners or team members that is important. Matching students of similar or equal ability is the responsibility of the physical education teacher. Negligence was found in the case of *Tepper v. City of New Rochelle School District* (1988) when mismatched students were placed in competitive drills for lacrosse. The lacrosse coach allowed an inexperienced player with a slight build (a member of a no-cut junior varsity squad) to go head-to-head against a 260-pound (118-kilogram) senior varsity team member. Mismatches can also occur by gender, as was the case in *Synder v. Morristown Central School District* (1990). In an eighth-grade physical education class, a female student and male student were matched in a game of touch football. The female student was injured during the game and filed suit against the school district. The case was dismissed when it was determined that despite the gender difference, the students were of similar ability. However, this case reminds us of the importance of considering all student characteristics before assigning match-ups. The creation of a respectful class atmosphere can also help prevent injuries when mismatches accidentally occur.

The establishment of class routines and clear articulation of rules and expectations are important in creating a motivating and respectful learning atmosphere. Students should practice class rules and routines, and these should include warnings about the inherent risk of the physical activity. Students should also be trained in behaviors specifically related to the instructional unit that can guard against injury (e.g., correct spotting technique in gymnastics). For example, in the case of *Livingston v. Wausau Underwriters Ins. Co.* (2003), a physical education teacher was charged with negligence when she failed to prevent a student from hitting another student while taking practice swings with a golf club. The students in question "had been instructed not to swing their golf clubs in the waiting area and the student had disregarded that instruction" (Conn, 2004, p.30). The case was dismissed and serves as an example of how one teacher proactively addressed how to handle risk in gamelike or practice situations.

Reasonable rules not only need to be established but also enforced in order to create a safe atmosphere. Failure to articulate expectations is difficult to justify. Van der Smissen (1990) concluded that if rules and routines are established but not enforced, it is as if there are no regulations for the activity. Rules and routines must be communicated, taught, and practiced to provide a safe learning environment that encourages engagement. Rules and routines, within or beyond class, provide structure for student behavior.

Let's face it: Not all students participate with the same level of enthusiasm and intensity. Unengaged students should never be forced or coerced to participate in activities that they are reluctant to try. If a court were to determine that the student had been coerced into participation, it would be considered willful and wanton negligence on behalf of the teacher. In one case, parents alleged that the school board and its employees acted negligently toward their child when she was made to participate in physical education class after complaining of leg pain (*Raymond and Wesley Raymond v. Orleans Parish School Board,* 2003). The student was also made to use her crutches to get upstairs after the injury had occurred. There was an elevator available, but she was not allowed to use it. By making her use crutches on stairs, the school now has ADA violations. In a similar case, *Goben v. School District of St. Joseph* (1992), an overweight, reluctant teenager was urged to jump over a hurdle. During an attempt, her foot caught the hurdle, and she was injured. These cases confirm that there is a thin line between motivation and coercion. It is best for teachers to refrain from second-guessing the actions of their students, and to create a behavior-management plan for student adherence.

With the implementation of a behavior model, such as the one designed by Don Hellison, an "at-risk" education expert, personal and social responsibility can be taught and promoted within the physical education curriculum. Hellison (2003) suggests teaching personal and social responsibility by developing an awareness of one's own behavior. Hellison uses the following ascending levels of social responsibility: irresponsible, respect, participation, self-direction, and caring. Initially, the teacher identifies the student's level of personal and social responsibility, but eventually it is the student who must have an awareness of his or her own personal and social behaviors (see the self-evaluation form on page 153). This model allows the teacher to separate potential issues of noncompliance from those identified by a student as potentially harmful. The establishment and enforcement of rules, through the implementation of a behavior model, will result in a positive learning environment in which many instructional strategies can be used. Planning, instruction, and preventive teacher decision making will be discussed further in chapter 9.

Supervising and Monitoring Students

Lack of supervision is the most common lawsuit filed against teachers. Adequately anticipating the hazards of a specific activity and monitoring all areas accessible to the students (e.g., locker rooms and hallways) are part of a teacher's duties. Supervision is more than simply observing; it requires action, including the care of facilities and equipment, adherence to school policy, and documentation of incidents. Supervision should be both proactive and reactive. The careful monitoring of students, regular inventory and care of equipment, care and inspection of facilities, and establishment of policy are preventive activities. The development and efficient enactment of an emergency plan is both proactive and reactive. When injury does occur, it is important that the physical education teacher knows how to respond and document the incident. As evidenced in the chapter vignette, a well-developed emergency plan can provide swift care when needed. Schools should have established emergency plans, and the teacher should be certified in basic first aid and CPR.

Teachers should position themselves so that they can see all students in order to monitor student behavior, physical ailments, overexertion, and other potential dangers. Allowing unsupervised participation in physical education is considered poor practice and a breach of teacher duties. The absence of a teacher is a common source of litigation. When the teacher "steps out of the classroom," if only for a second, it increases the likelihood that an incident could take place. Neglecting to supervise students during physical education in the locker rooms or in the hallway before and after class could lead to litigation. Being in close proximity to the students is the best way to perform the duty of supervision.

Self-Evaluation

Date _____

Self-control: How well did you control your temper and mouth today?

Effort: How hard did you try today?

Self-coaching: Did you have a self-improvement or basketball goal and work on it today?

Coaching: Did you help others, do some positive coaching, or help make this a good experience for everyone today?

Outside the gym:

Self-control?

Effort?

Goal-setting?

Helping others?

One comment about yourself today:

Reprinted, by permission, from D. Hellison, 2003, *Teaching responsibility through physical education*, 2nd ed. (Champaign, IL: Human Kinetics), 51.

Still, a teacher cannot see everything; therefore, training students to be supervisors is one way to increase the likelihood of quick intervention. For example, if during a swimming unit students are taught water safety techniques, a student might recognize the signs and symptoms of a classmate struggling in the water. Teachers and students alike should constantly scan the room for potential hazards, such as equipment on the floor or incorrect equipment use.

In the case *Grandalski & Grandalski v. Lyons Township High School District 204* (1999), an accident during the last day of a gymnastics unit led to submission of a lawsuit arguing that the school district was negligent because it had failed to provide the proper safety devices, directly supervise the activity, and maintain discipline within the class. The court ruled in favor of the school district because the child, an accomplished gymnast, had attempted to complete an advanced gymnastics maneuver beyond those planned for during a basic gymnastics unit in the physical education class. The injury took place while the teacher had been assessing the gymnastics skill of other students, which is common practice (not negligent practice) in physical education. Based on this case, Sawyer (2003) provides the following recommendations for steps toward prevention: (a) Have a written curriculum available at all times, (b) have school administrators review the curriculum and provide the necessary safety equipment, (c) provide in-service programs to help physical education teachers instruct new movement skills, (d) physical education teachers should clearly explain what their students can and cannot do during class, (e) students should be instructed not to engage in activities that are not part of the curriculum, and (f) physical educators should be trained to respond quickly and appropriately to medical emergencies.

Maintaining Equipment

A physical education teacher should select equipment that is appropriate for the age, ability, and maturation of the students. The equipment should be used only for its intended purpose. Students need to be taught how to use the equipment. For example, students using weight room facilities, whether experienced or inexperienced, need to be taught how to use each piece of equipment. Proper lifting technique should be communicated orally and in writing. To hold students accountable and to create documentation of a student's knowledge of equipment use, a cognitive assessment should be administered. Weight machines are generally safer than free weights; therefore, the cognitive demand of the assessment should reflect the level of risk. Providing evidence of student knowledge regarding safety techniques could be as simple as a multiple-choice question or as complex as a full demonstration of safety techniques.

Equipment in poor condition poses a risk to students.

Todd Gasper, participating in a summer conditioning (weight training) program, under the supervision of his coaches, attempted to lift 335 pounds from a squat rack without a properly fitting weight belt and without warming up. A fellow lifter had asked Gasper to wait and to put on a properly fitting weight belt; he did not. The court ruled in favor of the coaches because they had properly instructed Gasper on how to use the weights, how to inspect and care for the equipment, and how and when to use safety mechanisms (*Gasper v. Freidel,* 1990).

Sawyer (2003, p.13) suggests the following risk management tips relating to equipment: "(a) All equipment purchased [for educational use] should be approved by the school district, (b) all equipment should be evaluated for safety before it is purchased, (c) only purchase equipment from an approved vendor, (d) self-made equipment or equipment purchased from an unauthorized source should not be used at school, (e) all equipment should be inspected regularly for safety and repair, (f) all equipment should be inventoried and stored when not in use, (g) inform students of safety rules associated with the equipment, and (h) all equipment used in physical education should be the property of the school district." Moreover, the teacher needs to purposefully plan how the equipment will be used in a given space.

Students should be carefully spaced throughout the facility when working with implements such as rackets or golf clubs. It is through teacher planning and student practice that students come to learn how to work with one another in the given space. The physical education teacher must teach students how to practice under control and must enforce the guidelines. In the case of *Brahatcek v. Millard School District* (1979), tragedy resulted from improperly spaced students. A ninth-grade student missed the first day of a golf unit in which the teacher instructed the students on golf basics and safety techniques, such as where a student should stand in relation to other students when executing practice swings. On the second day of the golf lesson, the student moved into an area in which another student was performing practice swings and was subsequently struck by the golf club. The student later died from the injuries.

Inspecting and Maintaining Facilities

Teachers must regularly inspect the facilities to minimize risks related to improper setup (e.g., gymnastics mats) or poor condition (e.g., a basketball rim hanging from a backboard). Preventive maintenance should be conducted regularly. It is the obligation of the physical education teacher to regularly inspect the facilities. The inspection should cover structural defects as well as maintenance issues. Needed repairs should be requested immediately. Realizing that repairs may take a while to be completed, retain your documentation of the request. Areas waiting for repair or under repair should be clearly marked and avoided. Failure to inspect and repair the facilities can result in an intentional tort. If an inspection of the facilities reveals dried blood on a gymnasium floor, proper biohazard care should be taken immediately (see www.osha.gov for details of biohazard care).

In the case of *Catberro v. Naperville School District* (2000), a fourth-grader attempted to sue the school district because he had been injured jumping a rope in physical education class. One of the poles that the rope was tied to, a standard with a wide base, had been purchased at a garage sale and was in poor repair. The parents of the injured child suggested that the teacher was negligent because he had purchased the poles in such poor condition. Care of facilities and equipment is merely one example of teacher duties and actions, which, if not completed reasonably, are considered negligence.

School and Department Policy

Physical education teachers should be informed of district policy, such as emergency action, prohibited activities, and those related to footwear. Emergency plans describe the sequential procedures to be taken when an injury occurs. Emergency plans are designed to provide timely care to the injured party and to prevent litigation. Unless you are working at a brand new school, your school has created policies that are a result of litigation or threat of litigation. When the North Colonie Central School District No. 5 failed to enforced its own rule regarding the playing of softball during recess, they were found negligent (*Tashjian & Tashjian v. North Colonie Central School District No. 5,* 1975). The school district had created a policy prohibiting participation in the activity of softball during recess because of a previous injury from a bat. The injured third-grader in this case was awarded $37,100 in damages. A physical education teacher, whether in class or on recess duty, must be aware of district policy.

In a different scenario, an inexperienced teacher, new to the district, designed and implemented a floor hockey unit for his seventh- and eighth-grade students. However, he was unaware that floor hockey had been removed from the physical education curriculum three years earlier as part of an out-of-court settlement. The plaintiff, a dentist whose son had lost a tooth during a floor hockey unit in physical education class, alleged that the risk in the sport was inappropriately high. To avoid going to court, the school district offered to remove floor hockey from its physical education curriculum. These events were not communicated to the new teacher, and he implemented a floor hockey unit. The teacher was not alerted of this situation until the principal made an official evaluation observation. The bottom line is that the new teacher should have requested and been provided a copy of the physical education curriculum. The teacher then should have adhered to the activities in the curriculum, deviating only if the document was revised and approved by the local school board of education.

Physical education teachers need to familiarize themselves with the student conduct code. Many student handbooks include policy on proper footwear for participation in physical education. It is the responsibility of the physical education teacher to enforce the guidelines for proper footwear. Repeated offenses of the footwear policy should be documented. Chronic abuse of this policy should result in the physical education teacher contacting the student's parents or guardians as well as the school administration. In a case that was ultimately overturned, a student who suffered injury as a result of slipping on a gym floor was awarded $50,000. The student had been participating in his socks because he had forgotten to bring his tennis shoes to physical education (*Passafaro v. Board of Education of the City of New York,* 1974). The Athletic Equipment Managers Association (AEMA) provides guidelines for proper athletic footwear.

Documenting Incidents

Documentation should be not only reactive but also proactive. Everything done or created in the name of safety should be documented (e.g. class rules, lessons plans, practicing procedures and rules, general inventory and repair of equipment). Documentation should also include how abilities were matched and how mismatches were prevented. If a student were to file a lawsuit, documents generated by the teacher would serve as evidence of proper instruction, practice of safety techniques, proper scope and sequence, purchase and inventory of equipment, behavior management plans, or request for repair of equipment and facilities.

Teachers' Unions

Although best practice is the most important step to avoiding litigation, in many states teachers' unions serve as protection against litigation. The two most common are the American Federation of Teachers (AFT) and the National Education Association (NEA). These associations have national and state offices to help provide services such as liability coverage, advocacy for professional development opportunities, and advocacy for equitable pay and benefits. Teachers can pay dues to local, state, and national organizations to receive the benefits of membership.

> The AFT advocates sound, commonsense public education policies, including high academic and conduct standards for students and greater professionalism for teachers and school staff; excellence in public service through cooperative problem-solving and workplace innovations; and high-quality healthcare provided by qualified professionals. (American Federation of Teachers, *Who We Are,* n.d.)

Right-to-work laws (see table 8.1) secure the right of employees to decide for themselves whether or not to join or financially support a union; therefore, employees are entitled to receive some services without being forced to pay dues. For example, in South Carolina and 20 other states, employees have the right to be represented by a union for contract negotiations and to receive union wages and full benefits resulting from negotiations but do not have to join the union or pay for its services.

Table 8.1   State Right-to-Work Laws As of January 1, 2005

State	Year constitutional amendment adopted	Year statute enacted
Alabama		1953
Arizona	1946	1947
Arkansas	1944	1947
Florida	1968	1943
Georgia		1947
Idaho		1985
Indiana *only applicable to school employees*		1995
Iowa		1947
Kansas	1958	
Louisiana		1976
Mississippi	1960	1954
Nebraska	1946	1947
Nevada		1951
North Carolina		1947
North Dakota		1947
Oklahoma	2001	2001
South Carolina		1954
South Dakota	1946	1947
Tennessee		1947
Texas		1947
Utah		1955
Virginia		1947
Wyoming		1963

From U.S. Department of Labor.

SUMMARY

Physical education teachers must take steps to ensure a safe and equitable learning environment in order to reduce not only the risk of harm to their students but also the risk of liability. Physical harm is not the only potential by-product of negligence. Negligence can also cause psychological harm. And gender inequity and discrimination against students with disabilities can result when teachers do not exercise due care. Teachers who organize, allocate, manage resources (e.g., students, time, space, equipment, activities, and teacher attention) and adhere to educational policy are likely to create active and equitable learning experiences. These learning experiences require conscientious decisions by the teacher before, during, and after lesson enactment. Careful considerations must be given to selection, enforcement, and feedback for the students. It is important to realize that despite the use of many prevention strategies, teachers cannot completely prevent injuries. Being familiar with the national standards and practices supported by NASPE and AAHPERD will keep teachers current in their attempts to create safe learning experiences for their students.

Discussion Questions

1. Identify a situation in which a teacher might be considered negligent because of his or her actions or lack of action.

2. What types of decisions do teachers make to increase the safety of their students?

3. You have been given an opportunity to make revisions to the physical education curriculum. What activities would you add? What risks are associated with those activities?

4. You have to make a presentation to the school board regarding the addition of an adventure-based curriculum to physical education. How do you justify the change in curriculum and assuming the increased risk?

Professional Portfolio Contents

1. Research and critique a school emergency action plan, explaining what training is needed to carry it out effectively.

2. Videotape yourself or a peer teaching and determine if equal attention was provided to both male and female students. Include the coding sheet of student–teacher interactions in your portfolio.

3. Using a sample student profile, create physical education goals and objectives for an IEP.

Key Terms

breach of duty—The neglect or failure to fulfill the responsibilities of employment.

damages—Compensation awarded to those suffering loss or injury to themselves or their property caused by the negligence of another person.

duty—Obligation to fulfill the responsibilities of employment.

liability—When someone is legally responsible for loss or damage that occurs while performing the duties of teaching.

litigation—Any case, controversy, or lawsuit for the purpose of enforcing the law.

negligence—The failure to act reasonably or to exercise due care under the circumstance of the situation.

plaintiff—The person who brings action; the one who has been injured.

standard of care—Reasonable actions to prevent injury.

tort—"A civil wrong that does not involve a contractual relationship" (Wong, 1994, p. 9); intentional or unintentional harm resulting from unreasonable actions or negligence from a person.

Resources

Adapted Physical Education National Standards: www.cortland.edu/apens

National Center on Physical Activity and Disability: www.ncpad.org

National Consortium for Physical Education and Recreation for Individuals with Disabilities: www.uwlax.edu/sah/ncperid

Occupational Safety and Health Administration: www.osha.gov

PALAESTRA: Forum of Sport, Physical Education and Recreation for those with Disabilities: www.palaestra.com

References

American Federation of Teachers. (n.d.) *Who we are*. Retrieved October 3, 2006, from www.aft.org/about/index.htm.

Brahatcek v. Millard School District 273 N.W. 2d 680 (Supr. Crt. NB, 1979). Retrieved September 24, 2004, from http://web2.westlaw.com.

Brophy, J. (1985). Interactions of male and female students with male and female teachers. In L. C. Wilkinson & C.B. Marrett (Eds.), *Gender influences in classroom interaction* (pp. 115-142). Orlando, FL: Academic Press.

Catberro v. Naperville School District, 203, 317 Ill. App. 3d 150, 739 N.E. 2d 115; (App. Crt. IL, 2000). Retrieved September 24, 2004, from http://web2.westlaw.com.

Chase, M.A., Ewing, M.E., Lirgg, C.D., & George, T.R. (1994). The effects of equipment modification on children's self-efficacy and basketball shooting performance. *Research Quarterly for Exercise and Sport, 65(2),* 159-168.

Cohen v. Brown University, 991 F.2nd 888 (1st Cir. 1993). Retrieved September 24, 2004, from http://web2.westlaw.com.

Conn, J.H. (2004). *Civil liabilities in kinesiological settings.* Unpublished manuscript.

Davis v. Monroe County Board of Education (97-843) 526 U.S. 629 (120 F.3d 1390, 1999). Retrieved September 24, 2004, from http://web2.westlaw.com.

Dibortolo v. Metropolitan School District of Washington Township, 440 N.E. 2d 506 (App. Crt. 2nd Dist. IN, 1982). Retrieved September 24, 2004, from http://web2.westlaw.com.

Fosselman v. Waterloo Community School District 229 N.W. 2d 280 (Supr. Crt. IW, 1975). Retrieved September 24, 2004, from http://web2.westlaw.com.

French, J., & French, P. (1984). Gender imbalances in the primary classroom: An interactional account. *Educational Researcher, 26(2),* 127-136.

Gasper v. Freidel 450 N.W. 2d 226 (Supr. Crt. SD, 1990). Retrieved September 24, 2004, from http://web2.westlaw.com.

Goben v. School District of St. Joseph 848 S.W. 2d20 (App.Crt.MO, 1992).

Grandalski & Grandalski v. Lyons Township High School District 204 711 N.E. 2d 372 (App. Crt. IL, 1999). Retrieved September 24, 2004, from http://web2.westlaw.com.

Gray, G.R. (1992). Risk management behaviors related to the teaching of floor hockey in K-12 physical education. *Journal of Legal Aspects of Sport, 2(2),* 40-45.

Gray, G.R. (1995). Safety tips from the expert witness. *Journal of Physical Education, Recreation & Dance, 66(1),* 18-21.

Hart, J.E., & Ritson, R.J. (1993). *Liability and safety in physical education and sport.* Reston, VA: AAHPERD.

Hellison, D. (2003). *Teaching responsibility through physical activity* (2nd ed.). Champaign, IL: Human Kinetics.

Hulley, K.S. (2001). *Gender bias: What are the current issues?* Paper presented at the Annual Meeting of the Mid-South Educational Research Association, Little Rock, AK. (ERIC Document Reproduction Service No. ED460156).

Kelly, L. (1995). *Adapted physical education national standards.* Champaign, IL: Human Kinetics.

Landers v. School District No. 203, O'Fallon 383 N.E. 2d 645 (App. Crt. IL, 1978). Retrieved September 24, 2004, from http://web2.westlaw.com.

Livingston v. Wausau Underwriters Ins. Co., 658 N.W. 2d 88 (App. Crt., WS, 2003). Retrieved September 24, 2004, from http://web2.westlaw.com.

Passafaro v. Board of Education of the City of New York, 353 N.Y.S. 2d 178 (Supr. Crt. App. Div. NY, 1974). Retrieved September 24, 2004, from http://web2. westlaw.com.

Raymond and Wesley Raymond v. Orleans Parish School Board, 856 So. 2d 27, 181 Ed. Law Rep. 911, 2003-0560 (La. App. 4 Cir, 2003). Retrieved September 24, 2004, from http://web2.westlaw.com/.

Rink, J.E. (2005). *Teaching physical education for learning* (5th ed.). New York: McGraw-Hill.

Sawyer, T.H. (2003). Tort immunity. *Journal of Physical Education, Recreation & Dance, 74(6),* 12-13.

Scott v. Rapides Parish School Board, 732 So. 2d 749 (App. Crt LA, 1999). Retrieved September 24, 2004, from http://web2.westlaw.com.

Smith v. Vernon Parish School Board, 442 So. 2d 1319 (App. Crt. 3rd Cir. LA, 1983). Retrieved September 24, 2004, from http://web2.westlaw.com.

Synder v. Morristown Central School District, No. 167 563 N.Y.S. 2d 258; (Supr. Crt. A.D. 3rd Dept. NY., 1990). Retrieved September 24, 2004, from http://web2. westlaw.com.

Tashjian & Tashjian v. North Colonie Central School District No. 5, 50 A.D. 2d 691, 375 N.Y.S. 2d 467 (Supr. Crt. NY, 1975). Retrieved September 24, 2004, from http://web2.westlaw.com.

Tepper v. City of New Rochelle School District, 531 N.Y.S. 2nd 367 (A.D. Dept. 1988). Retrieved September 24, 2004, from http://web2.westlaw.com.

U.S. Department of Education, Office for Civil Rights. (2002). *Protecting students with disabilities.* Retrieved August 15, 2004, from www.ed.gov/about/offices/ list/ocr/504faq.html.

U.S. Department of Labor (2004). *Title IX, education amendments of 1972.* Retrieved September 14, 2005, from www.dol.gov/oasam/regs/statutes/titleix. htm.

Van der Smissen, B. (1990). *Legal liability and risk management for public and private entities.* Cincinnati: Anderson.

Werner, P. (2004). *Teaching children gymnastics: Becoming a master teacher* (2nd ed.). Champaign, IL: Human Kinetics.

Wong, G.M. (1994). *Essentials of amateur sports law* (2nd ed.). Westport, CT: Library of Congress.

CHAPTER

9

Decision Making

STANDARD 3: *Diverse Learners.* Understand how individuals differ in their approaches to learning and create appropriate instruction adapted to these differences.

OUTCOME 3.2: Use appropriate strategies, services, and resources to meet diverse learning needs.

STANDARD 4: *Management and Motivation.* Use and have an understanding of individual and group motivation and behavior to create a safe learning environment that encourages positive social interaction, active engagement in learning, and self-motivation.

OUTCOME 4.2: Organize, allocate, and manage resources (e.g., students, time, space, equipment, activities, and teacher attention) to provide active and equitable learning experiences.

The principal called, and the K-2 physical education job is yours if you want it. This job has been your first choice among those you applied for because the district has just built a new school to accommodate the recent growth in population. You will be the first and only physical education teacher in that building. The district has a physical education curriculum, however, and the principal has charged you with reviewing the document and making decisions regarding content. To the best of his knowledge, it had been about 10 years since the last revisions in the physical education curriculum, and it still needs to be aligned with the national and state physical education standards.

The principal has also asked you to complete two specific tasks: (1) Develop a character education focus, and (2) prepare a five-year budget for the district planning committee. This new school will educate students bussed in from five different neighborhoods of the city; thus, it is important to establish a positive, respectful learning environment beginning on the first day of school. Sixty-five percent of the enrolled students speak Spanish as their primary language. The school population, in general, represents vastly different socioeconomic statuses and ethnicities, making your task challenging. You are prepared to develop the character education curriculum because you are familiar with the idea of promoting social responsibility; however, you feel uncomfortable preparing a five-year budget because you have never been given such an opportunity.

SCHOOL CONTEXT

In this chapter, the authors address resources as they pertain to the ever-changing needs of the learner and how the context of teaching situations influences teacher decision making. Specifically, National Standards for Beginning Physical Education Teachers Outcome 3.2, "use appropriate strategies, services, and resources to meet diverse learning needs," is discussed in the context of the school, the family unit and societal change, and the influence of public health issues. Additionally, the second part of Outcome 4.2, "to provide active and equitable learning experiences," is also addressed through current issues in education, school, and curriculum reform. A discussion of specific decisions made during teaching and learning events relating to the use of resources (Mosston & Ashworth, 2002), as well as steps for preparing a budget, closes the chapter.

DIVERSITY AND LEARNER NEEDS

Today, the notion of society as a melting pot, in which all cultures are blended into one, has been replaced with a more pluralistic perspective, encouraging individuals to maintain their cultural heritage and personal identity. Collectively, many different cultures contribute to the fabric of the United States. Nearly one-third of our students can speak Spanish, and the study of language now includes sign language (for students with hearing impairments) and computer programming. Schools are a reflection of our community and therefore are culturally, academically, and economically diverse. Teachers are encouraged to provide learning materials that acknowledge and respect diversity and create a safe learning environment for all learners (see chapter 8, Reducing Risk and Liability).

Modern School Demographics

The U.S. Department of Education (USDOE) forecasts record levels of public elementary and secondary enrollment through 2013 (USDOE, 2005). Public school districts are organized in small and large groups in urban, suburban, and rural settings and are governed by their local school board. With regard to school size, findings suggest that moderately sized, as opposed to large, high schools provide a better environment for academic achievement, especially for economically disadvantaged students (Bickel, Smith, Eagle, & Hardman, 2001; Lee & Bryk, 1988, 1989). Interestingly, the majority of minority and economically deprived students are enrolled in larger schools, that most often reside in urban settings (USDOE, 2000). School size not only influences student behavior and academic achievement but also teacher attitudes and behaviors; teachers at large high schools are more likely to report apathy, tardiness, and absenteeism than teachers who work in moderately sized or smaller schools regardless of being located in a rural, suburban, or urban location (USDOE, 2003). Given the fact that class and school size influence learning, teachers must be prepared to creatively engage all students. For example, as confirmed by Hastie and Saunders (1991), the larger the class size the less time spent in practice and instructional activities. Size, as well as racial diversity of a class, should be considered during lesson preparation.

Despite recent increases in diversity among the student population, the ethnicity of the teachers has remained relatively stable. The majority of public school teachers in the United States are white, with 37 percent having well over 10 years of experience (USDOE, 2002). Unlike the early years of U.S. education, equal numbers of males and females are going into the teaching field, with first-year teachers making up approximately 16 percent of all public school teachers (USDOE, 2003). Also among beginning public school teachers, there is a much greater number of white than black and Hispanic teachers. Because of the disproportionate number of white versus minority teacher candidates, schools with the highest percentages of minority students and English language learners are more likely to be taught by white teachers (USDOE, 2003). Ethnicity, race, and cultural differences influence the student–teacher relationship. It is important to consider the group characteristics and responsibly select alternative instructional strategies to attain the highest possible achievement among the students.

In general, the student academic performance outlook is mixed. Reading scores among 9- and 13-year-olds and math scores among 9-, 13-, and 17-year-olds have increased since 1971 (USDOE, 2004). Yet, in science, there were either decreases or no detectable differences between 1970 and 1999. Internationally, the United States ranked 15th in both math and science testing (USDOE, 2004). School and teacher effectiveness influence academic performance, as do the family unit, public health issues, and poverty during childhood.

Family and Societal Behaviors

Over time, the family unit and its mobility rate have changed; the average American family moves every three years. The number of single-parent and blended families is increasing, while the number of families made up of married parents with children is decreasing (Parke, 2003). Within the family structure, the roles have also evolved, as evidenced by the increasing number of mothers within the workforce. Because of these family-unit changes, among other things, many children face emotional, social, and physiological issues that inhibit learning, thus forcing schools to expand curriculum related to health and social services (Swerdlik, Reeder, & Bucy, 1999). As a result, the lack of parental involvement in schools has become a serious problem (USDOE, 2003).

Although not directly a result of changes in the family unit, changes in societal behaviors, such as increases in school violence, drug use, absenteeism, and bullying, make it difficult to provide a safe environment for learning. *Bullying* refers to someone saying or doing something to gain power over another person (e.g., teasing, ignoring, or assaulting). Bullying affects all types of students, but not all students report the incidents. More males than females and more blacks than whites and Hispanics were likely to report incidences of bullying (USDOE, 2003). Families can play an important role if a student is bullied or feels unsafe because the more people who address the problem the more likely it is to be resolved.

Families also influence physical activity participation in young people (Sallis, Prochaska, & Taylor, 2000). Parents and siblings have been identified as important factors in how often young people are active. Parents who are active are likely to have active children. Physical education is not considered one of the top predictors of physical activity in U.S. youth. According to Sallis, Prochaska, and Taylor (2000), parents, physical activity preference, previous physical activity, perceived competence, and gender are the most common correlates of physical activity in children; therefore, it is important that physical education teachers attempt to relate school activities to factors beyond the school day in order to promote physical activity and lifelong prevention of disease.

Public Health Issues

Student performance in school is influenced by public health issues, such as childhood obesity and type 2 diabetes mellitus. There is a growing public health burden of inactivity among America's youth. Children are becoming increasingly inactive and therefore are at greater risk of being overweight and unfit (U.S. Department of Health and Human Services [HHS], 2000). Physical inactivity may continue throughout life and has implications for the increased prevalence of several chronic diseases (e.g., cardiovascular disease, colon cancer, diabetes) in adulthood. Those diseases specifically related to physical inactivity are preventable, yet 21 percent of adolescents and 24 percent of the adult population are sedentary (HHS, 2000). Table 9.1 illustrates the prevalence of obesity and overweight in the United States.

Table 9.1   Prevalence of Obesity and Overweight in the United States

	Males aged 2-5	Females aged 2-5	Males aged 6-11	Females aged 6-11	Males aged 12-19	Females aged 12-19
Average for all groups (%)	9.9	10.7	16.9	14.7	16.7	15.4
Non-Hispanic whites (%)	8.2	9.1	14.0	13.1	14.6	12.7
Non-Hispanic blacks (%)	8.0	9.6	17.0	22.8	18.7	23.6
Mexican Americans (%)	14.1	12.2	26.5	17.1	24.7	19.9

Physical education, in addition to other community-based physical activity programs, has the potential to produce multiple physical and cognitive benefits. With regard to the relationship between physical education and cognitive performance, a study of 65 high school physical education programs in South Carolina found that performance on state academic tests was significantly related to physical fitness (Mitchell, Castelli, & Strainer, 2003). Physical fitness has also been associated with better academic performance in children in several other large-scale interventions (California Department of Education, 2001; Dwyer, Sallis, Blizzard, Lazarus, & Dean 2001; Sallis & McKenzie, 1999; Shephard et al., 1984). However, until recently, few studies have adequately accounted for the influence of other related variables, such as socioeconomic status, ethnicity, and effectiveness of the school environment (Castelli, 2005), although these factors have also been found to influence both fitness and academic performance. Recently, Castelli (2005) showed that aerobic fitness has a strong association with performance on standardized mathematics tests. Thus, attainment of the National Association for Sport and Physical Education (NASPE) physical education standards related to physical fitness may not only provide physical health benefits but also cognitive benefits, regardless of socioeconomic status. Because schools contain fit and unfit children from a variety of socioeconomic levels, physical education teachers are encouraged to promote aerobic fitness in, during, and beyond class time, thus increasing the likelihood that the students will reap both physical and cognitive benefits.

Poverty During Childhood

Thomas Jefferson believed that in order to have a democratic society, people must be equally educated. It was also believed that education would help to eliminate poverty. Yet poverty continues to be a concern because children with low socioeconomic status are less likely to receive the same educational opportunities as others. For example, children who have experienced poverty are less likely to be physically active, and the incidences of childhood obesity and type 2 diabetes are higher among low-income households (Poulton et al., 2002) and among African American and Mexican American children (Kumanyika, 1993). Evidence suggests that a lower household income leads to fewer educational opportunities, as inequitable learning experiences continue to exist. Teachers must realize that their students come from diverse cultural, economic, and social backgrounds. Therefore, they should not make assumptions about students' experiences. Using a pretest (such as Fitnessgram, described in chapter 10), student interest surveys, and oral histories can help teachers understand the background of their students.

As our society becomes more diverse, the needs of our youth change. If schools are a reflection of society, then they must deal with more diverse societal issues and the different needs of their students. As the needs of a nation shape schools, the converse is also true: Schools can influence the nation, if progressive school reform is enacted.

ACTIVE, EQUITABLE LEARNING EXPERIENCES THROUGH REFORM

In 1983, the National Commission on Excellence in Education published *A Nation at Risk*. The report suggested that the state of education in the United States was in a "din of mediocrity" and set into motion the standards-based reform movement of today. The Reagan–Bush era forged several different committees to examine educational practice, establish national education goals as outcomes for all learners, and hold school administrators, teachers, and staff accountable for achieving such outcomes.

Although school reform has always been around, standards-based reform focuses on all learners achieving a specific outcome. Standards state what all students should know and be able to do (NASPE, 2004). Forty-seven states have published standards for K-12 education, which are adaptations or adoptions of national standards. Standards are not curriculum but do help to form a framework for both educational policy and practice. A joint presidential and gubernatorial summit in 1989 is believed to have been the first public acknowledgment and utilization of standards-based reform.

Recently, federal law required that student achievement results for schools provided with Title 1 funding must be publicly reported, thus holding schools and teachers accountable for attainment of basic reading, mathematics, and science standards. The federal mandate, No Child Left Behind (NCLB), requires each state to test reading, mathematics, and science in grades three through eight, demanding that all students meet the age-appropriate standards by the 2013-2014 school year. Because all children must meet basic standards in core academic subjects, it is believed that this federal legislation will lead to active and equitable learning experiences for all children. A by-product of standards-based reform and new federal mandates is the school report card. The school report card is a public document containing educational indicators that provide information about the performance of students (Johnson, Barton, & Muldoon, 1998). Indicators are usually categorized as school characteristics, teacher characteristics, and student performance. School report cards are designed to be a public measure of school effectiveness. All schools receiving Title 1 monies must publicly report student achievement scores on state and national tests. Initially, curriculum was governed only by local school boards of education; however, more recently, state and federal mandates are influencing school curriculum materials.

To meet the NCLB mandates, some school activities such as physical education and recess have been reduced or replaced by more academic activities (Pellegrini & Bohn, 2005). This practice is contrary to recommendations by the American College of Sports Medicine (2006), which suggests that schools provide enjoyable, lifetime physical activities, promote motor skills development, and reduce exemptions from physical education. This puts schools at odds with how to simultaneously address public health issues and meet basic academic achievement standards.

The application of standards-based accountability in physical education began in 1992 with the publication of *Critical Crossroads* and initiation of the NASPE Outcomes Project. This document called for changes in physical education and served as the impetus for defining a physically educated person (Rink, 1993). It also resulted in national physical education content standards (NASPE, 2004) to which students and teachers would be held accountable.

Before the initial publication of physical education standards, there was little consensus about what a physically educated person was, should know, or should be able to do. A call for reform in physical education (Locke, 1992; Rink, 1993; Siedentop, 1993; Stroot, 1994) suggested a "now or never" survival tactic. Although change in physical education has focused on vastly different points, reform efforts in physical education have commonly addressed curriculum and accountability.

The desire to create effective, active, and equitable learning experiences resulted in several large-scale physical education initiatives such as Sports, Play, and Active Recreation for Kids (SPARK); the Saber-Tooth Project; character education; and the South Carolina Physical Education Assessment Program (SCPEAP). More specifically, curriculum reform was the emphasis in the SPARK program, the Saber-Tooth Project, and character education. SPARK attempted to increase physical activity levels and health-related fitness knowledge of upper-elementary-school children through maximum participation (McKenzie, Sallis, Faucette, & Kolody, 1997). Instructional and participatory time in the program was equally divided between fitness and motor skill development and took place within physical education classes and outside of school.

The Saber-Tooth Project, involving Nebraska schools, attempted to make changes in physical education by using a university–school partnership (Doutis & Ward, 1999). Teachers in the Saber-Tooth Project, although initially frustrated, eventually recognized the importance of change and identified increased effectiveness in planning, assessment, and student accountability (Doutis & Ward, 1999). Findings suggest that despite districtwide curriculum reform, enactment and implementation looked different across schools and teachers (Doutis & Ward, 1999).

In 1985, while working with at-risk students in physical education, Don Hellison created a new curricular focus emphasizing Teaching Personal and Social Responsibility (TPSR), as introduced in chapter 8. Fitness and skill development are also integrated into this model. The reform took a social-learning approach and specifically delineated, through the use of a rubric, levels of student growth in physical education. Hellison's responsibility approach has been successfully enacted in elementary and secondary schools located in urban, suburban, and rural settings (Hellison, 2003).

Finally, the largest, sustained reform effort took place in South Carolina, in which implementation of a state-mandated accountability system—South Carolina Physical Education Assessment Program (SCPEAP)—resulted in sweeping changes among high school physical education programs. The SCPEAP represented a paradigm shift from autonomous and individual programs to mutual accountability and common goals (Lawson, 1998). In 2003, an in-depth study of high (n = 4) and low (n = 4) performing high school physical education programs revealed that all programs in the study, regardless of performance, had attempted to make positive change (Castelli & Rink, 2003). Three primary changes were (1) attempting to put standards into practice, (2) offering longer units of instruction, and (3) emphasizing student choice. Lawson (1998) concluded that if reform in physical education could be enacted, multiple benefits would result for all students.

As suggested by the findings of Ward and Doutis (1999), teacher decision making plays an important role in curriculum reform and enactment. Additionally, teacher decision making influences the provision of active, equitable learning opportunities and the awareness of and respect for diversity and learner needs. Use of available resources helps teachers make informed and effective decisions.

TEACHER DECISION MAKING AND ITS IMPACT ON STUDENTS

Teachers make *preimpact, impact,* and *postimpact* decisions regardless of the instructional style or sport activity (Mosston & Ashworth, 2002). The school context, student characteristics, and available resources, among other things, influence teacher decision making in each of these phases. Preimpact decisions include planning and preparation before instruction and help to establish and maintain a safe learning environment. Some of the teacher's preimpact decisions include (a) appropriately selecting and modifying activities, (b) matching students' abilities, (c) motivating and managing student behavior, (d) establishing rules and routines, (e) selecting instructional strategies, and (f) addressing safety issues.

Impact behaviors involve implementing the preimpact decisions in addition to supervising student engagement in the planned activities. Most impact decisions take place during or immediately following the enactment of the lesson. Because these decisions are made during instruction, they are often made quickly and based on student responses or behaviors.

Postimpact decisions include assessment and evaluation of student performance and implementation. A reflective teacher thoughtfully considers the effectiveness of the lesson and then returns to the preimpact decision-making phase as decisions are made and then revisited. The ultimate goal of teacher decision making is to establish a reflective cycle in which the teacher attempts to meet student needs, thereby motivating them to achieve.

TEACHER DATA-DRIVEN DECISIONS

Teacher decisions should be based on information received from the students. Regularly conducted formative (during the instructional unit) and summative (at the end of the instructional unit) assessments are a practical way to obtain information about students. For example, if students are asked to complete a pretest on the definitions of health-related fitness terms, the teacher would then be able to address misconceptions about the content. If a student is unable to score within the healthy fitness zone for the push-up test, it means that the student needs more opportunities to build upper-body strength. It is a best practice for a teacher to make instructional decisions based on formal and informal student performance data; however, workplace inhibitors, such as class schedules or large class sizes, cause many physical education teachers to view assessment as a luxury and not as a necessity (Kelly, Dagger, & Walkley, 1989). The data collected through student assessments should drive teacher decision making related to instruction.

Evidence supporting data-based teacher decision making was found among the literature that investigated student attitudes about physical education curriculum. Carlson (1993) found that physical education had little meaning to middle school students, perhaps suggesting that the curriculum contained activities that were not of interest to students. Confirming Carlson's findings, Tannehill and colleagues (1994) reported that more than 40 percent of physical education students liked physical education less than math, science, English, history, and foreign language. Additionally, only 31 percent of high school students perceived physical education as important or very important (Tannehill & Matanin, 1994). Evidence also suggests that males and females, in addition to students of different ethnicities, perceive physical education curriculum differently (Tannehill & Matanin, 1994). For example, many Asian American students and middle and high school boys are opposed to learning dance in physical education.

Findings from these studies suggest that physical education curriculum is perceived differently among students and therefore needs to be dynamic to be equitable for learners of different genders and ethnicities. Teachers need to consider these data when designing physical education curriculum. Data regarding student attitudes suggests that physical education curriculum should include progressive activities, such as rock climbing, that are both of interest to the students and facilitate attainment of the standards. Teacher *preimpact, impact,* and *postimpact* decisions should be data driven.

TEACHER PREIMPACT DECISIONS

According to the NASPE (2000a) guidelines, a high-quality physical education program includes the following components: (a) opportunity to learn, (b) meaningful content, and (c) appropriate instruction. This means elementary school students should spend 150 minutes per week in physical education instruction, and secondary school students should spend 225 minutes per week. Each instructional period should be led by a qualified physical education specialist (not a teacher with training in a different specialization).

Opportunities for children to learn are increased when developmentally appropriate content is presented in an organized fashion. Immediate and long-term teacher planning should consider how to maximize learning opportunities for all children regardless of gender, ethnicity, or socioeconomic status, as previously described. These opportunities should focus on improvement in social and cooperative skills from an inclusive, multicultural perspective.

Meaningful Content

The substance of the physical education curriculum needs to be meaningful to its learners. Content is most meaningful to young people when it includes instruction on a variety of motor skills designed to enhance the physical, mental, social, and emotional development of every child and engages students in authentic sport, physical activities, and assessments (i.e., replicating a lifelike sporting event or assessment of motor skills in a real-life situation). Teacher decisions should focus on the students' understanding of cognitive concepts related to motor competency and on health-related fitness.

Content is meaningful when it inherently addresses public health issues and when all children reap both physical and cognitive benefits from physical activity and fitness. To obtain these benefits, children must be provided with the skills to maintain or improve their health and well-being throughout their lives. The Physical Best series of materials provides a scope and sequence of content, activities that support learning, and printable worksheets to enhance the cognitive aspect of physical activity and fitness. The PE4Life and Coordinated Approach to Child Health (CATCH) curricula offer a K-12 perspective on enhancing physical activity and fitness among youth. Lessons should promote lifelong physical activity and should not use activity as a punishment.

Allowing students to have input in the selection of content is often motivational. As part of the preimpact or planning phase, teachers could administer a student interest survey, allowing students to identify the sport-related activities they are most interested in and appreciate the most. It may appear that the physical education budget will limit the creation of meaningful experiences; however, the student survey may show that some of the simplest activities, found within the community, are what the students want to focus on. For example, students may be interested in becoming proficient at in-line skating so that they can skate with friends on the weekend. Roller skating and in-line skating are very popular instructional units. Students are usually required to provide parental permission and a nominal fee ($2.00 for five sessions of skating). Students are permitted to bring their own skates if they meet safety specifications.

Appropriate Instruction

Various instructional models can be used to motivate students and meaningfully deliver content (Metzler, 2005). The selection of appropriate instructional strategies should be based on maximum practice and the inclusion of all students. Appropriate instruction in physical education incorporates the best-known practices, derived from both research and teaching experiences. Well-designed physical education lessons facilitate student learning and purposefully focus on the concepts and tactics related to specific tasks. High-quality physical education strives for all children to be active at learning centers or in small-sided games and uses technologies such as pedometers and heart rate monitors.

Instruction is most effective when physical education teachers encourage students to participate in physical activities beyond those required during the school day (e.g., YMCA programs, intramurals, community recreation). Physical education teachers should assign out-of-school assignments that support student learning—for example, asking students to conduct an Internet search for information about their favorite sport activity. This task could be assigned as homework and require students to find out how they could participate in that activity within their community. Numerous sport-specific Web sites exist, and many contain accurate information (see www.cln.org/subjects/pe_cur.html for a list of sites related to physical education). Perhaps the assignment could require students to select an activity that they have never participated in and research it on the *Great Activities* Web site. *Great Activities* is an online newspaper (http://greatactivities.net) for elementary and middle school physical education teachers, offering modern interpretations of traditional and creative activities. A teacher or school subscription is required. Whatever the task, be sure that it is age appropriate and is conducted in a manner that is consistent with district policy related to Internet use. Based on what the students find, the teacher can then make decisions about how to make physical education more meaningful. Of course, selecting content is only part of creating meaningful experiences for the students; the other half requires appropriate instruction.

An example of poor teacher decision making occurred when physical education student Steven Larson broke his neck while performing a gymnastic exercise (*Larson v. Independent School District No. 314,* 1980). A required activity during an eighth-grade physical education class gymnastics unit turned out to be harmful because of teacher negligence. The teacher conducting the activity was a first-year teacher and certified in physical education. Steven had not participated in the necessary progressions to develop enough skill to attempt the exercise, and the activity was not spotted correctly. The Supreme Court of Minnesota found that both the teacher and the principal were liable for failing to reasonably develop, plan, and administer the physical education curriculum. The principal was also at fault for failing to supervise an inexperienced teacher. The teacher should have considered his or her preimpact as well as impact decisions to promote a safe environment for student learning.

TEACHER IMPACT DECISIONS

Impact teacher decisions relate to the implementation of teacher plans: how the teacher organizes, allocates, and manages *resources* (e.g., students, time, space, equipment, activities, teacher attention) in order to provide active and equitable learning experiences. Teaching physical education classes has been compared to overseeing a three-ring circus or described as trying to supervise *organized chaos* because even though teachers have put considerable effort into making preimpact decisions, these decisions are only a small part of the process. As any PE teacher will tell you, he or she constantly makes adjustments—impact decisions—during the lesson, which can feel like trying to manage a circus.

Organizing Students During the Lesson

The enactment of teacher plans should be flexible enough to allow teachable moments and other spontaneous diversions from lesson plans that enhance student enjoyment and completion of challenging tasks. As discussed in chapter 8, several student characteristics (e.g., ability, gender, maturation) should guide how teachers pair or organize students for activities. During the lesson, there may be times when the physical education teacher finds that one team is much stronger than another. It then becomes the physical education teacher's responsibility to modify the lesson plan to create a more equitable learning experience. To encourage success, the teacher could modify the game, exchange players, or step back and reintroduce the task.

Students should take some responsibility for carrying out the lesson. Students who have ownership and take responsibility for their own learning are more likely to move the content into their long-term memory, resulting in a permanent change in behavior. There are several ways that students can contribute: (a) respectfully interacting with peers, (b) providing peer feedback, (c) safely and actively participating, (d) managing equipment, and (e) respecting space boundaries. The teacher cannot assume that students will possess these skills; they must be taught as part of the planned curriculum. Just as effective elementary physical education teachers practice the rules and routines, teachers of more mature students need to teach them which critical elements to observe in a peer teaching situation and remind them to respect boundaries.

Allocating Equipment, Space, and Time

Initially, allocation of equipment, space, and time is addressed during the preimpact decisions; however, addressing issues related to these resources is an ongoing process. The teacher must continually monitor the students' use of equipment, the condition of the equipment, and the inventory. The teacher who develops a system in which students also have responsibilities relating to these resources is one who has more time for instruction and assessment of student performance.

If students are taught how, they can help allocate equipment and space within a physical education lesson. For example, one or two students can distribute the rackets while the teacher introduces the task. Students can also help make their own boundaries for small-sided games. Ultimately, it is the teacher who must oversee and approve the student decisions; however, students can handle responsibilities related to the allocation of equipment, space, and time.

Limitations in space, facilities, or equipment may force the teacher into creative ways of keeping the students actively engaged. For example, the school weight room may only have 18 stations, but the teacher has 25 students in his or her class. As a preimpact decision, the teacher creates seven more resistance exercise stations to accommodate all students. On the day of the lesson, several students are absent from this class, so the teacher must adjust the lesson for the students who are present.

Managing Resources

Managing resources is an important component of effective teaching and is planned and enforced during each lesson. Because most elementary physical education teachers work in isolation, they establish unique management systems that are specific to their context (e.g., facilities, number of students). They are also more likely to seek information about different management strategies than high school physical education teachers (Garrahy, Cothran, & Kulinna, 2002).

Whether a teacher management plan is rigid or flexible, teacher time and attention are divided during the lesson. Teacher responsibilities include (a) supervising student behavior, (b) critically analyzing student responses, (c) watching for safety issues, (d) pacing the lesson so it is challenging and engaging, (e) providing enough opportunities for all students to practice and make progress, and (f) diverting attention to issues that arise. During the lesson, the teacher, as a manager, should enforce the rules of conduct and simultaneously provide knowledge of performance and results to his or her learners. It is the teacher's responsibility to manage the collection of assessment data (e.g., motor skill performance, student social responsibility, physical activity measures) during the impact phase of decision making. The teacher must find a way to collect information that will enable him or her to monitor student progress toward the state and national standards (see chapter 10 for technology hints).

For instance, a teacher may want to collect information about student performance at the end of a football unit. The teacher sets up several small football fields for three-on-three games in order to assess the passing and receiving skills of the students. The teacher positions herself at the end of the fields with a video camera to record game play on the field closest to her. She has planned to have the students rotate fields and change responsibilities during game play. During enactment of her planned lesson, she discovers that the space designated for the games is too small; players from different fields are entering into others' game space. Fearing that she may be endangering her students, especially because some of the games are competitive and strenuous, she addresses this immediately by providing adequate space between the playing fields. Although not in this particular case, overlapping boundaries are sometimes a result of having too many students in one physical education class, making the situation difficult to both manage and conduct student assessments.

Large Class Sizes

Large classes are inappropriate yet, unfortunately, a reality in physical education. According to the Council on Physical Education for Children (NASPE, 2000b), physical education class sizes should contain the same number of students as the elementary school classroom does (e.g., 25 students). Two classes of students are often combined and sent to the gym for a physical education class taught by a single teacher. Large classes are dangerous and put the teacher at a disadvantage because teachers of large classes spend more time on organization and discipline (Hastie & Saunders, 1991). Large physical education classes contribute to negative student attitudes (Layfield, 1995) and inhibit student learning (Silverman, 1988).

Physical education teachers should advocate for class sizes that are equitable with those of classroom teachers; however, this may be easier said than done. Curriculum reform and policy change can be a frustrating, drawn-out process. A study of three elementary school physical education specialists who taught classes ranging from 38 to 75 students found that these teachers worked under difficult conditions and experienced feelings of marginalization and hopelessness (Hastie, Sanders, & Rowland, 1999). The teachers felt "they were forced to teach under poor conditions with large classes, and hence, were forced to teach a certain type of curriculum based on class size" (Hastie, Sanders, & Rowland, 1999, p. 286).

TEACHER POSTIMPACT DECISIONS

Postimpact teacher decisions should include feedback on student performance, evaluation of the effectiveness of the instruction, and evaluation of "congruence between intent and the actions of learning experience" (Mosston & Ashworth, 2002, p. 25). However, this is often the most neglected phase of decision making. Postimpact teacher decisions involve gathering information about student performance and comparing this information to the performance criteria. This information should then be used to provide feedback to the learner and to design future lessons.

Feedback on student performance should be provided as soon as possible after the event. Students who can perform a motor task and then immediately watch themselves on videotape have the best chance of changing their performance based on the feedback. The teacher who does not return student cognitive tests or provide feedback on motor performance is neglecting to conduct one of his or her duties as a teacher. Feedback on student performance should be both direct and indirect.

Indirect feedback is provided to the learner through the teacher's planning for the next lesson. For example, if students are frustrated with a task, will the teacher move on to a more difficult task anyway, or will the teacher present the task again in a more effective way? The most important part of postimpact teacher decision making is gathering information from their supervision of the activity and making adjustments in their planning based on this information.

Postimpact decisions guide teacher preimpact decision making for future lessons and curriculum planning. The reflective teacher (see chapter 1) bases his or her decisions on the student performance data obtained from previous lessons. To establish an interactive loop between the decision-making phases, a teacher must use evidence-based practices. To provide evidence-based physical education, a teacher may need to obtain additional resources.

TEACHER DECISIONS REGARDING THE BUDGET

The amount of resources available to a teacher dictates the type of curriculum and instructional strategies he or she can employ. Recently, a new physical education teacher in the Chicago Public Schools arrived for her first day on the job to find that the only equipment available were six playground balls. She was told that she had to make do with the equipment she had been given because no funds were provided in this year's *budget*. Instead of becoming discouraged, this teacher got active. Immediately, she began planning the units that required minimal equipment, such as team building and walking. She simultaneously designed a budget that would provide one piece of equipment per student for the remainder of the units. When she created her budget, she had to make difficult choices about which activities would be most important for her students. Once her priorities were set and the budget of about $10,000 was designed, she began seeking alternative funding sources.

The teacher first approached the school's Parent Teacher Organization, who provided her $200 to begin purchasing equipment. She then contacted the Illinois Association for Health, Physical Education, Recreation and Dance, seeking information about writing a grant for her school, which she ultimately successfully secured. Then she contacted a local life insurance company and told them about her situation. Over time, the insurance company subsidized the purchase of $10,000 worth of equipment for the program. This is only one teacher's situation, but it prompts the question: Should physical education teachers have to work this hard to obtain the tools of their trade? The answer is no; however, this is sometimes the reality.

The amount of money and equipment available will drive the curriculum. When designing a budget, it is necessary to first tour the facilities and inventory the equipment. Teachers need to know what equipment they have and what condition it is in. The next step in making a budget is to find out how much money is likely to be available. Teachers must then review their long-term plans, identifying the specific instructional units that will be part of the curriculum. Based on their current inventory of equipment and the planned instructional units, teachers should identify a list of new, additional, and maintenance equipment (see *Guidelines for Facilities, Equipment, and Instructional Materials in Elementary Education* [NASPE, 2001] for a detailed budget). New equipment is equipment purchased for a new unit added to the curriculum. Additional equipment refers to the accumulation of more pieces for the existing instructional units. Maintenance purchases are made to replace broken equipment.

To help teachers prepare their budgets, Flaghouse has created an online budget builder (www.flaghouse.com/wl_login.asp?Category= Special%20Populations). Once the teacher has provided basic contact information, he or she can begin to select items from Flaghouse and create a budget. The online budget builder allows the teacher to e-mail a draft of the budget to an administrator or business manager for review and approval. This stage often requires several levels of approval (e.g., principal, business officer) and may take some time to complete. Alternative funding sources like those described earlier can help to provide additional resources.

Grant Writing

As stated earlier, teacher decisions should be based on evidence provided through student assessments. Student assessments can also be used as evidence to obtain extramural funding to help obtain resources for a physical education program. More and more teachers have turned to external funds to help obtain resources and thus create effective physical education programs. According to Johnson and Schilling (2001), there are three basic steps to securing external funds for a physical education program: "locating sources of funding, learning the application procedures and eligibility requirements, and writing and submitting a grant proposal" (p. 48). The grant-writing process is not easy, and the physical educator must be prepared to dedicate substantial time to the process.

Pros and Cons of Resource Availability

The news about the availability of resources is both good and bad. Recent economic constraints on school districts have inhibited the availability of resources. As fewer resources are financially supported, curriculum change results (Stroot, 1994). Facilities and equipment are among the most important perks to physical education teachers, and yet many districts are being asked to do more with less.

The use of the Internet to find resources and the opportunities to obtain external funds, such as the Carol M. White Physical Education Program grant, are positive trends related to resources. The Internet provides a plethora of resources to aid in teacher decision making. Elementary physical education teachers, once isolated from colleagues, can now use the Internet to obtain lesson plans, new activities, curricula, health-related physical fitness suggestions, and ideas to address specific societal issues that they encounter. The Carol M. White PEP grant focuses on providing federal funds for an organization to provide high-quality physical activity experiences for youth.

SUMMARY

The effective use of resources is necessary for meeting the needs of today's students by providing an active, equitable learning environment. Teachers should first consider the school context and student characteristics as they progress through the phases of decision making. Reflective teachers evaluate their own performance by monitoring student progress toward the attainment of state and national standards. Management of resources is more than simply inventorying equipment; it is also part of the reflective cycle. Considering that standards-based educational reform has suggested a revision in the physical education curricula, the reflective practitioner must revisit budget and curriculum to see if they are having the intended impact on students. To develop a curriculum that has impact, a teacher may need to secure external funds through grant writing.

Discussion Questions

1. What types of preimpact teacher decisions should be made to help provide active and equitable learning opportunities?
2. How can white, beginning teachers prepare themselves for teaching in predominantly black or Hispanic communities?
3. What types of evidence could help teachers make data-driven decisions?

4. What kinds of school contextual issues do teachers need to consider before making decisions?

5. Describe how teachers can make the curriculum and learning activities meaningful for students?

6. During a lesson, you discover that the boundaries for your small-sided games slightly overlap. How would you most effectively address this safety issue without disrupting the flow of the lesson?

7. Your physical education budget is $400. Create a list of equipment that you would like to purchase and justify your selections.

Professional Portfolio Contents

1. Include a student activity survey. Create and distribute a survey to the students at the school where you are conducting your field experience inventorying their likes and dislikes about specific sport activities included in the physical education curriculum.

2. Go to the Web site for the school where you will conduct your field experience and collect information about students' ethnicity, school context, facilities, physical education curriculum, and scheduling format. Summarize the information into a narrative about how these school and student characteristics will influence your preimpact and impact decisions as a teacher.

3. Create a budget for a local school district PK-12 physical education program.

Key Terms

budget—The financial planning for the purchase of equipment.

bullying—When someone says or does something to have power over another person.

resources—Materials used to support the implementation of the physical education program (e.g., online lesson plans, a professional library, equipment, extramural funding sources).

Resources

Association for Supervision and Curriculum Development (ASCD): www.ascd.org

PE Central: www.PECentral.com

PElinks4U: www.PElinks4U.com

PE4life: www.PE4life.com

References

American College of Sports Medicine. (2006). *ACSM's guidelines for exercise testing and prescription* (7th ed.). New York: Lippincott, Williams & Wilkins.

Bickel, R., Smith, C., Eagle, T.H., & Hardman T. (2001). *Poor, rural neighborhoods and early school achievement.* (OVID Accession No. ED450982). Retrieved on September 23, 2005.

California Department of Education. (2001). *Academic achievement and physical activity.* California Department of Education. (2001). *California physical fitness test: Report to the governor and legislature.* Sacramento, CA: California Department of Education Standards and Assessment Division.

Carlson, T.B. (1993). We hate gym: Student alienation from physical education. *Journal of Teaching in Physical Education, 14(4),* 467-477.

Castelli, D. (2005). Academic achievement and physical fitness in 3rd, 4th, and 5th grade students. *Research Quarterly for Exercise and Sport 76(1),* A-15.

Castelli, D., & Rink, J. (2003). Chapter 3: A comparison of high and low performing secondary physical education programs. *Journal of Teaching in Physical Education, 22(5),* 512-521.

Doutis, P., & Ward, P. (1999). Chapter 4: Teachers' and administrators' perceptions of the Saber-Tooth project reform and of their changing workplace conditions. *Journal of Teaching in Physical Education, 18(4),* 417-428.

Dwyer, T., Sallis, J.F., Blizzard, L., Lazarus, R., & Dean, K. (2001). Relation of academic performance to physical activity and fitness in children. *Pediatric Exercise Science, 13(3),* 225-238.

Garrahy, D., Cothran, D., & Kulinna, P.H. (2002). *Teachers' perspectives on classroom management in elementary physical education.* (ERIC Document Reproduction Service No. ED 467 768, 2-13.)

Hastie, P.A., Sanders, S.W., & Rowland, R.S. (1999). Where good intentions meet harsh reality: Teaching large classes in physical education. *Journal of Teaching in Physical Education, 18(3),* 277-289.

Hastie, P.A., & Saunders, J.E. (1991). The effects of class size and equipment availability on student lesson involvement in primary school physical education. *Journal of Experimental Education, 59,* 212-224.

Hedley, A.A., et al. (2004). Prevalence of overweight and obesity among US children, adolescents, and adults, 1999-2002. *JAMA, 291,* 2847-2850.

Hellison, D.R. (1985). *Goals and strategies for teaching physical education.* Champaign, IL: Human Kinetics.

Hellison, D. (2003). *Teaching responsibility through physical activity* (2nd ed.). Champaign, IL: Human Kinetics.

Johnson, D., & Schilling, T. (2001). Get the gold: A physical educator's guide to grant writing. *Journal of Physical Education, Recreation & Dance, 72(3),* 48-58.

Johnson, R.L., Barton, K., & Muldoon, J. (1998). *The selection of educational indicators for inclusion in school report cards: A report to the members of the South Carolina accountability project.* Columbia, SC: South Carolina Educational Policy Center.

Kelly, L.E., Dagger, J., & Walkley, J. (1989). The effects of an assessment-based physical education program on motor skill development in preschool children. *Education and the Treatment of Children, 12,* 152-164.

Kumanyika, S.K. (1993). Special issues regarding obesity in minority populations. *Annals of Internal Medicine, 119(7),* 650-655.

Larson v. Independent School District No. 314, Brahan, Minnesota 289 N.W. 2d 112 (Supr. Crt. MN, 1980).

Lawson, H. (1998). Rejuvenating, reconstituting, and transforming physical education to meet the needs of vulnerable children, youth, and families. *Journal of Teaching in Physical Education, 18,* 2-25.

Layfield, D.P. (1995). Relationship between class size and attitudes toward physical education in fifth grade students. *Masters Abstracts International, 33,* 714.

Lee, V., & Bryk, A.S. (1988). Curriculum tracking as mediating the social distribution of high school achievement. *Sociology of Education, 61(2),* 78-94.

Lee, V., & Bryk, A.S. (1989). A multilevel model of the social distribution of high school achievement. *Sociology of Education, 62(3),* 172-192.

Locke, L.F. (1992). Changing secondary physical education. *Quest, 44,* 361-372.

McKenzie, T.L., Sallis, J.F., Faucette, F.N., & Kolody, B. (1997). Long-term effects of a physical education curriculum and staff development program: SPARK. *Research Quarterly for Exercise and Sport, 68(4),* 280-291.

Metzler, M. (2005). *Instructional models for physical education* (2nd ed.). Scottsdale, AZ: Holcomb Hathaway.

Mitchell, M., Castelli, D., & Strainer, S. (2003). Chapter 2: Student performance data, school attributes, and relationships. *Journal of Teaching in Physical Education, 22(5),* 494-512.

Mosston, M., & Ashworth, S. (2002). *Teaching physical education* (5th ed.). Boston: Benjamin Cummings.

National Association for Sport and Physical Education. (2000a). *What constitutes a quality physical education program?* Retrieved August 12, 2005, from www.aahperd.org/naspe/template.cfm?template=qualityPePrograms.html.

National Association for Sport and Physical Education. (2000b). *Appropriate practices in movement programs for young children ages 3-5.* Reston, VA: Council on Physical Education for Children.

National Association for Sport and Physical Education. (2001). *Guidelines for facilities, equipment, and instructional materials in elementary education.* Reston, VA: Author.

National Association for Sport and Physical Education. (2004). *Moving into the future: National standards for physical education* (2nd ed.). Retrieved September 12, 2005, from www.aahperd.org/naspe.

National Commission on Excellence in Education. (1983). *A nation at risk: The imperative for educational reform.* Washington, DC: Author. Retrieved May 19, 2003, from www.ed.gov/pubs/NatAtRisk/title.html.

Parke, M. (2003). *Are married parents really better for children? What research says about the effects of family structure on child well-being.* Washington, DC: Center for Law and Social Policy. (ERIC Document Reproduction Service No. ED 476114).

Pellegrini, A., & Bohn, C.M. (2005). The role of recess in children's cognitive performance and school adjustment. *Educational Researcher, 34(1),* 13-19.

Poulton, R., Caspi, A., Milne, B.J., Thomson, W.M., Taylor, A., Sears, M.R., et al. (2002). Association between children's experience of socioeconomic disadvantage and adult health: A life-course study. *Lancet, 360,* 1640-1645.

Rink, J. (Ed.). (1993). *Critical crossroads: Middle and secondary school physical education.* Reston, VA: National Association for Sport and Physical Education.

Roblyer, M.D. (2003). *Integrating educational technology into teaching* (3rd ed.). Upper Saddle River, NJ: Prentice Hall.

Sallis, J.F., & McKenzie, T. (1999). Effects of health-related physical education on academic achievement: Project SPARK. *Research Quarterly for Exercise and Sport, 70(2),* 127-135.

Sallis, J.F., Prochaska, J.J., & Taylor, W.C. (2000). A review of correlates of physical activity of children and adolescents. *Medicine and Science in Sports and Exercise, 32(5),* 963-975.

Shephard, R.J., Volle, M., LaValle, H., LaBarre, R., JeQuier, J.C., & Rajic, M. (1984). Required physical activity and academic grades: A controlled study. In J. Ilmarinen & I. Valimaki (Eds.), *Children and sport* (pp. 58-63). Berlin: Springer-Verlag.

Siedentop, Daryl. (1993). Thinking differently about secondary physical education. In J. Rink (Ed.), *Critical crossroads: Middle and secondary school physical education* (pp.1-6). Reston, VA: National Association for Sport and Physical Education.

Silverman, S. (1988). Relationships of selected presage variables and context variables to achievement. *Research Quarterly for Exercise and Sport, 59,* 35-41.

Stroot, S. (1994). Contextual hoops and hurdles: Workplace conditions in secondary physical education. *Journal of Teaching in Physical Education, 13(14),* 342-360.

Swerdlik, M.E., Reeder, G.D., & Bucy, J.E. (1999). Full-service schools: A partnership between educators and professionals in medicine and mental health, and social services. *NASSP Bulletin, 83(611),* 72-79.

Tannehill, D., & Matanin, M. (1994). Assessment and grading in physical education. *Journal of Physical Education, Recreation & Dance, 13(4)*, 395-405.

Tannehill, D., Romar, J.E., O'Sullivan, M., England, K., & Rosenberg, D. (1994). Attitudes toward physical education: Their impact on how physical education teachers make sense of their work. *Journal of Teaching in Physical Education, 13*, 406-420.

U.S. Department of Education, National Center for Education Statistics. (2000). *Characteristics of the 100 largest public elementary and secondary school districts in the United States: 1999-2000.* Washington, DC: Government Printing Office.

U.S. Department of Education, National Center for Education Statistics. (2002). *The condition of education.* NCES 2002-2005. Washington, DC: Government Printing Office.

U.S. Department of Education, National Center for Education Statistics. (2003). *The condition of education.* NCES 2003-067. Washington, DC: Government Printing Office.

U.S. Department of Education, National Center for Education Statistics. (2004). *Highlights from the Trends in International Mathematics And Science Study (TIMSS) 2003.* NCES 2005-005. Washington, DC: Government Printing Office.

U.S. Department of Education, National Center for Education Statistics. (2005). *Projection of education statistics to 2014.* Washington, DC: Government Printing Office. Retrieved September 1, 2006, from http://nces.ed.gov/programs/projections/app-a.asp.

U.S. Department of Health and Human Services. (2000). *Healthy people 2010: Understanding and improving health* (pp. 1-25). Washington, DC: Government Printing Office, 22B.

Ward, P., & Doutis, P. (1999). Chapter 2: Toward a consolidation of the knowledge base for reform in physical education. *Journal of Teaching in Physical Education, 18(4)*, 332-340.

10

Addressing Technology

STANDARD 9: *Technology.* Use information technology to enhance learning and personal and professional productivity.

OUTCOME 9.1: Demonstrate knowledge of current technologies and their application to physical education.

OUTCOME 9.2: Design, develop, and implement student-learning activities that integrate information technology.

OUTCOME 9.3: Use technologies to communicate, network, locate resources, and enhance continuing professional development.

Before class begins, you set out rackets across the gymnasium floor. Balls of different sizes and textures are spread throughout the space. When you meet Mrs. Brown's class at the door, there is an air of excitement among the students. With a glance and a nod, the students enter the room, pausing to read the list of instant activities on the dry erase board. Quickly, each student selects an implement, an object, and a tool to measure physical activity. Some students choose a heart rate monitor, while others clip a pedometer to the waist; within minutes the activity begins. You weave through the bodies in motion and praise the students who have aligned their choices with their personal fitness goals. Through questioning, you prompt the students who are having difficulty making positive choices. Your daily routines and integration of technology have maximized time, achieved student-centered learning through technology, and given students the responsibility for creating an environment in which you can provide instant feedback.

Technology drives modern existence and influences the lives of both students and teachers. In many ways, the integration of technology into the educational setting has helped to facilitate students' problem-solving, inquiry, and communication skills. Technology has also manifested new learning theories and instructional practices. Yet inadequate funding, poor technology skills among teachers, accessibility issues, and the ever-changing nature of technology have slowed the comprehensive integration of technology into the educational setting. Despite the fact that 99 percent of all public schools in the United States are "hardwired" for technology, technology in education has had less of an impact than it has in other workplaces (National Center for Education Statistics [NCES], 1999).

Technology is a vehicle for educational reform; however, according to a study by the National Center for Education Statistics, only 20 percent of full-time public school teachers feel "very well" prepared to integrate technology into their grade level and subject matter (NCES, 1999). Take, for example, the notion of physical education teachers as advocates, as introduced in chapter 4. The likelihood of teachers acting as advocates is diminished if teachers do not have the skills to create newsletters, construct Web sites, or generate reports, such as those produced by Fitnessgram software. Technology integration has tremendous potential in physical education, but only if teachers have the skills and comprehension to use it.

TECHNOLOGY AS A PROCESS AND PRODUCT

When asked to define technology, many physical education teachers will reply, heart rate monitors, software, or computers; however, a more comprehensive perspective should result from effectively integrating technology into the educational setting. Technology is not just a product but also a process, a scientific method, or a new way of thinking that elicits particular outcomes.

Consider the elementary school students in the vignette: How do you think they responded when introduced to pedometers? The answer is, they wiggled, bounced, moved briskly, or even vigorously responded to the teacher's directives because they wanted to record as many steps as possible. After observing student responses (in this case, responses to the use of pedometers), teachers need to adjust their teaching to the new information about student performance.

One alternative pedagogical practice associated with technology is *constructivism,* or an indirect style of teaching that is based on the premise that students' previous experiences influence the construction of new knowledge. Constructivist theory suggests that control and initiative be placed with the student to make learning more authentic. A constructivist curriculum uses group activities designed in part to facilitate the acquisition of collaborative skills that are often required within contemporary work environments. Literature regarding teachers who use technology suggests that expert technology integrators teach using both direct and indirect methods (Dexter, Anderson, & Becker, 1999). Constructivist classrooms should be *student centered* and *student directed;* however, with state mandates and standards, the technology lessons often look like a hybrid of direct requirements and student-centered instruction (Ertmer, Gopalakrishnan, & Ross, 2001). In today's classrooms, teachers teach to the standards, thus narrowing the curriculum, leaving little room for experimentation with new teaching methods. There are few benefits when technology is applied only to traditional instructional methods; instead, the technological tools (i.e., computers) should be applied in conjunction with progressive teaching strategies.

As suggested in the previous chapter, effective teachers are those who make data-driven decisions. Technology such as heart rate monitors, pedometers, and video provide instant knowledge of performance. Both teachers and students are presented with additional information regarding the effectiveness and quality of movement. Viewing technology in terms of both process and product leads to greater impact on student performance. Currently, technology-rich physical education classes are in the early stages of development. Therefore, teachers should strive to use technology as a means of either enhancing teacher efficiency or providing information that could not be delivered without technology as the medium.

CHARACTERISTICS OF EXEMPLARY TEACHERS WHO USE TECHNOLOGY

Exemplary teachers plan with the standards in mind, create an environment for effective use of technology, have the necessary technology skills, and are willing to take positive risks in front of their students. National and state physical education standards provide a road map for instructional practice, with technology capable of facilitating both the product and the process of achieving those standards. Exemplary teachers who use technology in physical education might first select NASPE Standard 3, "exhibits a physically active lifestyle," as the standard to address during instruction (NASPE, 2004). Originally created in 1995, these student standards identify what a student should know and be able to do upon completion of his or her physical education experience. Specific age-appropriate performance outcomes are identified under each standard (go to www.aahperd.org to find out more). The teacher determines how best to deliver the content and identifies which technology would best facilitate the learning objectives. In this example, heart rate monitors or pedometers might be ideal facilitators.

An effective environment for technology integration begins with the teacher expectations that were generated during the planning stage. For example, when obtaining the technology (e.g., heart rate monitors), the teacher has an expectation that the students will care for the equipment. Physical education preservice teachers have cited "the potential of breaking the equipment" as a inhibitor of technology integration (Castelli & Fiorentino, 2004). Teachers with documented policies and clearly articulated expectations for equipment care have an easier time integrating technology into their classes. To facilitate classroom management, Polar, which makes heart rate monitors, has created a class-management system that facilitates, rather than inhibits, the use of technology in physical education lessons. Students simply enter the gym, find their numbered heart rate monitor, and begin physical activity. Certain heart rate monitors allow for upload of heart rate data at the conclusion of the lesson. Teachers who establish expectations, policies for equipment use, and class routines for technology integration are most likely to be successful in creating a positive, effective environment.

It is inappropriate to suggest that teachers need to know everything there is to know about technology. A teacher integrating technology for the first time should select one type of technology or tool that is accessible and that he or she is comfortable with. For example, a teacher could create a physical education newsletter using his or her word processing skills. This newsletter could both advocate for the physical education program and disseminate information (e.g., teacher expectations, policies, and procedures). Technology by itself will not enhance student learning nor replace the instruction of the teacher. Teachers who have skills in and knowledge of even one technological area can help stimulate student learning.

The integration of technology does not always go smoothly; there will be times when the technology will fail. A teacher once brought 30 sixth-grade students to the computer lab to review Web sites related to physical activity and health. Working in pairs, the students were asked to navigate three preevaluated Web sites to find specific information. This activity was scheduled for a day when the gymnasium was being used for voting purposes. During the Internet scavenger hunt, two of the three Web sites were unavailable because the Internet server was not functioning properly. After reflection and discussion with the media specialist, the teacher learned that she should have *cached* the Web sites (stored the Web sites on the hard drive) before the lesson. Exemplary teachers are not afraid to take positive risks in front of their students. They are courageous, well-prepared people who are comfortable with the technology, consider both the process and product, and create an atmosphere in which technology facilitates attainment of the standards.

For example, when the teacher attempted to display the Center for Disease Control Web site VERB (www.cdc.gov/youthcampaign) the page would not open. Instead of panicking, the teacher used pictures of the Web site as well as the PDF document that she had downloaded onto her laptop to explain the purpose of the page. The VERB Student Planner assists students in the selection of and participation in physical activity through the creation of a downloadable physical activity log. These materials endorse physical activity during and beyond the school day using parent and teacher signatures for *accountability*. If the teacher had relied exclusively on the school's server to display the CDC VERB Web site, the lesson could not have been completed efficiently.

APPLICATION OF SPECIFIC TECHNOLOGIES

National Beginning Teacher Standard 9 mandates that all teachers be able to identify and apply technology to physical education, integrate new learning strategies related to the technologies, and use technology as a form of communication. A teacher should first ask three questions when considering technology integration: (a) Will the technology improve teacher efficiency, (b) will the technology foster learning in the students, and (c) does the technology accomplish something that could not be accomplished previously without it? The teacher should begin by identifying which technology he or she is most comfortable with and then consider its implementation. The next section discusses the integration of basic technologies that preservice teachers in physical education are most comfortable with (Castelli & Fiorentino, 2004): the Internet, digital video, Fitnessgram/Activitygram, pedometers, and heart rate monitors. Additionally, student-designed Web pages and handheld devices are discussed.

Internet

The Internet is a means of meeting many benchmarks of NASPE Standard 9 of the National Standards for Beginning Physical Education Teachers through communication, information dissemination, and advocacy. Upon employment, teachers receive an e-mail account and are provided space on the school district's Web server for a Web page. These tools allow teachers to communicate with their students beyond the school day, connect with parents, create and implement technology-rich learning opportunities, and gain access to current information.

E-mail and teacher Web pages are powerful tools for communicating with colleagues and parents. As suggested in chapters 5 and 7, continued professional growth depends on networking with other professionals. A school district e-mail account should be reserved exclusively for conducting business. Professionals must avoid online shopping, personal e-mail communications, and spam mailings from their school computer and e-mail account, or they risk contaminating the school's network.

Web pages are a means of communication and should contain professional, up-to-date content. Departmental and personal Web pages should serve three primary purposes: (a) to communicate policies, procedures, and expectations to physical education students and parents (see chapter 8, Reducing Liability and Risk); (b) to promote independent and interdisciplinary learning; and (c) to increase Internet usage among the students. If the students are going to use the Internet, all district policies must be adhered to. For example, many school districts require written parental permission. Also, teachers should prescreen any potential Web site for age-appropriateness. Physical education teachers should collaborate with the media specialists because they can often provide Internet filters to link student access to only the selected Web sites. Although Web pages are valuable ways to rapidly disseminate information, teachers must use caution when including students.

The Internet represents both the positive and negative aspects of information access. For every piece of accurate information on the Internet, there are as many inaccurate materials. Most young learners are perceptive users of the Internet but lack the content knowledge to make wise decisions as consumers of this information. It is, therefore, the responsibility of the teacher to select accurate, age-appropriate content for the student viewing the information. An acceptable Web site for adults may not be an appropriate site for students. Web page content, visual design, navigation, security, and vocabulary must be evaluated before a page should be considered for student use.

A learning activity associated with Web usage is a WebQuest. WebQuests are a "series of interwoven activities theoretically grounded in cooperative learning, higher order thinking, authentic assessment, constructivism, and service learning" (Erwin & Castelli, 2004, p. 32). A *WebQuest* is an online scavenger hunt in which students complete a task, investigate information sources, participate in a specific learning process, navigate resources, and meet specific assessment criteria. For example, to illustrate the importance of nutrition and physical activity, a WebQuest might focus on caloric expenditure. The WebQuest titled "Healthiest Fast Food" (www.amphi.com/~psteffen/cheeseburger/index.htm) requires students to track their physical activity and record what they ate for a specific amount of time. WebQuests are an effective way to use the Internet to enhance student learning of physical education concepts.

The final task of a WebQuest sometimes requires small groups of students to create their own Web pages or WebQuests. A WebQuest might begin with a probing question, such as "Why are some people better jugglers than others?" The students must first respond to the question, then search Web sites that the teacher has evaluated to obtain information about eye–hand or eye–foot coordination and circus skills. Based on their findings, the students then physically practice the juggling tasks during physical education class. Outside of physical education class, the students continue to work on their project by developing their own Web page that provides hints for other students to improve their eye–hand or eye–foot coordination. Finally, the students place links to other Web sites on their page. At the elementary level (5th grade), this project would have to be integrated across the curriculum, in collaboration with other teachers. In middle and high school, a student would only need access to the Internet to complete the assignment because the software is free online and does not require the user to download it.

The demands of WebQuests or student Web page projects warrant a few cautions. Despite federal initiatives to hardwire every school and household within the United Sates, many students still do not have access to computers and the Internet. The information age has not provided equitable access and benefits to all students. The term *digital divide,* coined by Lloyd Morrisett (Hoffman & Novak, 1998), describes the access to technology resources across different levels of socioeconomic status. Roblyer (2003) found that not only socioeconomic status but also race and gender play a role in technology access. Although schools, libraries, and other public places provide free access to the Internet, many students lack the transportation necessary to use these resources. Teachers must be sensitive to students who may not have access to these resources. To ensure equitable access, physical education teachers may want to provide in-school time and resources to complete online assignments, or provide an offline option for completing the assignment.

Digital Video

Performance-based assessments to measure student learning are used in physical education, and digital video is ideal for increasing the efficiency and accuracy of assessing (Kimball, 1996; Lund, 1997). Qualitative analysis, also referred to as observational assessment in physical education, is "the systematic observation and introspective judgment of the quality of human movement for the purpose of providing the most appropriate intervention to improve performance" (Knudson & Morrison, 2002, p. 17). Performance assessments captured on video have unlimited replay, can be slowed for more in-depth analysis, can be edited and broken down into specific performance parts, can be viewed from multiple angles, provide instant feedback, and can be stored for future reference. Video can be used for, but is not limited to, any performance-based assessment. Video is also used to provide student choice and to examine teaching practice.

For qualitative analysis, the use of video is most effective when used with a student who demonstrates the skills of an advanced beginner (Mohnsen, 2004). The use of video has the greatest impact on student learning when it is shown immediately after completion, includes teacher feedback, and displays performance from different angles (Darden, 1999; Darden & Shimon, 2000; Doering, 2000). Immediately sharing performance assessments with advanced beginners helps the students understand the critical elements of the task and assessment criteria.

The use of video can assist the teacher in validating observational assessments. Originally, assessments focused on an individual completing a specific skill (e.g., a badminton serve) and were observed and recorded in a single session. You can envision a physical education teacher with a clipboard in hand and students waiting in line for their turn to be tested. The gymnasium with video cameras is vastly different. Teams or small groups of students collaborate while using the video camera to document their own competency. The teacher, once the assessment authority, now has the role of coaching or facilitating student performance. Peer critiques are also an effective way to integrate video technology into physical education.

Peer Critiques

The reciprocal style of teaching incorporates social interaction and feedback into teaching and learning. The learners form partnerships and assume the roles of *doer* and *observer* (Mosston & Ashworth, 2002). The *doer,* the *observer,* and the teacher form a triad whose responsibility is to immediately identify and correct errors in performance. The infusion of technology helps learners to play these roles. A person with a video camera is easily identified as an *observer* and so forth.

The presence of a video camera facilitates accurate peer observations. The role of the teacher using a reciprocal style is to monitor the observers, to give feedback to the observers, and to answer the observers' questions. Observers need training time to learn their responsibilities. The video camera allows for playback, thus promoting accuracy of feedback, understanding of roles, and identification of performance criteria.

Video and Student Activity Choices

You know that student choice in physical education has a positive impact on student learning (Condon & Collier, 2002). The use of video provides both the teacher and the student with significant choice: The teacher could provide specific testing protocols for assessment, allow students to videotape their own routines in dance or gymnastics, or allow students to tape what they believe to be their own best performances. When given the opportunity to choose, students are more motivated and tend to take greater responsibility for their own learning (Condon & Collier, 2002).

Choice is embedded in alternative curriculum models, such as Sport Education, which encourages participation in sport through affiliation and role-playing (Siedentop, 1994). During a Sport Education softball season, a student could be assigned the role of media specialist. The media specialist uses a camera and a notepad to record the events of the sport activity and creates press releases for the school. The media specialist could also be responsible for videotaping students' hitting technique. These series of images, generated over multiple opportunities in the batter's box, are used as an observational assessment. The teacher or the student playing the role of coach could watch the videotape and provide feedback to the hitter.

Video and Physical Activity

Few would argue the physical benefits associated with regular physical activity for both children and adults (U.S. Department of Health and Human Services [HHS], 2000). Additionally, recent research has demonstrated robust findings suggesting that physical fitness can result in improved cognitive functioning, such as attention and memory (Castelli et al., in press). Despite these benefits of physical activity and fitness, few adolescents are meeting the recommended guidelines (HHS, 2000). These trends have resulted in a large-scale attempt to promote physical activity.

The promotion and assessment of physical activity have become important outcomes of physical education programs. "Encouraging students and parents to assess their activity levels both in and out of class" (Darst, 2001, p. 27) should be a central focus of helping students meet National Physical Education Content Standard 3, "a physically educated person exhibits a physically active lifestyle" (NASPE, 2004, p. 1). Physical education is an ideal time to promote physical activity, and some would even argue that it is a responsibility of the physical education teacher to assess physical activity (Pangrazi, Beighle, & Sidman, 2003; Sallis & McKenzie, 1991). Videotape can be used to evaluate physical activity patterns.

McKenzie, Sallis, and Nader (1991) created the System of Observing Fitness Instruction Time (SOFIT) for teachers to monitor and evaluate the amount of time students are engaged in physical activity during physical education and the intensity of the activity. While viewing a videotape of a lesson, a teacher randomly selects students and assigns a level-of-physical-activity code to their activity (5 = moderate activity [like a light jog], 6 = vigorous activity [like jumping rope], and so on). At the completion of the lesson, the teacher calculates the total number of minutes all students spend in moderate to vigorous physical activity and calculates the percentage of class time spent at these activity levels. The students should have spent more than 50 percent of the time being physically active (McKenzie, Sallis, & Nader, 1991). This observational system offers teachers insight into the effectiveness of their planning.

Videotape can also provide a glimpse of teacher effectiveness beyond a simple measure of time spent in physical activity. Several observational systems, such as the Qualitative Measure of Teaching Performance Scale (QMTPS) (Rink & Werner, 1989), focus on specific teacher behaviors related to practice, management, and effectiveness of instruction. Videotaping allows teachers to review performance and examine how their teaching (Kimball, 1996) directly relates to teaching standards. Observational systems and video analysis of teaching behaviors result in collection of baseline behaviors, creation of short- and long-term goals regarding specific teaching behaviors, and the use of new strategies to increase teaching effectiveness. This use of video places the primary responsibility for assessment with the teacher, not the learner. Other technologies, such as the Fitnessgram and Activitygram, pedometers, and heart rate monitors, are student-centered means of promoting physical activity and fitness.

Fitnessgram and Activitygram

The Fitnessgram and Activitygram are comprehensive health-related fitness and physical activity assessments. The Fitnessgram and Activitygram were created by the Cooper Institute for Aerobic Research to promote enjoyable, regular physical activity. In addition, these assessments can positively educate youth and parents about their personal health status. The fitness assessment can be used for people aged 5 through adulthood, although clear criteria have not been established for all fitness tests until the age of 10. The implementation of the Fitnessgram focuses on the "achievement and maintenance of a health-enhancing level of physical fitness" (NASPE, 2004, p. iv). The intent of the physical education content standard is not only to inform the students of their current health status but, moreover, to help students "develop the knowledge, skills, and willingness to accept responsibility for personal fitness, leading an active life, and healthy lifestyle" (NASPE, 2004, p 33). The combined Fitnessgram and Activitygram help students develop an understanding of health-related fitness concepts by relating them to the data derived from the fitness assessments and activity logs.

The Fitnessgram consists of assessments of aerobic capacity, body composition, and muscular fitness. To assess a particular health-related fitness component, the teacher or student may choose from several tests. In the area of aerobic capacity, for example, the Fitnessgram materials recommend using the Progressive Aerobic Cardiovascular Endurance Run (PACER) but also support the use of traditional assessments such as the one-mile run or the walk test. Body composition allows the use of skinfold measurements or body mass index, which is extrapolated from height and weight measurements. The area of muscular fitness is divided into abdominal strength and endurance, trunk extensor strength and endurance, upper-body strength, and flexibility. The Fitnessgram materials require the curl-up (also known as a sit-up) and trunk lift. Unlike other versions of fitness tests, the curl-up and push-up tests are performed at a cadence. To gain a full understanding of the student's physical fitness, it is not necessary to complete all of the endorsed tests, but it is important to select tests from each of the identified health-related fitness areas.

To maintain test validity and reliability, the techniques specific to each assessment must be adhered to, and modifications must be avoided. This means that students need adequate practice time before the testing date. The amount of practice time should be directly proportional to student experience. For example, introduce second-graders to the curl-up technique during the spring activities in preparation for fitness testing involving the curl-ups in the third grade. The data generated from accurate testing is valuable to teacher lesson preparation.

The Fitnessgram kit comes with the Fitnessgram and Activitygram software. The software requires input of individual student data (by the teacher or the student) in order to generate a report specific to each student's fitness level. These data can then be used to communicate with the parent and to design individual physical activity plans. The Activitygram software allows students to record their physical activity during one weekday and one weekend day. They identify the type and amount of physical activity across the two days. After the information is entered into the computer, a report (similar to the one generated by the Fitnessgram software) is generated. Information contained in this report can be used to write individual fitness goals, design physical activity programs, and promote increased or continued physical activity based on student needs.

The Brockport Physical Fitness Test is a health-related, criterion-referenced fitness test designed for both the general and adapted population. Specific criteria are provided for students with mild mental retardation, visual impairments, spinal cord injuries, cerebral palsy, and congenital anomalies and amputations. Many of the fitness tests are administered in a similar manner as the Fitnessgram tests, with modifications only in the criteria. For example, a student who uses a wheelchair would complete the PACER test in the same way as someone who does not use a wheelchair but, because of the increased efficiency, would wear a heart rate monitor to detect levels of aerobic capacity. This version of the fitness test focuses more on functional capacity than attainment of the healthy fitness zone and beyond. The Brockport Physical Fitness Test also provides a training guide for specific disabilities.

Pedometers

Pedometers are another technology that teachers use to measure health-related fitness because they provide an inexpensive and time-effective way to measure a student's physical activity. Unlike the Fitnessgram, pedometers place more responsibility for physical activity on the learner than on the teacher. Pedometers measure physical activity in steps, distance, or caloric expenditure, depending on the model. Many different methods, such as self-reports or physical activity logs, can be used to measure physical activity (Beighle, Pangrazi, & Vincent, 2001; Trost, 2001), yet the pedometer works by simply attaching this noninvasive device to your waistband. The pedometer is designed to accurately measure physical activity during walking in both children and adults. Several studies have confirmed its reliability (Bassett et al., 1996; Gretebeck & Montoye, 1992). When the pedometer accuracy was compared to the observational assessment SOFIT and accelerometers, the pedometers were found to be equally accurate (Beighle et al., 2001; Kilanowski, Consalvi, & Epstein, 1999).

Accurate, affordable, and easy to use, the pedometer possibly represents the most successful integration of technology into physical education classes. Keep in mind that the recommended number of daily steps is different for children and adults. Typically, we hear 10,000 steps a day quoted as the magic number for a healthy, active lifestyle. For children, the average number of steps taken in 24 hours is approximately 13,000 for boys and 11,000 for girls (Vincent & Pangrazi, 2002). The average number of steps taken in a 30-minute physical education class is 1,600 for boys and 1,300 for girls (Morgan, Pangrazi, & Beighle, 2003).

Assessment of physical activity using a pedometer should begin by establishing a baseline. In the book *Pedometer Power,* Pangrazi, Beighle, and Sidman (2003) suggest that establishing a baseline begins with the calculation of stride length. By simply having students count the number of steps it naturally takes them to walk 100 feet (30 meters) and dividing 100 by the number of steps taken, stride length is estimated. Once stride length is calculated, pedometers can be set for each student, thus producing an accurate measurement of physical activity, estimation of distance traveled, and caloric expenditure.

Now that the pedometer is set to measure individual performance, it is time for the students to set individual goals for achievement. Students should use step-count logs or journals to write their goals in and monitor their progress toward those goals. Because goals should be reasonable, both in what will be accomplished and how long it will take, teachers must confirm the accuracy and appropriateness of student goals before monitoring progress. Physical activity logs can be used to monitor student progress, assess physical activity, and analyze student movement tendencies (Pangrazi, Beighle, & Sidman, 2003).

One advantage to using pedometers is the provision of immediate feedback regarding the volume of activity performed (Beighle et al., 2001). At any time, students can stop and look at the pedometer to gauge their progress toward their daily step goal. If the activity is bowling rather than pickleball, the student's number of steps might be smaller than anticipated or desired. The vignette at the beginning of this chapter describes how students can choose from a list of instant activities and equipment, thus selecting the activity that is most likely to help them meet their personal physical activity goals. These learning opportunities force the learner to discriminate between activities to find the one that promotes higher levels of physical activity. This outcome is directly aligned with the National Physical Education Content Standards (NASPE, 2004).

Heart Rate Monitors

Similar to what pedometers do, heart rate monitors measure physical activity; however, heart rate monitors provide information about the intensity of physical activity rather than information about quantity. Heart rate monitors help students identify and maintain a heart rate that is within their target heart rate zone by measuring the number of beats per minute. Heart rate monitors allow the student to focus on the task, but simultaneously monitor the intensity of the physical activity.

Unlike pedometers, heart rate monitors are a little more invasive, requiring the chest strap and monitor to be placed under the shirt, directly in contact with the skin. Despite the immense value of the heart rate monitor information, the invasiveness as well as cost may be a deterrent for use. Still, it would be ideal if all physical education students had a heart rate monitor. Creative planning can help teachers overcome potential barriers related to heart rate monitor use. For example, if the department can afford only 10 heart rate monitors, then 10 should be purchased and used every day on a rotational basis. Students should take turns wearing and using the heart rate monitors to be able to better understand the application of this information. A plan should be created to purchase 5–10 heart rate monitors a year, so ultimately every child has his or her own heart rate monitor to wear during the same class period.

The EZ600 model, made by Polar, stores information for up to eight different students and allows students to send their heart rate monitor data directly to a computer via an infrared beam. The data are logged electronically to track progression, analyze achievement of goals, and graphically illustrate the heart rate, thus creating a portfolio of individual student information. A technology-rich learning activity, found in the book *Lessons From the Heart* (Kirkpatrick & Birnbaum, 1997), takes an interdisciplinary approach to assisting middle school students with their understanding of heart rate monitor information. During the activity "Social Studies and Cardiovascular Fitness," pairs of students use the Internet to identify the leading cause of death in a self-selected country. The students then answer a series of questions about cardiovascular disease. An analysis of their own previously collected heart rate data (stored in their portfolios) helps the students compare physical activity levels across activities and across cultures. Finally, the students make physical activity recommendations for the country they have chosen. This pragmatic application of heart rate information increases the likelihood of applying the information to the students' own lives.

Using Pedometers and Heart Rate Monitors as Advocacy

Pedometers and heart rate monitors are an effective way to educate people about the importance of physical activity, making it easier for you to advocate for physical education. Parents often have stereotypes and negative images about physical education and sometimes pass these perceptions on to their children. Because teachers have included technologies such as pedometers and heart rate monitors, physical education is not what it used to be. Physical education knowledge and content are only valuable if extended beyond the school day and integrated regularly into students' lives. Parents and siblings have a tremendous amount of influence over a child's physical activity level. By requiring measurement of physical activity outside of school, teachers can promote lifestyle integration.

An assessment of physical activity outside of school can be conducted with or without a pedometer or a heart rate monitor. Of course, there is inherent risk that when sending a pedometer or heart rate monitor home it may not be returned or it may be broken; yet classroom teachers take that same risk every day sending home library books, textbooks, and workbooks for students to use to complete homework. Creating a school or district policy and training students to properly use the technology may help physical education teachers provide pedometers for assessment as part of a homework assignment—for example, using a pedometer to track the number of steps taken or distance traveled on foot over 24 hours.

Student-Designed Web Pages

Hypertext markup language (*HTML*) is commonly used in the design of Web pages. Originally, Web page development required understanding this language in order to design or create Web pages. Now, software can create Web pages, so you don't need to know HTML. Familiar Web page creators include freeware, such as Netscape Composer and Mozilla Suite, as well as the more expensive and advanced software like Macromedia Dreamweaver and Microsoft FrontPage. This software allows you to create Web pages from scratch or simply by editing an existing template. You can even use word processing software such as Microsoft Word and presentation software such as Microsoft PowerPoint to create Web pages. This increased simplicity has now made PK-12 students potential Web developers.

Because students have been introduced to technologies at a younger age than their teachers were, they are comfortable with and receptive to its use. Teachers need to guide the students, using worksheets or modules, to facilitate safe and accurate construction of a Web page.

As you can see in the module shown in figure 10.1, the students are given sequential directions and a template to work from. This assignment can be completed in the elementary classroom during indoor recess, lunch

Grades

6-8

Equipment

Computer work stations, Microsoft PowerPoint®

Teacher Directives

Reserve the computer lab well in advance.

Allow students to work independently or in pairs.

To prevent ineffective Web searching, provide a list of authoritative Web sites that promote and endorse participation in physical activity.

National Physical Education Standards

Standard 6: Values physical activity for health, enjoyment, challenge, self-expression, and/or social interaction.

Objective

To develop a PowerPoint presentation to be saved and uploaded to a server as a Web page that displays places in the community in which young people can be physically active. Details such as how to get started, location, contact information, cost, and benefits of participation will be included on the Web pages.

Set Induction

What is the definition of physical activity?

List some types of physical activities.

Where in our community can we be physically active?

What can someone do if he or she does not particularly enjoy participating in sports?

Are there alternative activities that require physical activity?

Instructions

As someone who is interested in being physically active within your community, use local Web sites to find information about potential opportunities for engagement.

1. Select a search engine and use the World Wide Web to gather information about where in your community someone could engage in physical activity. Try Web sites affiliated with schools, parks and recreation departments,

Figure 10.1 Student module: banner for a sport education season.

cities, or any others that come to mind. Some recommended search engines include the following:

AltaVista www.altavista.com

Ask.com www.ask.com

Dogpile www.dogpile.com

Excite www.excite.com

Google www.google.com

Hotbot www.hotbot.com

Lycos www.lycos.com

Yahoo! www.yahoo.com

Yahoo! Kids http://kids.yahoo.com

2. Identify content that might be important to include on the Web page.

3. Decide how the information should be distributed across the PowerPoint slides. For example, do you want to make a slide for each possible activity or make a slide that contains many similar activities?

4. Select a design template for the PowerPoint presentation. You can do this by going to "Format" on the top toolbar in PowerPoint. You will be presented with several options in the right-hand column. Preview the design templates and select one that best matches the content of your presentation.

5. It is important to remember to save your work periodically. You can do so by selecting "File" from the top toolbar, then selecting "Save." Be sure to save your presentation as a .ppt file in a location that you can access later.

6. Insert interactive elements. Select "Slide Show" from the top toolbar, then select "Custom Animation." The list of effects that you can apply to your text or pictures will appear in the right-hand column. It is best to apply only a few effects, as these can become distracting to the audience.

7. Save the Web page offline for peer review by another work group. This time, when you save your PowerPoint presentation, save it as a Web page. Go to "File" in the top toolbar, then select "Save As." Click the arrow next to the "Save as type" box at the bottom of the page and select the "Web Page" option. The page is now ready to present to your instructor. You can then upload it to the school's server or Web site if desired, or you can simply show the Web page as an offline document to your peers for review.

Assessment Criteria

The Web page reflects ways in which someone could choose to be physically active.

The Web page contains accurate information.

The colors and effects contribute to (and do not distract from) the importance of the content.

The materials illustrate the value of physical activity from the perspectives of health, enjoyment, challenge, self-expression, and/or social interaction.

Figure 10.1

time, or computer time. Although limited in function, the document can be *saved as* a Web page and uploaded to the school's server for display. These student Web pages can serve as evidence of students working toward attainment of social responsibility in addition to providing advocacy for the physical education program.

Handheld Devices

A personal digital assistant (PDA) was originally designed to store contact information for traveling business associates. Today, a PDA can also be a phone, a camera, a text messenger, or a form of entertainment or provide access to the Internet or all of these combined. The first-generation PDAs were limited by storage space, lack of expandability, and communication errors. Advances in the Palm OS platform have helped develop education-ally applicable software. When considering handheld technologies, there are two types: the Palm OS platform and the Windows-based platform. The screen of the Windows unit looks and acts just like the screen of a desktop computer. The discussion in this chapter focuses on the Palm OS platform.

The PDA has tremendous potential for physical education teachers. Physical education teachers often teach hundreds of students whom they see only one or two times per week. The inclusion of assessment and monitoring of student progress could become a logistical nightmare. Software now available for handheld devices allows teachers to take attendance, record assessment data, and store fitness-testing information by simply tapping on the screen of the PDA. The PDA provides mobility that desktops cannot. The physical education teacher can slide the PDA into his or her pocket and be ready to record assessment data on the track, near the pool, or in the gymnasium.

Data stored on the PDA can be transferred easily, via a docking cradle or infrared beam, back to permanent storage on a desktop or laptop computer, thus saving a teacher valuable time and increasing efficiency. Using a holistic scoring rubric, a teacher could easily store student performance data, such as the frequency and effectiveness of offensive tactics during game play. The teacher can store the information in an electronic format immediately following class or at the end of the school day. Specific Palm OS software and its integration are described further.

Record Book

Record Book is Palm OS platform software created by Bonnie's Fitware (www.pesoftware.com). It is grade book software specifically designed with the physical education teacher in mind. It is available in both Macintosh and PC formats, so it can be used at any school. The Record Book tracks attendance, observational assessments, and fitness test scores and can be customized to include other observational assessments. The screen is in a spreadsheet format for ease of entry and reading.

Documents to Go

DataViz software Documents to Go allows a teacher to create rubrics using Microsoft Word. Once saved in Word, it can be transferred to the PDA for reference and display in the field. Using Microsoft Excel, a teacher can take the scoring rubric and convert it into a spreadsheet complete with formulas for identifying student performance cutoffs for mastery, computing grades, or creating feedback documents. The psychomotor, cognitive, and affective domains could be assessed, depending on the scoring rubric developed by the teacher.

Presenter to Go

The effective integration of this software requires availability of additional devices: an LCD projector and Microsoft PowerPoint software. As part of the Documents to Go software series (which converts Excel and Word), Presenter to Go software allows PowerPoint presentations to be shown on handheld devices. PowerPoint is a user-friendly tool that can create and display task cards, pictures (JPEGs), presentations, Web pages, and more. The purpose of the Margi Presenter to Go software is to project a PowerPoint presentation from a PDA via an LCD projector in the gymnasium. If a desktop or laptop computer is unavailable or space is limited, the PDA can deliver the same PowerPoint presentations that are viewed in the classroom.

Margi Presenter to Go is not only an instructional tool but can also be used to check for understanding among the students. For example, you could create a presentation that asks small groups of students to demonstrate specific motor tasks or game tactics. Students could be asked to locate open space on a display of a court or a field with specific areas labeled. Or small groups or individual students could take an interactive quiz by reading tasks displayed on the screen—for example, transfer your weight up and down your mat using only low-level, steplike actions—and demonstrating correct responses. The teacher could then perform an observational assessment of the students. In this scenario, technology tools (PDA and LCD projector) offer an alternative assessment format that can immediately affect instruction.

Global Positioning Systems (GPS)

Global positioning systems are another handheld device that have potential use in school settings, including physical education. These systems have been developed to identify latitudinal and longitudinal positions, altitude, waypoints, compass directions, and rate of travel. Originally,

GPS units were developed for use by the military to map positions using accurate latitudinal and longitudinal coordinates. Since May 2000, the public has been allowed to use GPS units in their vehicles and for purposes such as estimating the distance to a hole in golf, marking waypoints on a hike, and locating and marking fishing spots, just to name a few.

In addition to the uses cited, a sport called geocaching—a high-tech version of hide and seek or orienteering—has evolved that uses GPS to locate points of interest and hidden items, or caches. Geocaching takes place in urban, rural, and natural settings. People who participate in the sport have set up geocaches, consisting of a logbook and sometimes other items, in most cities and in over 200,000 locations around the world. After setting up the cache, the hosts then post the coordinates at www.geocaching.com. Participants search the Web site for cache coordinates by country, state, city, or ZIP code, then use GPS to find the cache. Participants can search for caches located at points of interest near where they live or can search for caches while traveling. Since the initial geocache was set up in 2000, many variations have evolved. They include multicaches, virtual caches, event caches, mystery caches, Webcam caches, and locationless caches.

Using a GPS to geocache also has many implications in school or recreational settings. In physical education, teachers can set up orienteering courses for students by creating a puzzle or multistage cache. A puzzle or multistage cache gives clues or information to go to another set of coordinates. After visiting several sites, enough data is collected to lead to the answer or final cache of coordinates. Teachers could send students to coordinates for sites such as the flagpole, home plate on the softball field, soccer goal, or the starting line on the track. Clues could be given to discover a secret message that participants must decode. Teachers could turn this into a fitness experience by asking students to run or jog between points. As a homework assignment, a group of students or a student and parent could find sites in their community. Teachers could also give students a class assignment to develop their own geocache and post it on the Internet for others to find. In our experiences with geocaching, we have seen classes of students bussed to geocaching sites to complete geography, history, English, science, and mathematics assignments.

A possible roadblock to getting participants started in geocaching is the start-up cost of purchasing GPS units. Teachers can survey parents or adults to discover if they have a GPS unit they would be willing to loan. Teachers can also get small grants to purchase a few units and let participants work in small groups. Internet sites that can help teachers get started are www.geocaching.com, www.offroute.com, and www.garmin.com.

The Internet, video, pedometers, heart rate monitors, student-designed Web pages, and handheld devices provide straightforward ways to assess motor competency, the physical activity of physical education students, and social responsibility. Initial research on the effect of technology on teacher efficiency, student learning, and new ways of instructing is encouraging. When carefully planned management systems are used, teacher efficiency is increased because these technologies shift responsibilities to the learners. Learning is affected because instruction is student centered. The process focuses on student accountability for learning and application to their activity and fitness habits. Student learning is enhanced by the different instructional styles and the introduction of new instructional unit content. It's easy to see how using technology leads to student-centered learning. When a teacher uses technology with an eye toward both product and process, the technology produces knowledge—for example, the number of steps, distance traveled, or calories spent. It also leads to a process that shifts accountability from the teacher to the student and a process in which students apply their newly achieved knowledge to their activities and fitness habits. Technology has the potential, if handled effectively, to enhance student learning and produce physical, mental, and quality-of-life benefits.

FUTURE DIRECTIONS FOR TECHNOLOGY INTEGRATION

It is difficult to predict what technology in physical education class will look like in 10 years. Part of the problem is that computer technology changes quickly—soon after something is purchased it becomes obsolete. Storage capacity doubles every 12 months, processor speeds increase every 24 months, the Internet adds 77,000 new pieces of information a day, and microchips get smaller and smaller every year. Another factor that makes technology use in physical education difficult to predict is cost. A particular technology may be available but unaffordable in educational settings. For example, voice-activated software has been around for years; but because it requires hours of training, it is ineffective. High-definition television is also available; however, most schools cannot afford it.

Although it's difficult to predict which new equipment schools will find useful and adopt, the following new technologies are being integrated on some level. The iMovie software, available only for Macintosh computers (other programs are available for PCs) is user friendly and used for video capture and editing. Students can make their own movies to use for observational assessments, advertisements, or peer critiques. Students can break down videotaped images of motor skills to analyze specific movement elements.

Dartfish is software used in professional sports and in higher education that allows immediate field analysis of human movement. When a video camera is connected to a laptop computer, this software instantaneously displays feedback from multiple angles and provides frame-by-frame analysis, split-screen images, and an overlay of critical elements of movement. Although the price of the product is currently just out of the range of K-12 educators, the software has tremendous potential. Animation software, such as Poser, allows users to create animated figures performing advanced movement tasks, individually or in a sequence. This animation software or DVD-making software can help students create animated practice sessions demonstrating perfect execution.

DVDs are being used to provide ideal practice situations for middle and high school physical education students (Castelli & Fiorentino, 2004). Imagine going one-on-one with Michael Jordan or Kobe Bryant as a learning station in the gymnasium. An LCD projector projects a life-size, digital video image onto a wall of the gymnasium. The student faces the image, with equipment in hand, and physically responds to the action of the digital image. For example, the student, as a quarterback, executes a five-step drop then selects an open receiver and completes the pass. The receiver is a digital image, and the ball is simply thrown to the image on the wall. This scenario promotes student decision making, enactment of game tactics, and execution of motor skills.

The application of technology to the educational setting is only limited by one's imagination and budget. In the future we may see students practicing juggling while wearing virtual-reality goggles and gloves. Instead of attempting to juggle balls, which fall and roll across the floor, the students attempt to juggle imaginary rings of fire. The practice technique is the same, but the motivation is much higher. The gloves send student responses to the computer for analysis of their accuracy. For more information on such futuristic products, read *Using Technology in Physical Education* (Mohnsen, 2004).

A bold prediction for technology integration suggests that holograms and wearable computers will influence physical education. Using holograms, students in England could teach students in the United States how to play cricket. Students in U.S. classrooms could step inside the hologram to learn the task. Holograms would serve as both the demonstration and the teleconference. Wearable computers could provide noninvasive ways to regulate body temperature during exercise, provide measures of biofeedback, and examine cognitive responses in decision-making situations.

SUMMARY

Technology encompasses tools as well as the process by which individuals progressively solve problems. Such technology tools as the Internet, WebQuests, digital video, Fitnessgram/Activitygram, pedometers, heart monitors, handheld devices, and GPS systems each have potential to be integrated into physical education curricula to enhance teacher efficiency and foster student learning. The impact of technology in physical education is limited only by one's imagination and budget. The future technologies presented here may never reach physical education classes, but if a more efficient way of fostering student learning exists, is it not worth investigating? Using technology during student assessments enhances accountability, feedback, and effective evaluation when properly integrated. Keep in mind that before implementing a technology, the teacher should first ask (a) will the technology improve teacher efficiency, (b) will the technology foster student learning, and (c) does the technology accomplish something that could not be accomplished without it?

Discussion Questions

1. What is technology?
2. Some technologies promote physical inactivity; why should we consider using these types of technology in the physical education setting?
3. How do we get people to be comfortable with technology and assessment?
4. How can we respectully implement video in the physical education curriculum?
5. What are the two primary reasons for integrating technology into the physical education curriculum?
6. How could existing technology enhance teaching in your school?
7. What are ways, besides those discussed, that you could use each of the suggested technologies in this chapter in a physical education program?

Professional Portfolio Contents

1. Include examples of technology-rich lesson plans, a WebQuest, or a lesson submitted to PE Central.

2. Go to www.teach-nology.com/web_tools/web_quest and use the WebQuest Generator.

3. Include videos of student learning.

4. Include the URL for your Web page.

5. Design a module for the creation of student Web pages, design a basic orienteering lesson that integrates GPS technology, or design an interdisciplinary project with the media specialist at the school that provides evidence of online homework for students.

6. Generate a list of student-safe, age-appropriate Web pages.

7. Link a digital video of your teaching philosophy, a mock interview, or some sample lessons from your field experiences.

Key Terms

accountability—The state of being held responsible for meeting and maintaining an established standard of performance.

constructivism—An indirect style of teaching that is based on the premise that students' previous experiences are important and that they construct knowledge related to their experiences.

HTML (hypertext markup language)—The universal language used for Web site construction.

URL (uniform resource locator)—The address where a Web site is located on the Internet.

WebQuest—An online scavenger hunt requiring an interactive Web search to find information related to a specific task.

Resources

Cooper Institute for Aerobics Research. (1999). *Fitnessgram: Test administration manual.* Champaign, IL: Human Kinetics.

Dexter, S.L., Anderson, R.E., & Becker, H.J. (1999). Teachers' views of computers as catalysts for changes in their teaching practice. *Journal of Research on Computing in Education, 31(3),* 221-239.

Garmin: www.garmin.com

Geocaching: www.geocaching.com

Kirkpatrick, B., & Birnbaum, B.H. (1997). *Lessons from the heart: Individualizing physical education with heart rate monitors.* Champaign, IL: Human Kinetics.

Knapp, L.R., & Glenn, A.D. (1996). *Restructuring schools with technology.* Needham Heights, MA: Allyn & Bacon.

Mohnsen, B.S. (2001). *Using technology in physical education* (3rd ed.). Cerritos, CA: Bonnie's Fitware.

Offroute: www.offroute.com

PE Central: www.PECentral.com.

Whalen, S., & Fiorentino, L. (2004). *Teaming up with technology: Integrating technology into your classroom in health education and physical education.* Reston, VA: American Association for Health Education.

Winnick, J.P., & Short, F.X. (1999). *The Brockport physical fitness test manual: A health-related test for youths with physical and mental disabilities.* Champaign, IL: Human Kinetics.

References

Bassett, D.R., Ainsworth, B.E., Leggett, S.R., Mathien, C.A., Main, J.A., Hunter, D.C., et al. (1996). Accuracy of five electronic pedometers for measuring distance walked. *Medicine and Science in Sports and Exercise, 28(10),* 1071-1077.

Beighle, A., Pangrazi, R.P., & Vincent, S. (2001). Pedometers, physical activity, and accountability. *Journal of Physical Education, Recreation & Dance, 72(9),* 16-19, 36.

Castelli, D.M., & Fiorentino, L. (2004). The effects of different instruction on preservice teacher perceived ability and comfort with technology in physical education. *Research Quarterly for Exercise and Sport, 75(1),* 63.

Castelli, D.M., Hillman, C.H., Buck, S.E., & Erwin, H.E. (in press). Physical fitness and academic achievement in 3rd and 5th grade students. *Journal of Sport & Exercise Psychology.*

Condon, R., & Collier, C.S. (2002). Student choice makes a difference in physical education. *Journal of Physical Education, Recreation & Dance, 73(2),* 26-31.

Darden, G. (1999). Videotape feedback for student learning and performance: A learning stages approach. *Journal of Physical Education, Recreation & Dance, 70,* 40-45.

Darden, G., & Shimon, J. (2000). Revisit an old technology: Videotape feedback for motor skill learning and performance. *Strategies, 13,* 17-21.

Darst, P. (2001). Fitness routines for directing students toward a physically active lifestyle. *Journal of Physical Education, Recreation & Dance, 72,* 27.

Dexter, S.L., Anderson, R.E., & Becker, H.J. (1999). Teachers' views of computers as catalysts for changes in their teaching practice. *Journal of Research on Computing in Education, 31(3),* 221-239.

Doering, N. (2000). Measuring student understanding with a videotape performance assessment. *Journal of Physical Education, Recreation & Dance, 71,* 47-51.

Ertmer, P.A., Gopalakrishnan, S., & Ross, E.M. (2001). Technology-using teachers: Comparing perceptions of exemplary technology use to best practice. *Journal of Research on Technology in Education, 33(5),* 1-18.

Erwin, H., & Castelli, D. (2004). Building and facilitating physical education through WebQuests. *Teaching Elementary Physical Education, 15(5),* 29-32.

Gretebeck, R.J., & Montoye, H.J. (1992). Variability of some objective measures of physical activity. *Medicine and Science in Sports and Exercise, 24(10)*, 1167-1172.

Hoffman, D.L., & Novak, T. (1998, April 17). Bridging the racial divide on the Internet. *Science, 280(5362)*, 390.

Kilanowski, C.K., Consalvi, A.R., & Epstein, L.H. (1999). Validation of an electronic pedometer for measurement of physical activity in children. *Pediatric Exercise Science, 11*, 63-68.

Kimball, R. (1996). Collaborating on assessment. *Teaching Elementary Physical Education, 7*, 13.

Kirkpatrick, B., & Birnbaum, B.H. (1997). *Lessons from the heart: Individualizing physical education with heart monitors.* Champaign, IL: Human Kinetics.

Knudson, D.V., & Morrison, C.S. (2002). *Qualitative analysis of human movement.* Champaign, IL: Human Kinetics.

Lund, J. (1997). Authentic assessment: Its development and applications. *Journal of Physical Education, Recreation & Dance, 68(7)*, 25.

McKenzie, T.L., Sallis, J.F., & Nader, P.R. (1991). SOFIT: System for observing fitness instruction time. *Journal of Teaching in Physical Education, 11*, 195-205.

Mohnsen, B. (2004). *Using technology in physical education* (4th ed.). Cerritos, CA: Bonnie's Fitware.

Morgan, C.K., Pangrazi, R.P., & Beighle, A. (2003). Using pedometers to promote physical activity in physical education. *Journal of Physical Education, Recreation & Dance, 74(7)*, 33-38.

Mosston, M., & Ashworth, S. (2002). *Teaching physical education* (5th ed.). San Francisco: Benjamin Cummings.

National Association for Sport and Physical Education. (2004). *Moving into the future: National standards for physical education* (2nd ed.). Reston, VA: Author.

National Center for Education Statistics. (1999). *Indicator of the month: Teachers' feelings of preparedness.* Retrieved September 16, 2005, from http://nces.ed.gov/pubsearch/pubsinfo.asp?pubid=2000003.

Pangrazi, R.P., Beighle, A., & Sidman, C.L. (2003). *Pedometer power.* Champaign, IL: Human Kinetics.

Roblyer, M.D. (2003). *Integrating educational technology into teaching* (3rd ed.). Upper Saddle River, NJ: Pearson Education.

Sallis, J., & McKenzie, T. (1991). Physical education's role in public health. *Research Quarterly, 62*, 124-137.

Siedentop, D.E. (1994). *Sport education: Quality PE through positive sport experiences.* Champaign, IL: Human Kinetics.

Trost, S.G. (2001). Objective measurement of physical activity in youth: Current issues, future directions. *Exercise and Sport Sciences Review, 29(1)*, 32-36.

U.S. Department of Health and Human Services. (2000). *Healthy People 2010: Understanding and improving health* (pp. 1-25). Washington, DC: U.S. Government Printing Office.

Vincent, S., & Pangrazi, R.P. (2002). An examination of the activity patterns of elementary school children. *Pediatric Exercise Science, 14,* 432-441.

Werner, P., & Rink. J.E. (1987). Qualitative Measures of Teaching Performance Scale in Systematic Observation: Instrumentation for Physical Education. Champaign, IL: Human Kinetics.

CHAPTER

11

Professionalism
and Continued Growth

STANDARD 9: *Technology.* Use information technology to enhance learning and personal and professional productivity.

OUTCOME 9.3: Use technologies to communicate, network, locate resources, and enhance continuing professional development.

March Madness is fun for sports fans, but when you are a basketball coach, it takes on an entirely new meaning. Last year you were thrilled when River Ridge High School, where you had been teaching physical education, hired you as a varsity basketball coach. You enjoyed teaching physical education; however, it was your dream to coach a varsity basketball team. Your team has been more successful than you anticipated, and the school is alive with a spirit from that success. You feel obligated to give the team as much time as you can, to talk to the press and promote your program, and to provide extra practice sessions to address individual player needs. As the postseason approaches and expectations are rising, one of your physical education students catches your attention by stating, "I'm tired of playing team sports in PE. We always do the same thing in class. You only care about your basketball team." You suddenly realize that the demands of a first-year varsity coach have taken a toll on your quality of work as a physical education teacher. Before this year, you had always enjoyed teaching and spent quite a bit of time preparing lessons and interacting with your students. This year it has changed as you find yourself planning less and less, performing little student assessment and, as the student suggested, not caring about your teaching or students.

After graduating and securing employment, beginning physical education teachers are both excited and nervous about their first teaching jobs. Sensing that they have accomplished their goals and can now settle into the working world, first-year teachers often have the misconception that life will suddenly be a little easier. After all, there are no more mandatory reflections, teaching evaluations, or coursework assignments to complete. The reality of being a full-time physical education teacher is that these assumptions are invariably incorrect. Housner (1996) suggests that teachers' continued professional growth is developed through mentoring, reflecting, questioning one's own beliefs and practices, and changing teaching strategies. For first-year teachers to be successful, they need to continue many of the same tasks required during their undergraduate experience. Following a section on becoming a first-year teacher, each of these ideas will be discussed.

BECOMING A FIRST-YEAR TEACHER

Many things must take place for a person to make a smooth transition from successful student teaching to his or her induction year of teaching. The person is no longer simply a student, but for a brief time is identified as a teacher candidate. To complete the transition from student to teacher, the person must complete four important steps. First, he or she must fulfill the degree requirements, which globally are similar, but in reality are specific to the granting institution. Second, the teacher candidate must complete a professional portfolio containing evidence of how he or she has met the National Association for Sport and Physical Education (NASPE) National Standards for Beginning Physical Education Teachers. Third, the teacher candidate needs to successfully complete a student teaching experience, requiring the candidate to become the apprentice of a practicing teacher. During this experience, the teacher candidate gradually takes on all of the responsibilities of the cooperating teacher. Finally, each candidate must secure employment.

Beginning Teacher Standards

NASPE has published National Standards for Beginning Physical Education Teachers (see pages x-xi), which include acceptable outcomes for each standard. These standards, through the National Council for Accreditation of Teacher Education (NCATE), are used to grant accreditation for higher-education institution teacher education programs.

Beginning teachers are expected to present evidence of the requisite skills, knowledge, and dispositions, which are detailed in the standards. Among these skills are the ability to plan instruction, use technology, foster collaborations, assess student performance, and effectively communicate in multiple forums. Additionally, the teacher candidate must have knowledge of physical education content, an understanding of human growth and development, and responsive cultural sensitivity. To shift from attainment to application of these skills, the teacher candidate needs to be able to reflectively articulate his or her competencies in a single statement called a teaching philosophy.

Developing a Teaching Philosophy

While teacher candidates are attempting to master the outcomes identified by NASPE, they should be simultaneously developing their own philosophy of teaching. A *teaching philosophy* briefly describes one's personal conception of teaching and learning (e.g., personal goals for the teacher, goals for the students, beliefs about how students learn), a description of one's teaching style, and a justification of why someone would teach or assess in this manner. The philosophy statement is therefore an illustration of how the teacher candidate has reflected on his or her own growth and development. Yet the ultimate purpose of a teaching philosophy statement is to communicate to others how a person teaches and what the person values.

The most effective teaching philosophies are brief and to the point. Statements dealing with abstract thought are difficult for an administrator or potential employer to appreciate. Teaching philosophies are also specific to the discipline. If applying terms like multiple intelligence, it would be wise to consider using specific examples of what these theories would look like within a physical education lesson. It is also considered best practice for teacher candidates to demonstrate that they have reflected on their own experience and perhaps to highlight how those experiences have influenced how they teach. The teaching philosophy statement should represent the unique qualities of each person and can be written in first or third person (see figure 11.1).

Searching and Applying for Jobs

Writing a teaching philosophy is perhaps the most demanding part of the transition from student to teacher. In 2002, Senne developed a list of steps that are part of the *hiring process,* highlighting how people identify potential employment opportunities, apply for physical education teaching positions, conduct interviews, and ultimately accept employment (see figure 11.2).

The most important piece of advice for the teacher candidate regarding the application and hiring process is "Do your homework." First, the teacher candidate should find out if his or her university or college has a career planning and placement office. Remember, universities want their graduates to be employed, so they often provide numerous resources to support the student's hiring process. For example, these offices might help the teacher candidate develop a cover letter and resume. If the institution does not have a career planning and placement office, the teacher candidate will have to take the initiative to navigate these steps independently.

Today, many teaching vacancies are posted online in addition to appearing in more traditional listings such as those found in newspapers. Some employment listservs require candidates to register to access the site, and others can be accessed without formal commitment from the teacher candidate. Teaching job fairs are also commonly held on college campuses.

I believe the purpose of the physical education program is to contribute to each student's growth and development in the physical, cognitive, and social domains while exposing them to a variety of different curricula. This involves delivery of a sequential K-12 instructional program that prepares them for the basic skills of leisure and sport activity and fosters habits of a healthy and active lifestyle. The objectives that are met through the three domains (affective, cognitive, psychomotor) will provide an extensive base of knowledge for the student and will create a long-lasting backbone for their knowledge in physical education. It is important that students understand these components of physical education because it will be essential to apply in their everyday lives.

Health-related fitness should be the focus of any physical education curriculum. With the extensive obesity epidemic that appears in society today, it is in our nation's and our communities' best interest to educate our children on how to live a healthy and active lifestyle. However, fitness needs to be addressed according to what the student interests are. Students must be excited about what they are accomplishing, and this will guide them into healthy adult lifestyles. It will allow students the opportunity to be involved in many different kinds of activities that might interest them in the future.

In a physical education program it is also necessary to recognize the abilities and the needs of every student. Once these needs and abilities are recognized, one must adjust and plan accordingly in order to benefit every student to his or her full potential. As a teacher I must be prepared to develop appropriate instructional plans that include every student. After every lesson, I must reflect on my teaching and always be aware of what could have gone better. Reflecting is a key part of providing an education for students. Without reflection on a lesson I would not be able to determine how to make improvements or adaptations for the next lesson.

Staying involved in different professional organizations is a critical part of physical education. It is with these organizations that teachers obtain new ideas for curricula and lessons, and it allows teachers to keep up to date with the latest technology that they can use in physical education classrooms. Without organizations such as these, many teachers tend to follow in the footsteps of traditional, teacher-centered instruction, something that I believe should be banished from all schools.

I believe that by following these guidelines, a rich physical education program will emerge. It will lead students and the community to develop an appreciation for physical education and will help encourage a healthy lifestyle for the students' future.

Figure 11.1 Sample teaching philosophy statement.

Reprinted, by permission, from E. E. Nordmeyer, *Illinois State Board of Education Teaching Portfolio*.

Step 1: Candidate searches and locates teaching vacancies.

Step 2: Candidate requests teaching applications.

Step 3: Candidate submits cover letter, resume, and completed application.

Step 4: Candidate submits reference letters or forms.

Step 5: Candidate requests teaching credentialing file to be sent from the career services and placement office to the school system.

Step 6: Candidate confirms receipt of all teaching applications materials, credentials, and references.

Step 7: School system initiates review of applications and selection of interview candidates.

Step 8: School system conducts interviews and ranks candidates.

Step 9: Candidate accepts or rejects teaching offer.

Step 10: If candidate rejects offer, he or she starts again at step 2. If candidate accepts offer, candidate signs a teaching contract.

Step 11: Board of education approves teacher contract and teacher.

Figure 11.2 Application and hiring process.

Reprinted, by permission, from T.A. Senne, 2002, "Transition to teaching: Putting your best foot forward," *Journal of Phyiscal, Education, Recreation & Dance, 73(2):* 46-52.

Once a teacher candidate has identified a teaching vacancy that is of interest to him or her (e.g., right location, job responsibilities match goals and objectives), it is important for the teacher candidate to find out as much as possible about the schools and districts he or she is considering. Being knowledgeable about the characteristics of the school gives a job applicant a distinct advantage.

When completing an application, it is imperative that the teacher candidate follow the directions and guidelines set forth by the employer; failing to adhere to these procedures could eliminate the candidate from contention. A search committee is unlikely to consider generic and error-laden application forms. For example, an administrator reported reading a resume and cover letter from an applicant interested in coaching swimming and diving, yet the schools did not have a swim team or pool. That applicant was eliminated because he or she neglected to tailor his or her materials to the context of the job situation. Keep in mind that guidelines will be unique for each employer; however, generally speaking, the applicant must provide an application form, teaching philosophy, references, and letters of recommendation. It is the responsibility of applicants to do their homework and identify as many characteristics of the school district as possible.

After receipt of application materials, the school district will review them for potential matches between the job description and responsibilities and the applicants. There are often responsibilities related to the job that are not included in the job description that need to be considered. For example, female locker room supervision might be a job responsibility that isn't included in an advertisement. Teacher candidates need to understand that they might be eliminated from contention because of these additional responsibilities. So it is important to not give up on the job search if the first application does not result in employment.

Typically, school districts notify the applicants that their materials have been received and provide a tentative hiring timeline. Realize that these timelines are often arbitrary and could change. Because the teacher candidate does not receive a phone call within seven days does not necessarily mean that he or she has been eliminated from the candidate pool. Additionally, it may simply take time to schedule a meeting with all members of the search committee or to obtain school board approval for the hiring. Three to five candidates are usually selected from the pool of applicants for an interview.

Teacher candidates should be prepared for the interview phase of the process. The search committee no longer simply reviews the applicant's paperwork but now also critiques the candidate's dress, professional conduct, personality, potential as a colleague, physical fitness, and communication skills. A practice interview with a college professor, the career planning and placement office, or a peer is a valuable part of the candidate's preparation, especially before the first interview (see table 11.1 for suggestions for a successful interview). At the interview, it is

Table 11.1   Strategies for a Successful Interview

Grooming	Wear conservative, professional business attire.
Social etiquette	Use general courtesies; be polite and on time.
Preparation & organization	Bring a professional binder containing your teaching portfolio, a writing implement, paper, and a list of questions for the interviewer.
Body & verbal language	Be confident, make eye contact, avoid repetitive behaviors, and smile.
Responding to questions	Be confident, speak clearly, and be honest.
Handshake	Close the interview with a thank you and firm handshake.

Reprinted, by permission, from T.A. Senne, 2002, "Transition to teaching: Putting your best foot forward," *Journal of Physical Education, Recreation & Dance, 73(2):* 46-52.

appropriate for the teacher candidate to present his or her teaching portfolio. The teacher candidate should be prepared to leave it for review at a later time (this is where an electronic portfolio has advantages over a traditional portfolio, as will be discussed in chapter 12). After a successful interview, the search committee will likely contact the candidate's references, seeking confirmation of their observations.

At last, the phone call comes, and the teacher candidate must decide whether or not to accept this job. It is difficult to gauge whether the first job offer is the right one. Once the teacher candidate accepts the position, he or she must be approved for the position by the district school board. On occasion, something is discovered about the applicant that prevents him or her from securing employment. For instance, the applicant did not pass the criminal background check, teaching certification is pending, or a reference revealed a potential weakness. Most often, board approval is a formality, and the school board will trust the search committee and approve the candidate for hire.

INDUCTION YEAR OF TEACHING

The first year of teaching is the most difficult because new teachers are still learning how best to organize their lessons, present content, and refine management strategies. During this time, teachers are still in a probationary period of certification. To create a smooth transition for both the new teacher and the school, it is often mandated that a transition, or support, team be assigned to the teacher. This team usually contains one or two experienced teachers, representing several different subject areas. These teams are meant to support the teacher's reflective process of self-evaluation, not necessarily to directly determine if employment should be continued.

Finding a Mentor

It is important that new teachers find someone that they feel comfortable with and can trust to serve as a mentor. Preservice teachers look to college professors or cooperating teachers to mentor them, but in the workplace it is important to find a mentor who directly comprehends the context of the situation. This is of particular importance because the first-year teacher is subjected to a process of socialization in which some of the teacher training may be "washed out." An effective mentor can help ease the transition because he or she will have more knowledge regarding the history of the situation. Mentors can also help new teachers balance and prioritize their responsibilities.

Teaching and Coaching Role Conflict

Many physical education teachers struggle to balance the coaching and teaching roles because they are each one person being asked to simultaneously be competent at two different jobs. According to Figone (1994),

> Individuals may experience cognitive dissonance and physical tension when attempting to effectively fulfill the expressed expectations of both roles. In most cases, the teacher-coach either falls short of these expectancies of both roles or devotes time and energy toward one role, thereby neglecting the other (p. 29).

Initially, coaching jobs may provide more reward because additional stipends and public recognition are common incentives; however, as the vignette indicated, the teacher-coach may fall short of the expectations of his or her teaching responsibilities. Two major factors influence the teaching and coaching role conflict: (1) the idea that physical education is often marginalized and has a lower status than other subject areas and (2) the time demands related to athletics. Because of these factors, there is a tendency for inexperienced teacher-coaches to put more time and energy into their coaching responsibilities (Figone, 1994).

To overcome these factors, teacher-coaches must not give in to the notion that athletics has benefits for youth that are superior to those offered by physical education. The teacher-coach must take the approach that both physical education and athletics are beneficial. A teacher-coach can demonstrate this characteristic by imposing equally high expectations for students and athletes. Coaches typically have higher expectations for their athletes than for their students enrolled in physical education. Additionally, if a peer or formal evaluation were to reveal poor job performance, it is the responsibility of the teacher-coach to reflect on this feedback. If the feedback from the evaluation is disregarded, the professional growth of the teacher-coach discontinues.

EVALUATION, REFLECTION, AND CONTINUED PROFESSIONAL GROWTH

Probationary teachers are subject to an annual and semiannual formal review process. This often depends on the school, district, or even a specific administrator's style of leadership. Anecdotal reports suggest that some physical education teachers are regular participants in the formal evaluation process, and others have never been formally evaluated by an administrator. It is the suggestion of the authors that new teachers request a formal evaluation to be conducted by a school administrator. This evaluation can be valuable for continuing employment as well as for self-reflection. In poor economic times, a physical education teacher wants to be known as a competent, hardworking, and contributing member to the overall school community.

Self-Reflection as Evaluation

As a teacher gains experience, the amount of formal, written planning subsides; however, it is important for new teachers to maintain records of their instruction for both a liability defense and the iterative process of self-reflection. As stated in chapter 8, documentation of best practice can prevent litigation; but, moreover, it can act as an important part of the teacher's continued professional growth. Ideally, the first time a teacher enacts a new instructional unit, it will meet the needs of the students; however, what is more likely to happen is that the teacher will need to modify and revise the lesson scope and sequence, content, activities, and so on. For example, perhaps on the first day of a volleyball unit the students had better serving skills than anticipated, resulting in the teacher having insufficient activities to fill the class period. It would be important for the teacher to document this so there is reference for the next time the unit is taught.

Self-reflection should contain a judgment about both teacher and student performance. The reflective practitioner, as discussed in chapter 1, thoughtfully considers his or her planning decisions, interactions, student engagement, instructional climate, and teaching effectiveness. How a teacher reflects changes over time. This is because experienced and inexperienced teachers reflect in different ways (Griffey & Housner, 1991). Experienced teachers ask more contextual questions before planning, often make contingency plans, and have businesslike interactions that effectively provide information. Inexperienced teachers exhibit sudden shifts in activities, which indicates losing sight of long-term goals, and they lack specific knowledge about the complexity and context of the instructional situation (Griffey & Housner, 1991).

Successful impact decisions require the teacher to be knowledgeable in current teaching practice and alternative curricula and are expected of certified teachers. Remaining current in proper technique, methodology, and procedures is necessary. The football coach who does not remain current in proper tackling technique is considered professionally inadequate and is negligent. The same is true for physical education teachers who neglect to participate in professional development. Specific to physical education, necessary skills should be introduced before participation in the activity and in a progression from simple to complex. It is, therefore, valuable for inexperienced teachers to reflect on their practices and critically evaluate their own as well as the students' performance, thus questioning their own beliefs.

Peer Evaluation

Peer or mentor evaluations are often the most beneficial for new teachers. For example (hypothetically), an observational time analysis, SOFIT (described in chapter 10), was conducted for a new teacher, and it was discovered that the teacher had the students be physically activity for only 15 minutes of the 50-minute lesson. Additionally, this peer review revealed that the teacher spoke more to male students than to female students. This phenomenon that males receive more teacher attention than females, mostly because they exhibit disruptive behavior (Hulley, 2001), is confirmed among the physical education literature. Ineffective use of time and disproportionate interaction between male and female students make the difference between effective and ineffective teaching. A peer review is a nonthreatening means of continued refinement of one's teaching effectiveness.

One of the best ways to refine one's teaching effectiveness is to participate in continued *professional growth*—that is to engage in lifelong learning. Good teachers teach their students how to learn, not just what to learn. To stay current, particularly in information related to physical activity programming and training principles, one can continue education through formal graduate coursework and participation in local, state, and national conferences that specifically target the needs of the physical education teacher. These methods not only include new activities and different ways to present familiar content but also include the expansion of the knowledge base related to physical education.

Membership in professional organizations can help teachers continue their professional growth. Whether it's a teacher-coach struggling with performance resulting from a role conflict or simply an elementary physical education teacher who works in isolation, professional memberships offer a multitude of benefits. Please review the discussion in chapter 5 that addresses professional development training opportunities in professional organizations.

Professional organizations have also taken advantage of the Internet and produced helpful Web sites, such as www.PECentral.org, www.PE4life. com, and PElinks4U.com. The Teacher Institute has created a Web site (www.teacher-institute.com) and an online newsletter (*Better Teaching*) that provide research-based ideas for teachers. Additionally, many teachers use the Internet to introduce and promote their own programs, expectations, activities, and curriculum. From these formal and informal media, teachers can create and revise their personal goals in order to remain progressive and consistent with best practice.

Personal Goal Setting

For someone to be an effective teacher, he or she has to want to become one. For example, it is recommended that physical education teachers engage in research to inform their instructional practice. This has been referred to as evidence-based practice (EBP) and is promoted by the U.S. Department of Education, as well as NASPE. Personal goals should be based on evidence of proven practice and knowledge as well as be innovative and attainable. A new teacher may want to think in terms of short- and long-term goals. A short-term goal might be to implement more student choice in a rackets unit, and a long-term goal might be to secure funding to obtain heart rate monitors for student use. Goals are a means of challenging the status quo and furthering teaching effectiveness and may help minimize the potential effects of burnout.

Avoiding Burnout

Professionals often argue that one of the primary reasons for encouraging others to continue their professional growth is to avoid burnout (Austin, 1981). At some point in a teacher's career, he or she may ask, "Why am I doing this?" Sadly, "Fifty percent of America's beginning teachers leave the classroom within their first seven years of experience and never return" (Merseth, 1992, p. 679). With issues such as low pay, marginalization, and high demands, teachers may find themselves on the verge of burnout. The term *burnout* has been defined as the inability to function effectively in one's job as a result of stressful circumstance. This stress could stem from many sources but is called burnout because the teacher is so exhausted that he or she is no longer able to complete the responsibilities effectively (Dorman, 2003).

Teachers have reported that they thought burnout was a result of being too involved; instead it was often a result of isolation (Dorman, 2003). As stated earlier, involvement in a professional organization can be helpful when warning signs of stress or burnout appear. You may be burned out if you're feeling overworked, underappreciated, stressed out, bored, or overwhelmed by the everyday realities of your life (Byrne, 1998). The network of teachers created from organizational involvement can provide a support group to help navigate through stressful periods on the job. For a first-year teacher, these may come more frequently than they do for experienced teachers. The initial signs of burnout may hit within the third and fifth years if preteaching beliefs do not match the realities of the educational setting.

SUMMARY

The transition from student to teacher is a process that begins in the early stages of teaching training; however, the perception is that this transition begins with student teaching. During the apprenticeship opportunities embedded in student teaching, the teacher candidate is simultaneously engaged in the process of completing his or her portfolio, writing a statement of teaching philosophy, and applying for employment. Securing employment requires time, energy, and patience because the process can be initially disheartening, but eventually worthwhile.

Discussion Questions

1. How would you address the coaching and teaching role conflict in yourself? In your colleagues?
2. What are the warning signs of burnout?
3. What is the process of socialization, and can "washout" be avoided?
4. List professional organizations that physical education teachers might want to join. What do these organizations offer teachers?

Professional Portfolio Contents

1. Reflect on your personal goals and how you will proactively address the potential for a coaching and teaching role conflict.
2. Design a stress management plan. When will you find time for your physical activity and other personal needs if you teach all day and coach in the evening?
3. Include sample lesson plans in your portfolio that reflect your professionalism. Be sure that the lesson plans identify the standards being addressed, safety, references from professional journals, and activities that you obtained from state professional conventions.

Key Terms

hiring process—Searching for employment, interviewing, attending job fairs, and completing applications as a means of securing employment.

induction year—The first year of teaching.

professional growth—Questioning your beliefs through mentoring and reflection.

reflection—Retrospectively and critically evaluating teaching and learning events.

teaching philosophy—A personal conception of teaching and learning.

Resources

Fiersen, R., & Weitzman, S. (2004). *How to get the teaching job you want: The complete guide for college graduates, teachers changing schools, returning teachers, and career changes* (2nd ed.). Sterling, VA: Stylus.

Mentoring: www.imdiversity.com/Villages/Careers/articles/whitehead_find_a_mentor.asp

Mentoring: www.mentoring.org

PE4life: www.PE4life.com

PECentral: www.PECentral.org

PElinks4U: www.PElinks4U.com

References

Austin, D. (1981). Teacher burnout issue. *Journal of Physical Education, Recreation & Dance, 52(9),* 35-36.

Byrne, J.J.. (1998). Teacher as hunger artist: Burnout, its causes, effects, and remedies. *Contemporary Education, 69(2),* 86-92.

Dorman, J. (2003). Testing a model for teacher burnout. *Australian Journal of Educational and Developmental Psychology, 3,* 35-47.

Figone, A.J. (1994). Teacher-coach role conflict: Its impact on students and student-athletes. *Physical Educator, 51(1),* 29-33.

Griffey, D.C., & Housner, L.D. (1991). Differences between experienced and inexperienced teachers' planning decisions, interactions, student engagement, and instructional climate. *Research Quarterly for Exercise and Sport, 62(2),* 196-204.

Housner, L. (1996). Innovation and change in physical education. In S. Silverman & C. Ennis (Eds.), *Student learning in physical education: Applying research to enhance instruction* (pp. 367- 390). Champaign, IL: Human Kinetics.

Hulley, K.S. (2001). *Gender bias: What are the current issues?* (ERIC Document Reproduction Service No. ED460156).

Merseth, K.K. (1992). First aid for the first-year teachers. *Phi Delta Kappan, 5,* 678-683.

Senne, T.A. (2002). Transition to teaching: Putting your best foot forward. *Journal of Physical Education, Recreation & Dance, 73(2),* 46-52.

12

Creating Your Professional Portfolio

STANDARDS: This chapter addresses all standards.

Collecting evidence of your growth as a professional seemed like a "busy work" assignment. You had to reflect on each micro and peer teaching experience and then place the reflection in your electronic portfolio (e-folio); it was a lot of work with little return. Then, today, you previewed a video clip of one of your first teaching experiences. You laughed aloud as you thought about how nervous you had been standing in front of those middle school students for the first time. Although not specifically seen on the video clip, you tell your roommate about how you told the students to go play catch, and then suddenly there were objects flying in all directions. You had neglected to tell the students to throw in the same direction in order to promote safety. Suddenly, you realize just how much you have learned and how you have grown from your initial early field experiences. You continue to collect artifacts for your portfolio as you prepare to upload the e-folio revisions to your personal Web site so that potential employers can visit your Web site. Your e-folio, created over several years, now represents your best work, with video and audio clips, PK-12 student work, student assessments, and a philosophy statement, each artifact reflecting your enthusiasm and teaching effectiveness.

A *portfolio* is a collection of student work evidencing growth over time. Each piece of work is called an artifact. Portfolios are created to promote better understanding of purpose, professional socialization, and student accountability in meeting state and national standards for attainment of teacher certification. Portfolios are used as alternative assessments to identify student learning and growth over time, thus validating a person's knowledge, skills, and competencies (Senne & Rikard, 2002). This form of assessment is different from traditional forms (e.g., written tests, achievement tests) because it is an authentic display of learning covering a broad range of skills and competencies related to a single focus. For example, preservice teachers will likely have constructed a professional portfolio requiring collection and selection of pieces of work as evidence of meeting the professional teaching standards. It was also likely required that preservice teachers reflect on their personal growth and why they believe they have met specific standards. The portfolio is important for both preservice and in-service teachers because it serves as a comprehensive representation of their accomplishments (Gallo,

2005).

Portfolios are a form of authentic assessment that is an alternative to more traditional means of evaluation. This allows the preservice teacher to have input on the external judgment of achievement of the standards. As Herman and Winters explain (1994),

> Well-designed portfolios represent important, contextualized learning that requires complex thinking and expressive skills. Traditional tests have been criticized as being insensitive to local curriculum and instruction, and assessing not only student achievement but aptitude. Portfolios are being heralded as vehicles that provide a more equitable and sensitive portrait of what students know and are able to do. (p.48)

The recent inclusion of authentic assessment, like the portfolio, is believed to be advantageous because it (a) highlights the importance of actual work within and beyond the classroom, (b) provides the student with decision-making power in assessment, and (c) meets accountability concerns (Chittenden, 1991). Some of the disadvantages of the portfolio process are that preservice teachers are concerned about time-management issues (e.g., when are we going to have time to work on our portfolios?) and the need to be introduced to the portfolio process early in their teacher certification program (Senne & Rikard, 2002; Wood, 2002). Beyond these findings, little is known about how the portfolio process (e.g., collection and selection of artifacts, reflection) influences preservice teacher learning (Lynn, 2006; Novak, Herman, & Gearhart, 1996).

Artifacts found in a professional teaching portfolio can include sample lesson plans, graded coursework, long-term plans, systematic observations, curriculum materials, pictures, videos, drawings, K-12 student work, and assessments (see figure 12.1). The portfolio may also include a professional philosophy or mission statement. Typically, a resume reflecting work experience is also included in the portfolio (although this depends on the purpose of the portfolio). Some preservice teachers have also included a professional development plan highlighting how they will continue to grow after earning their bachelor's degree. In New York state, it is mandated that teachers begin working on a master's degree related to the subject matter that they are teaching within two years of initial teaching licensure. In this case, it may be important to detail professional growth plans for a future employer because it is required to maintain teaching certification.

Sample artifacts for inclusion in your own portfolio have been identified at the conclusion of each chapter in this textbook. Building your professional portfolio is a progressive, long-term process, not a single event.

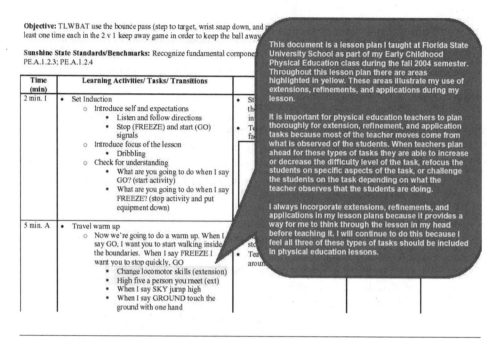

Objective: TLWBAT use the bounce pass (step to target, wrist snap down, and p[...]) least one time each in the 2 v 1 keep away game in order to keep the ball away[...]

Sunshine State Standards/Benchmarks: Recognize fundamental compone[...] PE.A.1.2.3; PE.A.1.2.4

Time (min)	Learning Activities/ Tasks/ Transitions	

2 min. I	• Set Induction
	  o Introduce self and expectations
	    ▪ Listen and follow directions
	    ▪ Stop (FREEZE) and start (GO) signals
	  o Introduce focus of the lesson
	    ▪ Dribbling
	  o Check for understanding
	    ▪ What are you going to do when I say GO? (start activity)
	    ▪ What are you going to do when I say FREEZE? (stop activity and put equipment down)
		• St
		  th
		  in
		• Te
		  fa

5 min. A	• Travel warm up
	  o Now we're going to do a warm up. When I say GO, I want you to start walking inside the boundaries. When I say FREEZE I want you to stop quickly, GO
	    ▪ Change locomotor skills (extension)
	    ▪ High five a person you meet (ext)
	    ▪ When I say SKY jump high
	    ▪ When I say GROUND touch the ground with one hand
		• st
		• Te
		  aroun

This document is a lesson plan I taught at Florida State University School as part of my Early Childhood Physical Education class during the fall 2004 semester. Throughout this lesson plan there are areas highlighted in yellow. These areas illustrate my use of extensions, refinements, and applications during my lesson.

It is important for physical education teachers to plan thoroughly for extension, refinement, and application tasks because most of the teacher moves come from what is observed of the students. When teachers plan ahead for these types of tasks they are able to increase or decrease the difficulty level of the task, refocus the students on specific aspects of the task, or challenge the students on the task depending on what the teacher observes that the students are doing.

I always incorporate extensions, refinements, and applications in my lesson plans because it provides a way for me to think through the lesson in my head before teaching it. I will continue to do this because I feel all three of these types of tasks should be included in physical education lessons.

Figure 12.1   Examples of artifacts in a professional teaching portfolio.

Portfolios are not created overnight by simply discovering old course assignments and unifying them in one location, either electronically or as a hard copy.

BUILDING A PURPOSEFUL AND PROFESSIONAL PORTFOLIO

To begin construction of the portfolio, the preservice teacher must first decide what type of professional portfolio he or she needs. This sometimes is predetermined by the primary and secondary purposes designated by the teacher preparation program (Melograno, 1999); if given the choice, the preservice teacher could select (a) an introductory portfolio, (b) a standards-based performance portfolio, (c) an employment portfolio, or (d) a PK-12 student performance portfolio. The introductory portfolio focuses on the initiation of preservice teachers into the profession of teaching. The introductory portfolio "serves as the catalyst for self-reflection and continual sharing of ideas and insights throughout the teacher education experience" (Melograno, 1999, p. 4). An additional intent of the introductory portfolio is to require beginning teachers to use a process of inquiry (e.g., to question, then apply) related to their subject matter.

The standards-based assessment portfolio is designed to reflect how a preservice teacher has met the National Standards for Beginning Physical Education Teachers (which are based on the National Council for Teacher Education [NCATE] requirements for teacher preparation) or state teaching licensure standards (see pages x-xi). The portfolio content focuses specifically on artifacts and reflective statements that evidence the competency of performance for a particular standard. For example, a lesson plan, a brief video clip showing delivery of the lesson plan, and a written self-reflection could act as evidence of attainment of NASPE Standard 6, planning and instruction.

The employment portfolio is designed for an audience of administrators and potential employers. These portfolios focus on the display of competencies related to the job that the preservice teacher is attempting to obtain. Because employment at schools usually requires competencies beyond teaching, the portfolio may extend into other realms, such as coaching. A portfolio emphasizing coaching skills might include documentation of coaching experience, a reflective analysis of coaching philosophy, abilities, current practices, or plans for future program development (Hubball & Robertson, 2004).

The PK-12 student assessment portfolio is very different from the employment portfolio. This type of portfolio relies on PK-12 student-generated artifacts (e.g., a written cognitive test, a videotape of students dancing a folk dance, the design of a gymnastics routine that reflects specific elements, a student's physical activity log, student heart rate monitor data) to represent the teacher's effectiveness. A PK-12 assessment portfolio is most often used by practicing teachers, although your preservice program will require you to document your ability to assess PK-12 student achievement and make lessons or curriculum decisions based on that data. The construction of the portfolio is broken into the stages of *decide*, *design*, *develop*, and *maintain*.

Organizing the Portfolio

The first stage of portfolio construction is to make decisions related to (a) identification of the purpose of the portfolio and type of portfolio, (b) selection of organizing features within the focus, and (c) choice of portfolio format. A preservice teacher must first *decide* who will review the portfolio. Determining why the portfolio is being created and the membership of the audience reviewing its contents are important tasks because they help define the final product. This process forces the preservice teacher to think of the end first, before designing the actual portfolio structure, similar to a backward design approach in curriculum development. A portfolio for a future employer looks different from that designed to provide evidence of attainment of teaching standards.

Purpose

The purpose of the portfolio must be clearly identified before the collection of artifacts can begin. As mentioned previously, the primary and secondary purposes may already be determined for preservice teachers (e.g., standards-based performance portfolios); however, if they are to use portfolios for the intent of securing employment or tenure, they must clearly define the purpose themselves. A preservice teacher might ask himself or herself, "What is the purpose of creating this portfolio? What role will this portfolio play in securing employment? How will this portfolio support ongoing learning and professional development?" Despite the fact that a portfolio can serve multiple purposes, when beginning, it is easier to prepare a portfolio for a single purpose and a well-defined audience.

Organizing Features

Once the purpose of the portfolio has been determined, the preservice teacher can then identify the *organizing features* (e.g., standards, work experiences, student assessments). The most common organizing feature, and the one we have been supporting throughout each chapter, is standards. Preservice teachers can organize their portfolios based on the achievement of the NASPE teacher standards.

A preservice teacher's portfolio could also be organized by his or her experiences. Some portfolios are organized chronologically by highlighting each work experience the preservice teacher has engaged in. These read more like a reflective journal. For example, a preservice teacher makes an entry into a journal capturing his or her feelings about a practice-teaching experience.

> I thought the lesson went very well today. I was pleased with how the students responded to activities. I still have to figure out how to get Pat involved. She has been resistant to participating in the activities for a couple of lessons now. First, I had to ask her to get off of the bleachers, then I overheard her teammates say that they did not want her on their team any more because she wasn't helping. I have learned to organize a lesson so that almost all of the students are engaged and enjoy the activity. I still seem to lose one or two students. Perhaps I need to talk with her individually. I am not sure how I can motivate her.

No matter what the organizing feature, it should be clear to the reader of the portfolio. Using bold, centered text, or a brief introduction to the portfolio will help orient the reader to the organizational features of the portfolio. For example, in a standards portfolio, an administrator would

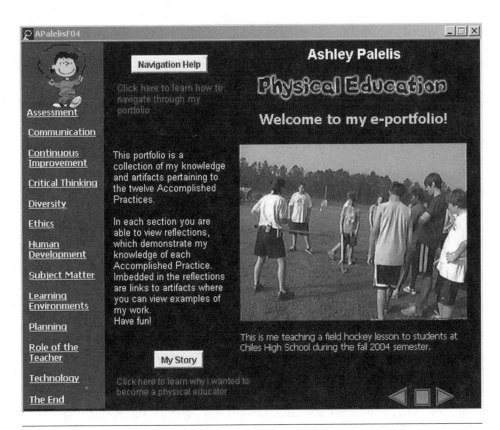

Figure 12.2 Example of portfolio organization.

navigate from standard to standard, not event to event. The organizing features influence the selection of portfolio format (see figure 12.2).

Format

Preservice teachers have many formats to choose from when *deciding* how to present their portfolios. Among the formats are (a) hard copy, (b) electronic, (c) Web-based, and (d) blog (Weblog). Many people still choose to organize their portfolios in a traditional format like a three-ring binder. The hard-copy format is most efficient for practicing teachers who are creating a K-12 student assessment portfolio, because many of the artifacts for this type of portfolio (e.g., written assessments for students, physical activity logs) would be difficult, although not impossible, to store electronically.

An electronic portfolio (*e-folio*) is constructed and stored on a computer or some form of media (e.g., CDs, DVDs, Web pages). The most common property of the e-folio is that it is organic. Using word processing software, the e-folio is easily revised. The greatest benefit of an e-folio is that it is a *living* document. An e-folio can be easily revised and updated. An e-folio is also advantageous because it can include a video component, whereas the hard copy format only allows still images.

A Web-based portfolio is the best for disseminating information to a large audience because the Internet is easily accessible to many people. The portfolio information is housed on a server and is typically interactive. Beginners use HTML editor software (e.g., Mozilla Suite, Netscape Composer, Microsoft FrontPage, Macromedia Dreamweaver, LiveText) to revise a portfolio template, which already has the organizing feature in place. Those with advanced technology skills often embrace this format because they can easily customize the organizing features while retaining the purpose.

A *blog* is a new portfolio format and is defined as any Web page with content organized according to date. Originally, blogs were Web pages designed to help keep track of a user's discoveries on the Internet. Since that time, the definition has expanded to encompass personal diaries, summaries of current events, and reflective portfolios (Tosh & Werdmuller, 2004). This format for portfolios uses a storytelling approach to track growth over time. For example, the preservice teacher can describe chronologically how he or she met the state and national standards for attainment of teacher certification. Artifacts can be included in the blog, but the focus is more on reflection.

The portfolio format dictates the presentation of the artifacts. For example, if it is important to the preservice teacher that videotape be included in the portfolio, then hard copy is an unacceptable portfolio format. A Web-based format may also be limiting for videotape, depending on the size, quality, and length of the video clip. Preservice teachers may need to revisit their format selection as new types of artifacts that they did not identify in their initial planning become available.

Before a preservice teacher can begin to design his or her portfolio, he or she needs to decide the type and purpose, identify the organizing features, and select a format. Portfolios are intended to reflect the uniqueness of each person, so these decisions should not be made lightly. Thoughtful decisions early in the portfolio process result in fewer revisions and a better product.

Designing the Portfolio

The presentation and organization of the portfolio content are highly individual. The *design* stage of portfolio construction requires the preservice teacher to make decisions about the display of the content, collection of artifacts, and tracking of portfolio work. The display of the portfolio content must be professional. Some content is inappropriate for portfolios, such as a glamorous self-portrait in unprofessional dress. Portfolios often contain a self-portrait; however, these pictures must portray the image that the preservice teacher will display while teaching. The use of overly casual or stylized fonts like Jokerman are also inappropriate and unprofessional. The preservice teacher needs to remember that the display should contain enough white space (this is, areas absent of text and graphics) to make the portfolio inviting and easy to read.

The best way to get started is to set up a template that reflects the portfolio's focus and distinctly identifies the organizing features. If using a Web format, this is a single page that contains one standard, a place to upload artifacts, and an area for reflection (see figure 12.3).

By using a template, each page of the portfolio will have a consistent and professional look that will help readers navigate the document. For preservice teachers, this is the ideal time to conduct a peer review of the portfolio template. One or two peers looking at the portfolio should

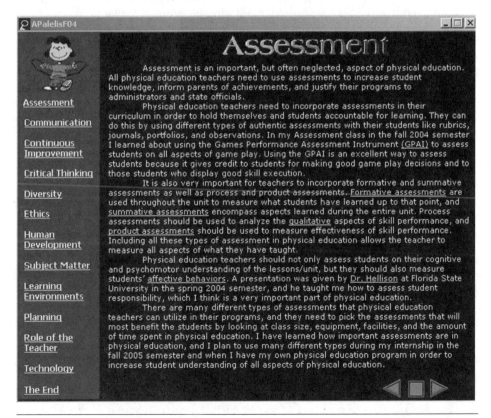

Figure 12.3 Example of a portfolio template.

result in timely feedback regarding the portfolio design. It would be inefficient to wait until the portfolio has been completed to seek a peer review because, by then, the revision would be tedious.

Once a template has been designed, the preservice teacher can consider which artifacts will best represent the attainment of each standard. The preservice teacher should consider, "Which artifacts, documents, and video and audio files belong in each category?" This is also the stage in which the preservice teacher should sequentially map how the artifacts are linked to each other and to the focus. Tables 12.1 and 12.2 list potential artifacts.

For a long-term project such as the construction of a portfolio, a working log should be kept to show the evolution of the portfolio. This tracking technique allows preservice teachers to pick up where they left off after brief layoffs. The log can be simple, such as a list of dates, decisions made, and activities completed. Some people use sticky notes to track progress over time. A log helps protect and preserve the original intent and purpose of the portfolio. Additionally, preservice teachers also need to develop a system for maintaining potential artifacts. Teacher candidates have busy schedules, and it may not always be feasible to

Table 12.1 Recommended Artifacts for a Professional Portfolio

Artifact source	Artifact type
Academic coursework	Article summaries/critiques, case studies, computer programs, curriculum plans, essays, goal statements, instructional materials, journals, projects, technology resources, unit plans
Professional development experience	Professional organization membership list, honors, Red Cross first aid and CPR certification, WSI certification, photographs, professional readings list
Field experiences	Anecdotal records, evaluations, instructional materials, journals, lesson plans, photographs, technology resources, unit plans, videotapes & audiotapes, K-12 student assessments
Work experiences	Evaluations, honors, resume
Student teaching	Curriculum plans, long-term planning, evaluations, goal statements, honors, instructional materials, journals, lesson plans, photographs, technology resources, unit plans, videotapes & audiotapes, K-12 student assessments

Adapted, by permission, from V.J. Melograno, 1999, *Assessment series physical education teacher preparation: Preservice professional portfolio system*. National Association for Sport and Physical Education (NASPE). AAHPERD Publications, Reston, VA.

Table 12.2   Potential List of Artifacts

Standard	Artifact Examples
Standard 1: Content Knowledge	• Lesson plans that show development of content in games, gymnastics, dance, and fitness for different grade levels • An interdisciplinary lesson plan • Video clip of you extending the content • Scanned copy of a quiz from a class that shows your knowledge of the content • Scanned copy of your passing score on the PRAXIS or state certification test • PowerPoint presentation on soccer skills • Block plan for a high school personal fitness class • Photograph of a poster listing instructional cues used in a dance class • Video clip of you performing a gymnastics sequence • Scanned copy of a feedback analysis sheet you completed on a lesson • Scanned copy of your cooperating teacher's evaluation of your knowledge of this standard

immediately place an artifact within the portfolio. If you've been introduced to creating an electronic teaching portfolio from the beginning of your preservice program, you may be required to burn a copy of your portfolio each semester in order to document your progress.

Developing the Portfolio

The *development* of the portfolio is the stage in which the preservice teacher gets to actualize the potential of the portfolio process. The preservice teacher must focus on two things in this phase: (1) collection and selection of artifacts, and (2) *reflection* and rationalization. As with each previous stage, many decisions need to be made about presenting the artifacts, the reflective rationalization justifying the artifact selection, and the critical evaluation of the work.

Collection and Selection of Artifacts

Preservice teachers should begin to collect potential artifacts once they have decided to pursue teacher certification. At this point, it is imperative that they develop a storage and retrieval system. Some preservice teachers store hard copies of all of their coursework in notebooks. Others choose to store information on a computer, perhaps in folders labeled by course titles, type of artifact (i.e., images, video clips, Word documents, etc.), or standards (i.e., Technology, Communication). If you choose to organize by standards, remember that some artifacts can be evidence for multiple standards. Each of these methods can be effective, but only if the method is aligned with the format of the portfolio. For example, many preservice teachers save only the hard copies of class assignments with instructor's feedback and not the original electronic copies of the assignments. If these preservice teachers decide to use a Web-based portfolio format, they must scan all of their documents so they can be viewed on the Web. Therefore, the recommendation is for preservice teachers to save *all* of their work in *all* possible formats, because it may not be immediately clear which portfolio format they will use.

It can be intimidating for preservice teachers to weed through all of their potential artifacts. In some physical education teacher education programs, the construction of a portfolio does not begin until the final year of the program. In this case, a preservice teacher may have four or five years of information from which to select artifacts (see table 12.1 for a list of potential artifacts).

What artifacts should preservice teachers select? It depends. Preservice teachers should select artifacts that best demonstrate attainment of a specific standard and illustrate growth over time. To display growth, a preservice teacher may want to provide an example of an early teaching experience or an initial lesson plan design and then compare and contrast it with an example of higher quality. The selection of the artifacts is driven by the format of the portfolio and the provision of evidence.

Reflection and Rationalization of Artifacts

As artifacts are being collected, a preservice teacher must reflect on each one's importance and rationalize its selection for inclusion in the portfolio. Here are three simple questions you can ask that will ignite the reflective practice: (1) "What?" (2) "So what?" and (3) "Now what?" (Campbell, Melenyzer, Nettles, & Wyman, 2000); see figure 12.4. Preservice teachers must ask themselves, "What artifact can I select as evidence for a particular standard?" Because there must also be justification of why this piece of work best represents the standard, a preservice teacher would then ask himself or herself, "So what? How did this artifact help me to grow professionally?" This is often difficult for preservice teachers to answer because it requires recalling their feelings during the creation and implementation of the artifact. This is where a blog is more advantageous, because the preservice teacher's personal growth is entered immediately after the event.

The final reflection question is "Now what?" Once the preservice teacher has selected the artifact, justified its selection, and described how he or she has grown from the experience associated with the artifact, he

What?

"The lesson was moving along just fine when all of a sudden the Goodyear blimp flew overhead! Everyone (including me!) stopped and screamed 'LOOK'…and there went my lesson!"

So What?

"For a moment I thought I'd never get them focused again, but I didn't panic. I quickly called them in, had them sit down, and for a few moments we watched it float by. We talked about it a bit and then I said, 'OK, that was fun, now let's get back to work' and everyone scooted off and picked up right where we had left off."

Now What?

"I had learned that sometimes it's best to just acknowledge the distraction… whew was I glad it worked. Teaching PE outside brings all kinds of distractions—bugs, wind, lawnmowers, the sun, and, yes, even the GY blimp. I think I made the best decision and if a blimp flies by again I know exactly what I'll do!"

Figure 12.4   Sample reflection questions.

or she must consider the future. Much like when they were developing a professional development plan, preservice teachers now need to express how this learning will affect their teaching.

A reflection should accompany each artifact included in the portfolio. The reflection should be in narrative form, flowing between and among the three probing questions and not read like a bulleted list. It is imperative that this communication be professional, clear, and concise. To promote reflection across the entire teacher training experience, online chats and discussions, blogs, and lesson plan evaluations should be engaged in regularly. A preservice teacher should acknowledge the importance of these early reflections and keep this information. Often it is discarded as unimportant, and thus a potential resource is lost.

During the development phase of the portfolio process, a preservice teacher should seek a critique or evaluation. When seeking a critical evaluation of the portfolio, a preservice teacher should consider the quality of presentation (organized, clear, creative), consistency throughout the portfolio (connection between philosophy, artifacts, and practice), quality of the evidence (originality, credibility, and reliability of artifacts), and quality of the analysis (rigorousness of the reflections and planning) (Hubball & Robertson, 2004). The evaluation can be formal or informal and can be conducted by a peer, instructor, or an experienced member of the field.

Maintaining the Portfolio

Because the portfolio is a measure of one's accomplishments, it is imperative that a preservice teacher take an active role in updating and maintaining it. Maintaining a portfolio could become overwhelming if the preservice teacher has not efficiently stored artifacts and has not tracked progress by keeping a log of work.

As stated previously, the easiest portfolios to maintain are stored electronically. Storage of the original template in its unedited state makes adding information smooth and efficient. If the template is placed on a Web server, the revisions can be posted to the general audience immediately upon completion. With this particular format, it is important that others feel like they know you, because there may never be face-to-face contact. The inclusion of a picture and brief biography may help the reader get to know you. The drawback of using a Web-based format is that the storage space is limited, which forces choices about what content to include.

An inadequately maintained online portfolio reflects poorly on a preservice teacher and can inhibit future employment. Preservice teachers should schedule regular maintenance of their Web-based portfolio or consider removing it from the Internet and selecting an alternative format if they don't have regular access. Because the skills of preservice teachers become more and more refined with each experience, it is important that they update their portfolio so there is representation of their best work.

Maintaining an accurate portfolio is a duty of a practicing teacher. A properly maintained portfolio, reflecting regular professional development, is an important part of reducing liability and risk related to teaching physical education (see chapter 8 for more information). Additionally, a portfolio can aid in the receipt of merit pay, attainment of recertification, and career advancement. A practicing teacher may want to consider a PK-12 student performance portfolio format because they have already provided evidence of attainment of standards required for certification.

ROLE OF TECHNOLOGY IN PORTFOLIO CREATION

The use of technology can enhance a teacher's portfolio, thus requiring a preservice teacher to think beyond the traditional portfolio process. Instead of simply collecting artifacts, a preservice teacher can use technology to create an archive of artifacts to be recalled as needed (table 12.3). Electronic archives, such as those found in libraries, allow artifacts to be stored in a single location and compressed to save storage space.

Table 12.3   Using Technology to Enhance a Professional Portfolio

Traditional portfolio processes	Enhancement through technology
Collecting	Archiving
Selecting	Linking, thinking
Reflecting	Storytelling
Projecting	Collaborating
Celebrating	Publishing

Data from Barrett, 2005.

Table 12.3 identifies several ways that the use of technology can enhance a teacher's portfolio. The use of Web-based technology also allows more interaction from audience members by linking artifacts to text in narrative reflections. This process encourages the audience to view designed links to display definitions, additional evidence, and the entire artifact rather than a section (e.g., curriculum materials) and allows the audience to unite pieces of evidence from different locations (e.g., personal Web site and a school's Web site).

Storytelling, which is often found in the blog format of portfolios, can also be enhanced by technology. Digital storytelling software can support the creation of Web-based or blog portfolios, which primarily focus on reflection. The Digital Storytelling Association provides the following definition:

> Digital stories use images, music, narrative, and voice together, thereby giving deep dimension and vivid color to characters, situations, experiences, and insights. This rich perspective can provide valuable evidence of attainment of teaching standards as well as evidence of effective teaching and learning.

In this context, learners create a two- to four-minute digital video clip using first-person narrative in their own voice, illustrated by (mostly) still images, with the addition of a music sound track to add emotional tone (http://electronicportfolios.org/digistory/).

The use of Web-based portfolios, particularly those that include access to archives, links, stories, and video, promotes collaboration and the building of networks because people with similar interest will access this information. These materials generated through the use of technology are in a publishable format and can easily be shared with future employers or networks of colleagues. Technology has the potential to substantially enhance portfolios.

PORTFOLIOS AND EMPLOYMENT

Think of a preservice teacher who has worked hard to develop a portfolio and has begun sending out cover letters and resumes as application to physical education teaching jobs. An administrator notices that the teacher has listed a Web site on his resume. She goes to the Web site to discover a professionally organized site, full of evidence of effective teaching. She is most impressed by a link to the school in which the preservice teacher did his student teaching, which displays student writing samples. Because writing excellence is a theme of her school, the administrator is immediately impressed. She then moves on to the next resume, only to view similar qualifications but no link to a Web site. If you were the administrator, which one would you interview? The portfolio can be used in several ways to help secure employment.

Portfolios and Job Searching

Using the Internet, a preservice teacher can search for jobs anywhere in the world. Several online organizations are specifically oriented to the recruitment of teachers. These online listservs may require you to register, thus allowing for mutual exchange of employment information. When inputting personal information, you may also find a space for a Web-page address, thus permitting your e-folio to be directly linked to your job application. Of course, more traditional methods of job searching, such as the newspaper, college job placement office, and campus job fairs, still exist. In these situations a CD-ROM of your portfolio can be mailed or handed to the employment contact.

Portfolios as an Interviewing Tool

Arguably, the most important factor related to a successful job interview is the preparation put into the task. Being unprepared for a job interview is inexcusable because it wastes the time of the teacher and the entire interviewing committee. Because 99 percent of the schools in the United States are wired to the Internet, it is important that preservice teachers use these resources to find out as much as they can about the school and the community. For example, does the school also have coaching vacancies? Are there clubs or intramurals that might be of interest? Collecting as much information as possible up front makes the candidate organized and well prepared. Obtaining this information will help you to determine which artifacts from your portfolio should be highlighted during an interview.

As previously suggested in chapter 11, to prepare for a job interview, a preservice teacher should consider a role-playing or mock interview. Role-playing is sometimes conducted as part of the teacher training process; however, some people will have to rely on friends or family to conduct a mock interview. These forms of practice should be taken seriously and made as authentic as possible. The portfolio can also be a point of discussion included in the interview. For example, the interviewee could say, "In my portfolio I have examples of how I set up a Sport Education basketball unit called March Madness at Seaside High School." The interviewee might also say, "In my professional plan, you will see that I would like to use my experience in football to someday obtain a varsity coaching position." This alerts the interviewer to the fact that the preservice teacher has more evidence of his or her abilities available in the portfolio. The interviewee should bring a CD containing the portfolio or the Web address where the portfolio can be found. It should not be left up to interviewers to find the information themselves, because they do not have the time to do so.

Portfolios and Coaching

Coaching portfolios should be specifically tailored to the position the preservice teacher-coach is seeking. The coaching portfolio, unlike the employment portfolio, does not necessarily contain information related to all of the experiences of the teacher-coach. If someone is seeking a varsity swimming coach position, all of the contents of the portfolio should support the attainment of this job. The coaching portfolio should include a philosophy statement, a handbook for athletes, and sample practice plans. By reviewing the coaching portfolio, someone should be able to determine how players will be evaluated and teams selected as well as how the coach will establish regular communication with the parents. Player and parent expectations should be clearly stated. For example, if the coach expects players to attend camp or be part of a summer program, it should be clearly articulated during and after the coach's hiring.

As previously stated in the job interviewing section of this chapter, it is important that the portfolio match the school's athletic philosophy. Does the school value participation so much that they are willing to add a subvarsity team to avoid making "cuts"? Does the school have a long-standing tradition, such as a girls' cross country team that has qualified for the state meet since its inception? Schools want assurances that the incoming coach will maintain these traditions as well as advance the skills and performance of the athletes participating in them. A coaching portfolio is quickly becoming an important factor, particularly for inexperienced coaches, in the attainment of full-time and upper-level coaching positions.

SUMMARY

During teacher training, it is often difficult for a preservice teacher to understand the importance of the portfolio process. This process is sometimes embedded across the curriculum of a teacher preparation program, and sometimes it is an external task to be completed independent of course assignments. Regardless of the methodology used to introduce portfolios, multiple levels of decision making are required for preservice teachers. The ultimate decision is, "How can I use this information to secure employment?" This chapter encourages preservice teachers to start collecting artifacts during their first year of teacher training and to update their materials regularly. The use of technology provides enhancements that hard copy formats cannot provide and therefore should be a consideration in the portfolio process.

Discussion Questions

1. What type of portfolio would best reflect your talents and competencies related to the teacher certification standards?

2. In a small group, investigate the technology tools available for portfolio building in several local school districts. Discuss which portfolio types and formats should be used by the physical education teachers as evidence of their own effectiveness.

3. List three different organizing features and discuss the advantages and disadvantages of these features.

4. Trade your portfolio with one other preservice teacher and conduct a peer evaluation of the portfolio. First list the five strengths and four limitations of the portfolio, and then discuss these with the portfolio designer.

5. As a class, brainstorm a list of questions that might be asked during a job interview. Have five members of the class act as the administrators and practicing teachers, who are part of an interview team. Conduct a mock interview during class for at least two preservice teachers.

Professional Portfolio Contents

1. Add a storytelling video about yourself to your portfolio (see Role of Technology in Portfolio Creation). Consider the format of the portfolio carefully. If you have access to the Internet, find out how much space (e.g., 100 MB, 50 MB) is available on the server for your e-folio.

2. Add a statement about your coaching philosophy to your teaching portfolio in case a coaching position becomes available.

Key Terms

artifact—An original piece of work created by a preservice teacher that acts as evidence of professional growth (e.g., lesson plans, cognitive tests, student assessments, video clips of teaching).

blog or Weblog—An online journal containing reflections related to the events of teacher training.

e-folio—An electronic portfolio that is stored on a computer, server, or storage media (e.g., CD, DVD).

organizing features—The elements by which the portfolio is structured (e.g., standards, work experiences, student assessments).

portfolio—A collection of preservice teacher work evidencing growth over time; an authentic assessment to evidence attainment of the NASPE teacher standards.

reflection—The process of critical consideration of key events that have taken place during teacher training (more evaluative in nature than simply recalling the events of the experience).

Resources

Rolheiser, C., Bower, B., & Stevahn, L. (2000). *The portfolio organizer: Succeeding with portfolios in your classroom*. Alexandria, VA: Association for Supervision and Curriculum Development.

References

Barrett, H. (2005). *Researching electronic portfolios and learner engagement*. The REFLECT initiative. Retrieved July 17, 2005, from www.taskstream.com/reflect/whitepaper.pdf.

Campbell, D., Melenyzer, B., Nettles, D., & Wyman, Jr., R. (2000). *Portfolio and performance assessment in teacher education.* Boston: Allyn & Bacon.

Chittenden, E. (1991). Authentic assessment, evaluation, and documentation of student performance. In V. Perrone (Ed.), *Expanding student assessment* (pp. 21-33). Alexandria, VA: Association for Supervision and Curriculum Development.

Gallo, A.M. (2005). Developing an A+ professional portfolio. *Strategies, 18(5),* 30-33.

Herman, J.L., & Winters, L. (1994). Portfolio research: A slim collection. *Educational Leadership, 10,* 48-55.

Hubball, H., & Robertson, S. (2004). Developing a coaching portfolio: Enhancing reflective practice. *Strategies, 18(2),* 16-18.

Lynn, S. (2006, October). *A longitudinal look at teacher candidate growth using the teaching portfolio.* Paper presented at the meeting of the 2006 NASPE Conference on Physical Education Teacher Education: Directions for the 21st Century.

Melograno, V.J. (1999). *Assessment series physical education teacher preparation: Preservice professional portfolio system.* Reston, VA: National Association for Sport and Physical Education, AAHPERD.

Novak, J.R., Herman, J.L., & Gearhart, M. (1996). Issues in portfolio assessment: The scorability of narrative collections. (CSE Technical Report No. 410). Los Angeles, CA: National Center for Research on Evaluation, Standards, and Student Testing assessments in large-scale testing programs. *Educational Evaluation and Policy Analysis, 19(1),* 1-14.

Senne, T.A., & Rikard, G.L. (2002). Experiencing the portfolio process during the internship: A comparative analysis of two PETE portfolio models. *Journal of Teaching in Physical Education, 21,* 309-336.

Tosh, D. & Werdmuller, B. (2004). *ePortfolios and weblogs: One vision for ePortfolio development.* Retrieved June 2, 2004, from: http://elgg.net/bwerdmuller/files/61/178/ePortfolio_Weblog.pdf.

Wood, S. (Summer, 2002). *The perceptions of preservice teachers and teacher education faculty regarding the e-portfolio process.* Unpublished doctoral dissertation. Tallahassee, FL: Florida State University.

About the Authors

Susan Lynn

Susan K. Lynn, PhD, is associate professor and program coordinator in physical education teacher education at Florida State University at Tallahassee. Dr. Lynn has received the Florida State University Teaching Incentive Award twice; was named three times as a nominee for the Taylor Dodson Award by the American Alliance for Health, Physical Education, Recreation and Dance Southern District; received the Founder's Award for Teaching Excellence from the South Carolina Association for Health, Physical Education, Recreation and Dance (SCAHPERD); and was named to Who's Who Among Students in American Universities and Colleges. Dr. Lynn has served as the coeditor in chief of *Physical Activity Today,* and her work has appeared in numerous publications, including the *Journal of Sport Management, Teaching Elementary Physical Education,* and *Research Quarterly for Exercise and Sport.*

In her spare time, Dr. Lynn enjoys participating in numerous social justice and community projects, going to the beach or the mountains with family and friends, and sipping coffee in a good bookstore.

Darla Castelli

Darla M. Castelli, PhD, is an assistant professor in the department of kinesiology and community health at the University of Illinois at Urbana-Champaign. Dr. Castelli's honors include the Teacher of the Year Award from the Maine Association for Health, Physical Education, Recreation and Dance (MAHPERD); the Past-Presidents' Scholar Award from the Illinois Association for Health, Physical Education, Recreation and Dance (IAHPERD); the International Young Scholar Award from the International Association for Physical Education in Higher Education (AIESEP); and the Hally Beth Poindexter Young Scholar Award from the National Association for Kinesiology and Physical Education in Higher Education (NAKPEHE). In addition, Dr. Castelli has published in the *Journal of Teaching in Physical Education, Research Quarterly for Exercise and Sport,* and *Medicine and Science and Sport and Exercise.*

When away from her work, Dr. Castelli enjoys physical activity, photography, and outdoor pursuits.

Peter Werner

Peter Werner, PED, is a professor in the Physical Education Center at the University of South Carolina at Columbia. In his 35-year career, Dr. Werner has authored or contributed to five books and more than 100 journal articles related to pedagogy or physical education for children. In addition, he has supervised numerous student teachers, chaired the Physical Education Institute Assessment Project Training Team in South Carolina from 1999 to 2000, and served as senior editor for *Teaching Elementary Physical Education* from 2000 to 2003.

Dr. Werner has received numerous awards, including a Presidential Citation from AAHPERD in 2004, an Enright Distinguished Alumni Service Award from Indiana University in 2003, and the Margie Hanson Distinguished Service Award from AAHPERD in 2002. He has also served as a NASPE reviewer for undergraduate program standards and is currently on the editorial review board for *Strategies*. In his leisure time, he enjoys making hand-crafted brooms, competing in marathons and triathlons, and whitewater canoeing.

Stephen Cone

Stephen L. Cone, PhD, is a professor in the department of health and exercise science at Rowan University in Glassboro, New Jersey. He has spent 35 years preparing teachers at the university level and teaching in K-12 schools, and in that time he has made numerous presentations and contributed to many publications in the areas of physical education and dance. Dr. Cone served as AAHPERD president and coauthored *Interdisciplinary Teaching Through Physical Education* and *Teaching Children Dance.* In addition, he has served as a dean of graduate and professional studies and chair of the physical education department. He has received several awards, including an AAHPERD Honor Award, a New Jersey AHPERD Honor Award, the New Jersey AHPERD University Professor of the Year Award, and Teaching Wall of Fame Awards from Rowan University in 2002, 2003, and 2004. He was named a fellow of the American Council on Education in 1993. Dr. Cone's favorite leisure pursuits include travel, photography, and family.